CHRISTOPH POETSCH
CONCEPTUAL PATTERNS IN PLATO'S PARMENIDES

CHRISTOPH POETSCH

# CONCEPTUAL PATTERNS IN PLATO'S PARMENIDES

VITTORIO KLOSTERMANN

Research and print have been generously supported by the
*Fritz Thyssen Stiftung.*

Bibliografische Information der Deutschen Nationalbibliothek

Die Deutsche Nationalbibliothek verzeichnet diese Publikation in der
Deutschen Nationalbibliografie; detaillierte bibliografische Daten sind
im Internet über *http://dnb.dnb.de* abrufbar.

Meinem Lehrer

Jens Halfwassen
(1958–2020)

# CONTENT

# 1. INTRODUCTION

Imagine we were given a text by a certain author that we could divide with some certainty into separate sections. The number of these segments would therefore be quite clear, while there might be one section about whose status and separateness we were unsure. Imagine further that we were uncertain what these sections are all about, whether they share a single subject or deal with different subjects, whether there is any subject to them at all, or whether they might ultimately be a mere joke. Imagine that we had other texts by the same author – earlier as well as later ones than the one we are concerned with –, whose systematic intentions and whose concepts are significantly clearer to us than the text in question. In fact, we might have even further hints: for instance, if the passages preceding the segmented text raise some systematic problems (which we understand more or less), and claim that the segmented text somehow provides solutions to these problems. To any decipherer of an unknown script or to any archaeologist trying to understand an incomprehensible inscription, a situation similar to this one would come close to paradise.

One very natural thing would be to carefully study the segmented text with regard to the occurrences of concepts which we know are likely to be significant from the other texts of this author. Of course, this could reveal that these crucial concepts are randomly spread through all the sections and hence that there are no distinct patterns observable with regard to their distribution. From this we would probably conclude that the different sections are likely not to deal with different aspects of this author's thoughts. However, this analysis could also reveal significant conceptual patterns. It could reveal, for instance, that crucial concepts are not randomly scattered throughout the sections, but that their occurrences form characteristic patterns because of varying degrees of density and concentration in the various sections. In their overall appearance, these patterns might even be systematically meaningful to us. This would doubtlessly be a very strong indication how to understand these different sections and their relation to one another. Additionally, these patterns might even provide a hint as to the status of that one special section about whose status we are unsure.

The present study attempts to prove that such conceptual patterns in fact exist in Plato's *Parmenides*. In the first part of this dialogue we famously find a young Socrates who advocates what at least appears to be very similar to Plato's Theory of Forms in dialogues likes the *Phaedo* and the *Republic*. And famously we find this young Socrates perplexed and completely unable to defend his position against a number of objections raised by an old Parmenides. But instead of bidding farewell to the forms, Parmenides provides, in the second part of the dialogue, an exercise by help of which he claims to enable one to counter these objections. This notoriously obscure exercise consists of eight (or nine) sections, within which Parmenides develops myriads of arguments about what he calls τὸ ἕν and τὰ ἄλλα. As it is well-known, it is all but obvious what these sections are in fact all about – even the status of one of them as a section in its own right remains controversial. Nor is it, subsequently, in any sense clear how this exercise and its arguments should actually be able to provide help in saving the forms against the objections in the first part of the dialogue.

Plato's *Parmenides* is hence a text to which – obviously – all the characteristics mentioned at the outset apply, while roughly 2,400 years of intense discussion and careful research have not brought us anywhere close to a broader scholarly consensus. I dare not claim to end these discussions (I suspect they never will, which is in fact a good sign in some sense). But I claim to provide some evidence by help of the conceptual patterns that might be of general interest for every approach to this difficult text. In the following, I shall therefore try to clearly distinguish between, on the one hand, observations on these patterns and conclusions I consider as fairly uncontroversial with regard to the evidence (chapter 3) and, on the other hand, such arguments and conclusions that imply more far-reaching claims and a more concrete interpretation of the given evidence (chapters 4–5). Thus, I hope, the evidence and results of the former will still be valuable to those who will not follow every aspect of my further interpretation in the latter chapters. Those are the two first main steps of this study. Subsequent to them, in a concluding third main step, I shall then exemplarily address the question as to how these results might actually be able to tackle the difficulties and problems that are raised in the first part of the dialogue with regard to the Theory of Forms (chapter 6). Hence, this study aims to address, in a general manner, the two main questions that scholars are facing with regard to Plato's *Parmenides*: What is its second part all about? How can the second part provide a solution to the problems in the first part?

By implementing the method that I shall describe in chapter 2, the first main step of this study will prove that the second part of the *Parmenides* appears as a surprisingly coherent whole in its bigger picture (chapter 3). The conceptual patterns strongly suggest that there is a kind of vertical 'ontological shift' through the eight (or nine) sections (§§ 5–7). This shift, however, is not a simple linear, but a more complex one (§ 11). These results will, at least, prompt the assumption that there is indeed some thematic shift in the sections and that Parmenides speaks of different subjects or aspects of reality throughout the exercise. In the sense of this more complex shift, these investigations in the first step will show that there is a special connection between the notorious corollary of the second section and the fifth section (§ 8). This connection has, to the best of my knowledge, remained largely unnoticed so far. Besides that, the investigations of the first main step will point out that there is a striking tripartition of being, becoming/passing away, and appearance to be observed (§§ 5–7; 10–11), while one commonly expects only a bipartition of these general ontological realms and a coincidence of the latter two in Plato.

The second main step of this study will then provide a more systematic and more far-reaching interpretation of the evidence (chapters 4–5). Within this step, I shall argue that a coherent way of interpreting the totality of the conceptual patterns is to suppose four main subjects to be treated in the second part of the *Parmenides*: the physical cosmos, the (World) Soul, the realm of forms, and a first principle of the forms (§ 12). A concise geometrical analogy will be provided to explain how the sections of the exercise relate to these four main subjects (§ 12). This account will thereby propose that the sections of Parmenides' exercise can be divided into two general types: those sections that circumscribe a certain subject *in itself* and those sections that do not introduce a new subject, but instead describe the *relation* between two subjects (§ 13). In this important respect, the present study differs significantly from all those approaches that tried to locate some kind of linear arrangement of different ontological subjects or realms in the sections of the exercise (§ 13). Within this context, it will also be argued that the famous corollary of the second section is not to be understood as one main section in its own right since it is concerned with the same subject as the fifth section (§§ 12; 16–17). The corollary thus fulfils a crucial task in connecting the first and the second half of Parmenides' exercise. By providing additional

conceptual patterns that support the proposed interpretation, I shall furthermore show that the given statistical results strongly suggest a different
and more complex systematic understanding of Plato's ontology in general,
and the crucial concept of participation in particular. By taking up the remarked tripartition from the first step, I shall argue that the second part of
the *Parmenides* suggests not a bipartite, but a *tripartite* ontology for Plato,
wherein becoming/passing away as such happens primarily on the level of
the soul, while it is only then mirrored or displayed in the physical realm
of appearance (§ 19). It will furthermore be shown that this also prompts a
more nuanced understanding of participation (§ 19).

In order to build all these results on firm ground, a more extensive elabo-
ration of the method is needed beforehand – a method which in its aim to
identify patterns in a given large amount of data resembles the core thoughts
of today's data science (chapter 2). Explaining this method will include
some technical details in statistics (§§ 1–2). These might be a little bit dry,
but they will decisively strengthen the objectivity of the present approach.
Hence I hope the results and their objectivity will justify this μακροτέρα
καὶ ἀκριβεστέρα ὁδός. To those who are either unfamiliar or in general un-
comfortable with statistics, the arguments of this study will however remain
accessible throughout. All that is needed will be intuitively graspable and will
ultimately boil down to two questions (§ 2). Those who are not primarily
interested in the technical details of the argument and want to delve right
into the more systematic results are therefore advised to read the introducing paragraphs of § 1 as well as § 2 for a rough overview of the approach,
and then to leap right to § 5 and maybe read the more technical details in
§§ 1; 3–4 afterwards.

The third main step of this study will ultimately address the question
of how the evidence of the conceptual patterns is actually able to provide
an answer to the objections that Parmenides raises in the first part of the
dialogue (chapter 6). This will be done by an analysis of two exemplary
and well-known aporias: the objection that Parmenides himself labels the
'Greatest Aporia' (§§ 24–25) and the one that is known as the first 'Third
Man Argument' (§§ 26–27). It will be argued that in the case of the latter
the terminology, among others, provides a decisive link between the aporia
in the first part of the dialogue and the conceptual patterns in the exercise. It
will hence be reconstructed how a Socrates who is instructed by the exercise
is able to counter the argument (§ 26). With regard to the Greatest Aporia it
will especially be shown how the special relation between the corollary and
the fifth section may play a decisive part in overcoming this problem (§ 24).

This comes down to the crucial intermediate position of the World Soul, which – as will be argued – is also Plato's systematic answer to this problem both prior to and after the *Parmenides* (§ 25). Ultimately, it will also be sketched in outline how the other aporias may be addressed by help of the present approach (§ 28).

Before starting by introducing the method in the next chapter, let me add one crucial remark on the scope of this study. Its aim is to introduce *in general* a new approach to Plato's *Parmenides* and to argue for its productivity in an *overall* perspective. This means that it neither provides a line-by-line commentary of the dialogue's text nor does it claim exhaustiveness in every respect. Instead, it introduces and puts up for discussion an approach to the *Parmenides* which I consider to be new. Its most innovative feature is, in my eyes, that it provides significant new evidence on the 'bigger picture' of this dialogue. As I shall argue, the bird's-eye view permits a fruitful perspective on a notoriously obscure text which was doubtlessly very influential throughout the history of philosophy, but which remains controversial and stimulating until today.

*

This book and the research behind it owes a lot to many persons. First of all, I would like to especially thank Benedikt Strobel for the many conversations we had on this project during the last few years. Even though – or perhaps: just because – our approaches to the *Parmenides* are quite different, I have benefitted immensely from our discussions on various chapters and on my method in general. I would furthermore like to thank him for the invitation to discuss some first results at the 'Philosophisch-Philologisches Colloquium zur antiken Philosophie' in Trier. Jakob Brüssermann has made the great effort to read the whole manuscript and with his superb sense of precision and language has provided many very valuable suggestions. I am very grateful for these improvements, which have enhanced the overall argument a great deal. Furthermore, I would like to thank Martin Avenarius, Diego De Brasi, Bill Engels, Lukas Fuhr, Andrew Gregory, Vittorio Hösle, Béatrice Lienemann, Alex Long, Winfried Lücke, Peter McLaughlin, Gustav Melichar, Andrej Miotk, Carl S. O'Brien, Sebastian Odzuck, Anna Pavani, Ron Polansky, Tim O. Roth, Pauline Sabrier, Thomas A. Szlezák, Jonathan Vandenburgh, and Denis Walter for supporting this project through discussions, criticism and in many other respects. Needless to say that I remain solely responsible for the remaining shortcomings.

Science is nothing without time and σχολή, and time runs short without money. Therefore, I would like to thank the *Fritz Thyssen Stiftung*, which generously funded the present project. In particular, I am very grateful to Hendrikje Gröpler and the whole foundation for their sympathy and understanding when this project was unforeseeably going through tough times. In addition, I am very grateful to this foundation for providing a generous subsidy to the printing costs.

Once again, I am very happy and I feel indeed very honoured that Vittorio E. Klostermann immediately agreed to include this study into his publishing programme. His whole team, and especially Anastasia Urban, has once more done an excellent job, both personally and professionally. I am very grateful for this trusting cooperation.

My parents and my brother have been constant support ever since the very beginning. I am afraid I cannot estimate how much. Not the least do I feel able to express what I owe to my wife, whose backup and encouragement, not only during this study, is simply invaluable, and to our son, whose gaze has turned the standards completely upside down.

There is only one to whom this book can be dedicated: my teacher Jens Halfwassen, who died all of a sudden, at the age of only 61, in February 2020, shortly after this project had taken its very first steps. He knew its main theses, had encouraged it several times and was looking forward to the results. To those who are familiar with his work, it will be obvious what the present study owes to him. In those places where I disagree with him, I am sure he would have welcomed the dissent: he himself time and again referred to the highly discursive context of the Old Academy, which left pretty much no theorem of its founder unquestioned. This Academic context always was his paradigm of philosophical συνουσία and διαλέγεσθαι.

## 2. THE PRESENT APPROACH

This chapter provides an overview of the method which forms the basis of the present study. This includes a few remarks on the textual basis and an explanation of the technical details. I shall first state some preliminaries (§ 1), then give an account of the statistical approach (§ 2). After that, I provide an overview of previous research which is of interest with regard to the present study (§ 3). Those who are primarily interested in the systematic results rather than in the technical details of the argument are advised to have a quick glance at the first paragraphs of § 1 and at § 2, and then to take a leap right to § 5. In order to evaluate the argument in its full depth, a closer reading of the present chapter is of course required.

### § 1. Method and Preliminaries

In the jungle of arguments that forms the second part of the *Parmenides* it is doubtlessly easy to lose sight. While one tries to cautiously follow Parmenides' arguments – which sometimes seem to be quite strange or simply fallacious – one easily loses sight of the bigger picture and risks to miss the forest for the trees. The present approach tries to contribute to this bigger picture by 'zooming out', as it were. This will be done by what I call 'conceptual patterns'. By this I mean the quantitative result, particularly its visual appearance in a bar plot, that is provided by the method (which I describe below) of tracking the occurrences of several concepts throughout the sections of Parmenides' exercise. These results may provide more or less distinct regularities and more or less meaningful peculiarities with regard to the distribution of different concepts. Obviously, the decision whether this is actually the case or not is not always clear-cut and binary, but implies varying degrees of markedness. It is thus quite difficult to determine when exactly a distinct, non-random peculiarity is actually given in a pattern (which would then provide firm ground for interpretation). Fortunately, there is an objective statistical way to decide and evaluate whether one is only chasing some phantom in the evidence, undistinguishable from mere coincidence, or whether a pattern provides in fact a non-random distribution, whose characteristics may then be legitimately interpreted (§ 2).

The main idea of the present approach is therefore to trace the occurrences of several concepts that are likely to be of systematic relevance in Plato and to evaluate whether these occurrences form patterns with non-random distributions. The only thing that will be done besides recording the occurrences as such is to evaluate whether a concept is affirmed or negated and, at times, to draw clearly discernable distinctions in the meaning of a few concepts.

The motivation behind all this is the following: we may, at least heuristically, suspect that Parmenides, throughout his exercise, might in fact address different things through his arguments and understand different things by τὸ ἕν and τὰ ἄλλα. We therefore try to get hints of what his unknown subject matter(s) might actually be by evaluating the affirmation and negation of a range of concepts that he employs. To explain this more vividly with a heuristic example: if someone predicates the concepts 'red', 'subject to gravity', 'fruit', and 'sweet' of some under- or undetermined subject called, say, τό τι, but negates through arguments the concepts 'able to fly' and 'blue' of it, we might suspect that he or she is talking about an apple. And if this someone – in another section of his or her exposition – talks again of a τό τι, but now predicates 'able to fly' and 'blue' of it, while 'red' and 'fruit' are negated, and 'subject to gravity' is affirmed somehow only with hesitation, we might suspect that τό τι in this second section is not the same as in the first, but might be a different subject, say, perhaps a blue macaw. In the same vein, the present approach tries to narrow down and determine what Parmenides might be talking about in the different sections by evaluating where he employs some crucial concepts and how he does so.

Besides evaluating single concepts, I shall furthermore group similar and related concepts in 'conceptual fields' in order to get an even more general picture of the dialogue's second part. The results of these investigations are, as mentioned above, analysed with statistical methods and are thus comparably objective in their statements. The patterns are displayed graphically by bar charts. This also provides the opportunity to visually and hence intuitively grasp the characteristic pattern of each concept or conceptual field. This is loosely analogous to the way in which Fraunhofer lines reveal their characteristic patterns for chemical compositions.

Let us begin with some formal preliminaries. The sections of the second part are labelled 'S1' to 'S8',[1] the corollary in 155e4–157b5[2] is addressed by 'S2C'. The preliminary summary ('PS') in 160b2–4 and the final summary ('FS') in 166c2–5 are not considered as parts of S4 and S8 respectively since they obviously summarise more than only these two sections. In the same way, the transitional passage ('TP') 160b5–d2 is not regarded as a part of S5 specifically since it discusses the approach in the *whole* second half (S5–8) on a more general level, while S5 itself starts at 160d3.[3] PS, FS, and TP are thus not taken into statistical account. This account concentrates solely on the sections S1–8.[4]

The textual basis is J. BURNET's OCT-edition with a few minor changes.[5] The Stephanus-pages and lines are used in accordance with this edition. Since Parmenides is without any doubt leading the whole discussion – in fact, his dominance is second to none in this regard in Plato's dialogues[6] –, the investigation concentrates solely on his contributions, which make up roughly 91 % of the second part. In total, Parmenides' part in S1–8 (without IS, FS, and IP) consists of $w_{total}$ = 10,272 words. For the single sections we get

[1] I use the term 'section' in a heuristic manner to refer to the eight (or nine) segments of the second part as neutrally as possible. There has been some debate whether the traditional way of speaking of eight (or nine) 'hypotheses' is ultimately correct or not. Some (such as ROBINSON ²1953, 241; ALLEN ²1997, 212; DORTER 1994, 51 N. 37; PETERSON 1996, 168; SCOLNICOV 2003, 3 N. 14; 26; FERRARI ⁸2019, 110–111) have argued that there are in fact only *two* hypotheses – 'if (the) One is' and 'if (the) One is not' – and S1–8 should thus rather be called 'arguments', 'deductions' or alike. This is in some sense correct in my view, although it is incorrect (or at least: imprecise) that there are only two hypotheses in that sense; Parmenides in fact employs *four* (cf. § 13). On the concept of ὑπόθεσις cf. the important remarks by VON FRITZ ²1969, 101.

[2] Stephanus-pages without any further qualification refer to BURNET's edition of the *Parmenides* throughout this study. All other dialogues are likewise quoted according to this edition by short title and Stephanus-page.

[3] The sections are thus: 137c4–142a8 (S1), 142b1–155e3 (S2), 155e4–157b5 (S2C), 157b6–159b1 (S3), 159b2–160b2 (S4), 160d3–163b6 (S5), 163b7–164b4 (S6), 164b5–165e1 (S7), 165e2–166c2 (S8).

[4] If I write 'S1–8' in the following, this always includes S2C. I use a slash (e.g. 'S2/3'), if S2C or any section in between is excluded.

[5] In 141e2, I read τοῦ μέλλοντος (with DIÈS) instead of [τοῦ μέλλοντος] (BURNET); in 144c6, I read ἑκάστῳ τῷ τῆς οὐσίας μέρει (with DIÈS) instead of [ἑκάστῳ] τῷ τῆς οὐσίας μέρει (BURNET, MORESCHINI); in 162a6, I read αὖ εἶναι ᾖ (with DIÈS) instead of αὖ [εἶναι] ᾖ (BURNET, MORESCHINI); in 162a8, I read τοῦ εἶναι (with DIÈS, MORESCHINI) instead of τοῦ <μὴ> εἶναι (BURNET); in 162b2, I read εἶναι μὴ ὄν (with DIÈS, MORESCHINI) instead of εἶναι [μὴ] ὄν (BURNET); and in 164a1, I read μετέχον <τοῦ> ὄντος οὐσίας (with MORESCHINI) instead of μετέχον [ὄντος] οὐσίας (BURNET). For the manuscripts of the *Parmenides* cf. LUCARINI 2021.

[6] The second half of the *Parmenides* is thus for sure the most asymmetrical of Plato's 'asymmetrical dialogues'; cf. SZLEZÁK 1988 on this issue.

the following word-counts: 1,619 (S1); 4,998 (S2); 531 (S2C); 688 (S3); 379 (S4); 1,003 (S5); 328 (S6); 514 (S7); 212 (S8); cf. also T.A.5 (p. 150).

The general method is as follows: the whole investigation is based on a selection of concepts that appear at least once in S1–8 and are potentially of systematic interest. These concepts are then counted in their occurrences within the slots of S1–8, resulting in word-counts $n_{S1}$, $n_{S2}$, …, $n_{S8}$ for every concept. This step uses, as additional support, the digitised text of the *Parmenides* with its search functions in the *Thesaurus Linguae Graecae* as well as the sources provided by the *Perseus Digital Library*. Besides this quantitative record, I evaluate every single instance of a given concept qualitatively: each occurrence is judged individually as to whether the concept is affirmed (+) or negated (–), or has a positive (o+) or negative (o–) tendency in one or the other direction. Occurrences judged as o+ are statistically counted as positive (+), those judged as o– are counted as negative (–). The differentiation o+/o– is, however, introduced for two reasons: on the one hand, to make the decision process more transparent; on the other hand, to better reproduce Parmenides' tendency to, at times, build arguments in a rather hypothetical or general manner while still adequately depicting the quantitative amount of a concept's instances within these arguments.

Here are the exact criteria (and some examples) of the four categories. An occurrence is judged *positive* (+) if a) the concept is affirmed,[7] or if b) a concept is generally employed in the argument without any negation.[8] An occurrence is judged *negative* (–) if the concept is negated.[9] An occurrence is judged as having a *positive tendency* (o+) if a) the concept is implemented in a general or hypothetical consideration or a definition, and is affirmed elsewhere in the section,[10] or if b) the concept is used within a general question, but obviously affirmed,[11] or if c) the concept is used within a rhetorical statement or question with a positive tendency.[12] An occurrence is judged as

---

[7] In 157e4, for instance, ὅλος and μόριον are affirmed and hence counted as +.

[8] A good example for this is the concept ὄγκος that occurs – quite out of a clear sky – in 164d1 (and subsequently in S7) as a concept of the argument, but without any traces of negation or negative tendency.

[9] In 137d2, πόλυς is clearly negated and thus counted as –.

[10] In 143c5–8, three instances of οὐσία are included in a general consideration, which is affirmed in 142c5–6; 142d9–e3. The three instances in 143c5–8 are thus counted as o+. In 156a6, for instance, ἀπόλλυμι is included in a general definition and is affirmed later in 156b1. Thus, 156a6 is counted as o+ (and 156b1 as +).

[11] Cf. e.g. 145e7, where κινέω is included in a general question and is later affirmed in 146a6–7. Thus, 145e7 is counted as o+.

[12] In 162b9, μεταβάλλω is, for instance, included in a rhetorical question, with a clear positive tendency and the occurrence is thus counted as o+.

having a *negative tendency* (o-) if a) the concept is implemented in a general or hypothetical consideration or a definition, and is negated elsewhere in the section,[13] or if b) the concept is used within a general question, but obviously negated,[14] or if c) the concept is used within a rhetorical statement or question with a negative tendency.[15] Everywhere, and especially in difficult cases, the intention is to depict most faithfully the implied tendency and attitude that in a given argumentation and its context is shown towards a concept.[16]

In APPENDIX B there is a complete list that documents each single decision. In difficult cases as well as for o+ and o- this is accompanied by a short explanation. Admittedly, language is a complex phenomenon that allows for nuances that are sometimes hard to categorise. And there is little doubt that others would judge differently in a few difficult and ambiguous cases. However, I do not think that this ultimately affects the overall statistical account or the patterns significantly. In any case, APPENDIX B provides a maximum of transparency for these decisions. In this appendix are marked a few instances (e.g. φαίνω), where only a specific meaning of a concept is actually counted. Since the approach ultimately focuses on the systematic significance of the patterns, sometimes two or three of them are grouped together, e.g. ὄναρ and ὕπνος. APPENDIX B (and C) however still permits discerning their counts. The pure quantitative amount and the qualitative account are each counted in two ways: in absolute numbers and in relation to the size of the section.[17] This ends up in the four tables T.A.1–4 in APPENDIX A.

---

[13] In 137e6, for instance, μετέχω is included in a hypothetical consideration, which is negated explicitly in 137d8–e1. The occurrence in 137e6 is thus counted as o- and the one in 137e1 as -. In 137c6–9 for example we find a general definition and hypothetical consideration with several instances of ὅλος, which is then explicitly negated in 137c5–6; 137d2–3. The former are counted as o-, the latter as -.

[14] In 138b7–8, κινέω is included in a general question, but it is later explicitly negated in 138c3; 139a2–3; 139b3. The first occurrence is thus judged as o-, the latter three as -.

[15] Cf. e.g. 138d1, where μέρος is included in a rhetorical question with a clear negative tendency, which is thus counted as o-.

[16] This implies that not every explicit affirmation or negation relates directly to τὸ ἕν or τὰ ἄλλα. One reason for this is that Parmenides talks about a bunch of subjects in that sense (e.g. τὰ μὴ ἕν in 146e6–147b3). But more importantly, many explicit statements refer only indirectly to the main subject(s) of the section: cf. e.g. 144a6, where πλῆθος (in the second instance) is affirmed explicitly for ἀριθμός, which is in turn closely related to the One in 144a7–9. The overall intention is therefore to grasp the affirmative or negative attitude towards the concepts (in this case: πλῆθος) in order to characterise what Parmenides might be talking about in his arguments; these mediate instances are thus taken into account as well.

[17] The relational size of a given word-count $n_{wordSX}$ in a section SX is calculated by $(n_{wordSX} / w_{SX}) \times 100$. The factor 100 is included only to get numbers with less decimal digits that are more easily manageable (e.g. 0.21 instead of 0.0021). Since this factor is applied to all relative word-counts, it does not effect their relation.

Grouping several concepts in a conceptual field (as described above) is, on the one hand, of course limited to the vocabulary that Parmenides actually uses throughout his exercise. On the other hand, selecting the concepts for a field may imply, at least to a certain extent, subjective nuances. In order to make this process as transparent as possible, APPENDIX C provides a full list of all concepts that Parmenides makes use of and the respective counts of their occurrences in the different sections. This list is based on a fully lemmatised text of 137c4–166c5 that was created for this study. The lemmatised text was then analysed by a programme written in C++ for these purposes.

## § 2. Statistical Evaluation

The occurrences of the concepts under consideration are tested with regard to their statistical significance. This is of great importance because it permits an objective evaluation of a concept's given distribution (apart from our subjective impression whether or not some distribution provides significant peculiarities).[18] For each single concept or conceptual field under consideration it is therefore calculated how much the given distribution in S1–8 differs from a fully random distribution. If this result (stored in the 'p-value') is lower than a specific level (the 'significance level $\alpha$'), we are justified to regard this distribution as statistically significant. The lower the p-value gets, the more unlikely it becomes that we wrongfully regard a concept's distribution as non-random. In short, as a rule of thumb: the *lower* a given distribution's p-value gets, the more confident can we be in regarding this distribution as non-random. If $p < 0.01$, we are – according to general statistical methods – on the safe side; commonly, already $p < 0.05$ is regarded as sufficient.[19]

---

[18] GREGORY 2012, 158–160; 173–174; 178 is therefore right in my eyes to criticise the absence of this important feature – a test of statistical significance – in KENNEDY 2010.

[19] Cf. e.g. MULLER 1973, 93; GRIES ³2021, 29; WINTER 2020, 168–169. Cf. also BRISSON ²1977, 17 who uses $\alpha = 0.05$ (= 5.0 %). This standard goes back to R. A. FISHER (cf. KIRK 2003, 83). This is surely not the place to discuss this extensively – but one has to be aware that there has been increasing discussion in other disciplines on the methodological value of null hypothesis significance testing, the convention of the significance level, and p-values (e.g. KIRK 2003; CUMMING 2014; WASSERSTEIN/LAZAR 2016; WINTER 2020, esp. 171–179). Let me name at least a few points of criticism in relation to the present approach. Firstly, it has been argued that using null and alternative hypotheses and rejecting the former according to a fixed (and conventional) threshold leads to dichotomic thinking (cf. KIRK 2003, 87–88; CUMMING 2014, 11). I agree in principle, especially since $\alpha$ is ultimately a matter of convention and thus in some sense arbitrary (cf. KIRK 2003, 88). Therefore, I would prefer – and will try to do to some extent throughout this study – to not regard the p-value as a simple dichotomic value, below or above $\alpha$, but as a *continuous* indicator of *how far* a given distribu-

Likewise, the *higher* the $p$-value gets, the less we can distinguish a given distribution from a random distribution. To explain this more vividly, let us say we find a certain concept c 28 times in S1–8. Now imagine that we build a dartboard with nine sections that differ in their relative size according to the size of the sections of the *Parmenides*. Imagine furthermore that a chimpanzee is given 28 darts to throw them randomly at this dartboard (and is supplied over and over with each dart that misses the board until it sticks). According to the different sizes of the nine sections, many more darts will end up, say, in S2 than in any other section. In the same sense, more will end up in, say, S5 than in S8. Were it close to perfect randomness, we would get from our chimpanzee for 28 occurrences a distribution of 4 (S1); 14 (S2); 1 (S2C); 2 (S3); 1 (S4); 3 (S5); 1 (S6); 1 (S7); 1 (S8).[20] Now the *given* distribution of c's 28 instances in the text is compared to such a perfectly random distribution, and, roughly speaking, it is then calculated how (un)likely it is that c's given distribution results from such a random spreading. This is (mediately) expressed by the $p$-value. If we find in the text, say, a distribution $c_1$ with 3 (S1); 10 (S2); 2 (S2C); 3 (S3); 1 (S4); 4 (S5); 0 (S6); 5 (S7); 0 (S8), we can calculate that this does not differ sufficiently from the random distribution to consider it securely as non-random since the exact $p$-value is $p = 0.134$ and

---

tion is away from a distribution that is not distinguishable from a mere random distribution. I therefore always provide the exact $p$-value instead of only stating whether or not $p < a$ is the case. Besides that, we will have DP (see below) as an additional indicator of how distinct a certain pattern is. Secondly, the objection was made that a rejection of the null hypothesis "doesn't allow any direct conclusions about the alternative hypothesis" (WINTER 2020, 171). As far as I can see, this is not correct in those cases where the null and the alternative hypothesis are *contradictory*. For in this case one of them must be true and the rejection of the null thus implies the correctness of the alternative hypothesis. In the present case, one has good reasons, I think, to regard random vs. non-random (or: not distinguishable from random distribution vs. non-random distribution) as a suitable contradictory pair. Thirdly, it was objected that a common significance level of $a = 0.05$ only "ensures that you make correct decisions 95 % of the time in the long run" (WINTER 2020, 171) and hence no strict certainty is reached (with $a = 0.01$ it is 99 % of the time). Again, this is true. However, with regard to the present case, it is still *relatively much more* objective to have such an objective value than – as it is commonly done when interpreting texts (cf. p. 25 for a general example) – to simply rely on one's gut feeling whether or not a certain pattern or clustering of a term is worth an interpretation. Fourthly, it has been shown that very strong variations and oscillation in $p$-values are possible with regard to sample sizes and replication (cf. CUMMING 2014, 12–13). This point does obviously not apply to the present approach since I draw no samples, but deal with the complete population.

[20] These are of course rounded values. The exact $p$-value of this distribution is $p = 0.990$. 'Perfect randomness' means in this case: the more often we let our chimpanzee throw those 28 darts on the board, the closer the average result comes to 4.42 (S1); 13.64 (S2); 1.46 (S2C); 1.88 (S3); 1.03 (S4); 2.74 (S5); 0.90 (S6); 1.40 (S7); 0.59 (S8). In order to avoid a possible bias, one could also have a large group of chimpanzees perform the experiment.

0.134 > 0.01 (i.e. $p > a$). In other words: from a statistical point of view, we could still not distinguish Plato's distribution $c_1$ with sufficient certainty from a chimpanzee that just randomly scatters these 28 occurrences across the sections. But if we find a concept distributed, for instance, in the following way: 1 (S1); 9 (S2); 0 (S2C); 1 (S3); 1 (S4); 8 (S5); 1 (S6); 7 (S7); 0 (S8), we can regard this distribution $c_2$ as non-random with enough confidence since the exact $p$-value of this distribution is $p = 0.000273$ and hence $p < a$. In general, calculating the $p$-value thus allows us to objectively evaluate how (un)likely it is that we wrongfully consider a given distribution as non-random. This is motivated by the following: we might, by intuition, judge perhaps correctly without calculation that a distribution like the one resulting from our chimpanzee above is not distinguishable from a random distribution. And we will probably also judge correctly by intuition that, if all 28 occurrences were to be found in S8, for sure this can be no random result. But things become much more difficult when in-between cases are concerned, as, for instance, with the distributions $c_1$ and $c_2$. This is the reason why the $p$-value is helpful.

The given distribution of a concept in Plato's text is thus tested against the case that someone like our chimpanzee had simply randomly scattered the same number of occurrences across S1–8.[21] The *less* a given distribution differs from this random distribution (and accordingly the *higher* $p$ gets), the more insignificant it is in that sense. In fact, we find a near perfect example of this distribution with regard to the particle μέν ($p = 0.985$). Plato's distribution of μέν – which supposedly does not follow any intentional pattern – is thus not in the least distinguishable from a random distribution.[22] Likewise, the *more* a given distribution differs from the random distribution (and accordingly the *lower* $p$ gets), the more significant it is in that sense.

---

[21]  To explain this once again in other, more exact terms: the $p$-value indicates how likely it is that we fail in regarding a given pattern as non-random, while it is *in fact* a random result. For instance, if we get $p = 0.001$, this means that we would fail in only 1 of 1,000 cases. Accordingly, if we have, say, $p = 0.1e–05$, it means that we would fail in only 1 of 1,000,000 cases. Note that the standard statistical procedure with $a = 0.05$ (which is still commonly employed in the majority of scientific studies with statistical evaluations) regards it already as sufficiently secure if we only fail in less than 1 of 20 (!) cases. Note furthermore that the $p$-value does not, as such, express the likelihood that a given distribution is produced by random chance (cf. WASSERSTEIN/LAZAR 2016, 131).

[22]  Cf. § 4 below for further details on the particles. Another interesting example is the quantitative distribution of Aristotle's hesitations throughout the sections that DORTER 1994, 50 presents (following BRUMBAUGH 1961, 14). Their distribution is not distinguishable from a random distribution ($p = 0.285$). This is no definite proof that these hesitations' distribution *is* insignificant, but the statistical consideration (not implemented by K. DORTER) objectively supports his claim that "[t]here is no conspicuous pattern" (IBID.).

|        | S1    | S2    | S2C   | S3    | S4    | S5    | S6    | S7    | S8    | $p$       | DP    |
|--------|-------|-------|-------|-------|-------|-------|-------|-------|-------|-----------|-------|
| μέν    | 15    | 44    | 4     | 6     | 4     | 7     | 1     | 5     | 1     | 0.985     | 0.054 |
|        | 0.926 | 0.880 | 0.753 | 0.872 | 1.055 | 0.698 | 0.305 | 0.973 | 0.472 |           |       |
| $c_1$  | 3     | 10    | 2     | 3     | 1     | 4     | 0     | 5     | 0     | 0.134     | 0.239 |
|        | 0.185 | 0.200 | 0.377 | 0.436 | 0.264 | 0.399 | 0.000 | 0.973 | 0.000 |           |       |
| $c_2$  | 1     | 9     | 0     | 1     | 1     | 8     | 1     | 7     | 0     | 2.73e-04  | 0.400 |
|        | 0.062 | 0.180 | 0.000 | 0.145 | 0.264 | 0.798 | 0.305 | 1.362 | 0.000 |           |       |

T.2.1 SOME EXAMPLES

Since the conceptual patterns are more easily graspable in a graphical way, a plot of the relative and absolute occurrences is provided. The plots for the relative counts have filled bars and are marked with the letter 'A'; the absolute counts are displayed by outlined bars and are marked with 'B'. Let us compare in that sense the two exemplary distributions $c_1$, $c_2$, and the pattern of μέν.[23] The results are given in table T.2.1 and diagrams D.2.1A–3B (p. 24). These examples allow of further remarks to get more familiar with these diagrams and the method. D.2.1A shows vividly how a nearly perfectly random distribution results in a balanced overall picture of the bars (especially when compared to the patterns we shall find later). Looking at D.2.2A, we can see how tempting it might be to latch a more detailed and far-reaching interpretation onto $c_1$'s remarkable peak in S7. However, the $p$-value (0.134) deters us from ascribing any significance to this pattern and its single peak. But in D.2.3A the situation is different. If we are able to find a plausible interpretation for the peaks in S5 and S7, this interpretation would rest on firm statistical ground, since $c_2$'s distribution is objectively proven to be non-random by its low $p$-value (0.000273).[24]

To those not very familiar or comfortable with statistics, all this basically means the following: all one needs to do is to intuitively approach the bar charts (especially the relative A-charts with the filled bars), but it is crucial to check the related $p$-value beforehand in order not to base any far-reaching interpretation on what is ultimately not distinguishable from mere accident. Hence, as I promised in the introduction, all boils down to two questions: is the $p$-value of a given distribution low enough, i.e. is it below 0.1?[25] And if so, are there any peculiarities observable in the bar charts that allow of a plausible systematic interpretation?

[23] In this example there is no differentiation between positive and negative occurrences.
[24] Note also how furthermore DP (an additional measure that will be introduced below) increases distinctly through these three examples.
[25] In a more comparative sense (cf. p. 20 n. 19), one may also ask *how* low the $p$-value is.

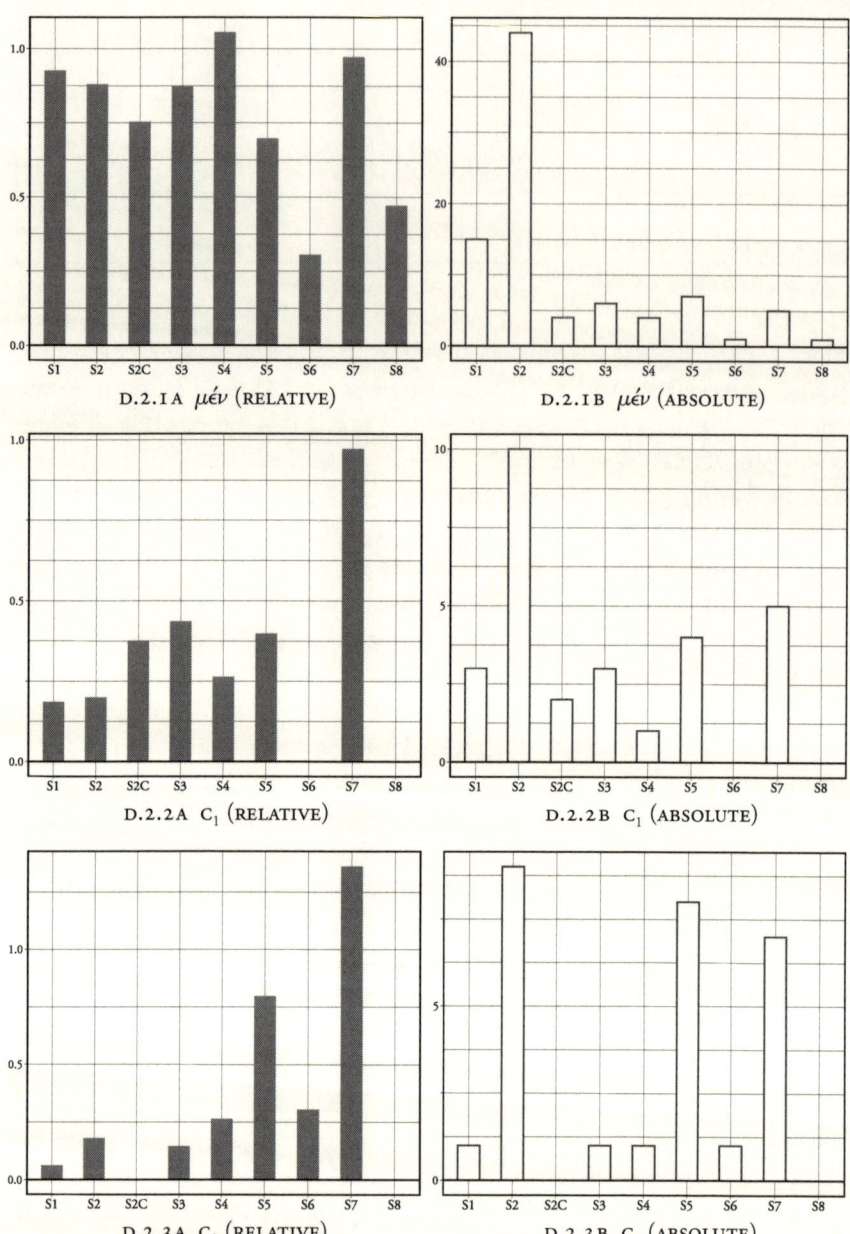

D.2.1A $μέν$ (RELATIVE)

D.2.1B $μέν$ (ABSOLUTE)

D.2.2A $C_1$ (RELATIVE)

D.2.2B $C_1$ (ABSOLUTE)

D.2.3A $C_2$ (RELATIVE)

D.2.3B $C_2$ (ABSOLUTE)

Let us note one more important thing: by evaluating also the *relative* number of occurrences and by integrating different probabilities for each section when calculating the *p*-value, we include the individual length of each section in the evaluation of each distribution. The investigation thus takes into account the fact that Parmenides shortens his explanations in the later sections. This implies in turn that if we still find a significant distribution, this fact cannot be discounted by pointing to the abridgments in the later sections. For these reasons, the diagrams with the relative counts (the A-charts) are thus decisively more valuable and sounder than the ones with absolute counts (the B-charts).

One possible misunderstanding needs to be addressed right away. Of course, I do not claim that Plato himself made any of these statistical considerations when composing the *Parmenides*. Neither do I claim that he intended his readers to approach the dialogue in this manner. However, it is still perfectly possible to grasp some truth of the text itself by applying contemporary scientific methods. Similarly, it is for instance obviously possible to properly apply modern statistical (and other) means to an undeciphered ancient script, such as the Indus script,[26] without presupposing that the ancients themselves thought about their script in this way or intended its readers to do so. However, this does not exclude that we could in principle arrive at some truth about this script by help of these modern methods.[27] In a sense, the present method is thus an objective version of a hermeneutical praxis that we very commonly apply when interpreting texts (philosophical or other). Quite often we state something like 'This concept c occurs x times in this passage – this must be significant and may hence serve as a basis for how to interpret this passage!'. However, strictly speaking, such a statement is incomplete as long as one does not properly test whether this frequency differs sufficiently from the frequency in other passages[28] to exclude a random concentration of c in the passage in question. In that sense, the present method is much closer to our common approaches than it might seem at first glance.

To state in more technical terms what has been said so far and with regard to the exact statistical details: the null hypothesis $h_0$ consists in a perfectly random distribution of each concept c and its given count $n_{total} = n_{S1} + n_{S2} + \ldots + n_{S8}$. The alternative hypothesis $h_1$ is non-directional and proposes a non-random distribution of c.

[26] Cf. e.g. PARPOLA ³2009, 99–101.

[27] To a large extent this is in accordance with an important hermeneutical distinction between what V. HÖSLE calls 'noematic' and 'noetic understanding' (cf. HÖSLE 2018, esp. 159–179). The former concentrates on the object of thought *in itself*, while the latter refers to a certain subject's (mental) grasp of and intention towards this object.

[28] Admittedly, it is usually much more difficult to objectively divide a text into sections than it is in the case of the *Parmenides*. However, this is still no objection to the present argument (cf. p. 135 n. 1).

A non-random distribution is regarded as (potentially)[29] intentional. The probabilities $p_{S1\ldots8}$ for S1–8 result from their size $w_{SX}$ in relation to the total word-count $w_{total}$, which means that $p_{SX} = w_{SX} / w_{total}$. We thus get $p_{S1} = 0.158$; $p_{S2} = 0.487$; $p_{S2C} = 0.052$; $p_{S3} = 0.067$; $p_{S4} = 0.037$; $p_{S5} = 0.098$; $p_{S6} = 0.032$; $p_{S7} = 0.050$; $p_{S8} = 0.021$. The significance level is set to a strict level of $\alpha = 0.01$ (= 1.0 %). Then the probability $P_c$ of a given distribution $n_{S1}$, $n_{S2}$, ..., $n_{S8}$ of c with a total count of $n_{total}$ is calculated according to the standard formula of multinomial probabilities:

$$P_c = \frac{n_{total}!}{n_{S1}! \times n_{S2}! \times \ldots \times n_{S8}!} \times p_{S1}{}^{n_{S1}} \times p_{S2}{}^{n_{S2}} \times \ldots \times p_{S8}{}^{n_{S8}}$$

All probabilities that are lower than or equal to the given one (i.e. all probabilities of those distributions of $n_{total}$ in S1–8 that differ equally or more significantly from the random distribution) are summed up. The $p$-value resulting from this is compared to $\alpha$ in order to determine whether or not we are allowed to refuse $h_0$ in favour of $h_1$. This exact multinomial test is implemented in R by using the package 'XNomial' by B. Engels.[30]

Additionally, a measure of dispersion is provided in order to objectively grasp how diverse and scattered a given distribution actually is. This measure, DP, was developed by S. Th. Gries for corpus linguistics and has been adapted to the present task.[31] DP always attains a value between 1.0 and approximately 0.0, thereby expressing numerically how much a given distribution differs from the expected distribution (based on the different sizes of the

---

[29] I add 'potentially' since this still depends to some extent on the question whether or not we are able to ascribe, in our interpretation, any meaningful systematic intention to a given distribution whose $p$-value is low enough. In that sense, one has to keep in mind that a certain pattern may be the result of a *direct* intention or only *mediately*. For the latter case, one could imagine for instance that Plato intended to use a certain concept $c_1$ and a (non-random) pattern of a concept $c_2$ may only be the mediate result of that direct intention since e.g. $c_2$ often comes along with $c_1$ or since $c_2$ occurs in the logical deduction that follows the treatment of $c_1$. But in any case – direct or indirect intention – using the described method helps not to draw on distributions that are not distinguishable from random distributions.

[30] Cf. R Core Team 2020 for R and Engels 2015 for the package 'XNomial'. This very helpful package permits calculating the exact multinomial $p$-value as well as two further tests, a log-likelihood-ratio and a classic $\chi^2$-test. Throughout this study, the function 'xmulti()' in Engels 2015 is used unless otherwise stated. The bar plots are done with 'ggplot2' in R, cf. Wickham 2016.

[31] Cf. Gries 2008; Gries 2010; Lijffijt/Gries 2012. The abbreviation 'DP' stands for 'deviation of proportions'. In order make it fitting for our purposes here, I treat the single sections of Parmenides' exercise as corpus parts.

sections).[32] DP may therefore be regarded as a kind of objective measure of how marked and diverse a given distribution is. DP ranges from completely evenly distributed (0.0) to the opposite (1.0).[33] As a rule of thumb: the more a given distribution diverges from the random distribution and the more the occurrences are concentrated in only some (or even only one) section(s), especially the small ones, the higher DP gets. DP is calculated in the following way, taking into account the word counts of each section ($w_{S1\dots S8}$, $w_{total}$) and the occurrences of the concept in question ($n_{S1\dots S8}$, $n_{total}$).[34]

$$DP_{norm} = \frac{\dfrac{1}{2} \sum\limits_{i=1}^{8} \left| \dfrac{w_{Si}}{w_{total}} - \dfrac{n_{Si}}{n_{total}} \right|}{1 - \dfrac{w_{S8}}{w_{total}}}$$

Finally, two more general comments on the present approach. Firstly, in dealing with different concepts and their distributions in S1–8, I am not engaging in evaluating the specific quality of the arguments in which they are involved. A careful examination of these is definitely a necessary step, but it is a later step of my approach.[35] It is therefore beyond the scope of the present study since it would ultimately imply a line-by-line approach to the exercise. In that sense, what I am trying to figure out is whether or not Parmenides is trying to *circumscribe* a kind of systematic structure or entity with his arguments, and if so what kind, regardless of whether those arguments are all ultimately sound or not. And secondly, since I am dealing with the 'bigger picture' of the dialogue's second part in total, one can obviously create objections regarding single lines or statements in this second part; I am well aware of that.[36] However, within a study of the present scope it simply is neither

---

[32] To provide an example: the pattern of μέν (which comes very close to a pure random distribution) has a very low DP-value of 0.054 while the very distinct pattern of the field of appearance has a very high DP-value of 0.877 for its positive occurrences. Cf. §§ 4–5; 7 for these two patterns respectively.

[33] Cf. LIJFFIJT/GRIES 2012, 147.

[34] Cf. LIJFFIJT/GRIES 2012, 148. I use the normalised form ($DP_{norm}$); for brevity's sake I do not add the index.

[35] Cf. the outlook in chapter 7.

[36] To name one instance: one could perhaps argue that 162d1–5 (the non-being One does not rotate) contradicts the claim in §§ 12–13; 16 that S5 ultimately may be understood as dealing with the World Soul, since the World Soul – as TIM. 36c2–d7 describes it – is rotating. One way of countering this, I think, would be to point out that S5 describes this entity solely in itself (§§ 12–13) while the rotation in the *Timaeus* is obviously closely linked to the physical cosmos (TIM. 36e2–5).

possible to anticipate every single objection of this kind nor to deal with all of them. What I am proposing is a *general* account for understanding S1–8 in total that finds, as I shall argue in chapters 3 and 5, decisive support in conceptual patterns and further evidence. And, as will be discussed in chapter 6, it shows a way in which Parmenides' exercise actually helps to counter the objections which he raises in the first part of the dialogue.

## § 3. Previous Research

As far as I can see, the statistical method just described has never been implemented so far in any research on the *Parmenides*.[37] There is, however, one example of a statistical approach to this dialogue. In the late 1970's and 80's, L. Brisson, in cooperation with J. Meunier, S. Lusignan, and J.-P. Benzécri, published a series of articles which employ statistical methods to approach specific aspects of the second part of this dialogue.[38] Two of them, Brisson ([2]1977) and Brisson/Benzécri (1989), are more or less exclusively concerned with the status of S2C. In addition to that, the latter article contains some more general observations. The claim of Brisson ([2]1977) is that S2C should not be understood as a separate section in its own right.[39] The main statistical arguments for this will be discussed in § 17. Brisson/Benzécri (1989) argue for the same claim, though this time based mainly on an analysis of correspondences. Brisson (1978) concentrates solely on the distribution of negations to which I shall pay no special attention in this study. Brisson (1984) is exclusively concerned with the answers of young Aristotle, which will not be taken into account either in my approach (neither did L. Brisson in his other articles). These works are without any doubt pioneering with regard to the method they employ. However, they – and especially the initial article – do not seem to have received the atten-

---

[37] There have been, of course, stylometric studies, such as Lutosławski 1897, 64–193, including *inter alia* the *Parmenides* (cf. also Dorter 1994, 5–9), but these are quite different with regard to their method and their goals. Brandwood 1992 provides a good overview of these studies. For a recent study in stichometry cf. e.g. Kennedy 2010 (but cf. also p. 20 n. 18 above).

[38] Cf. Brisson [2]1977; Brisson 1978; Brisson 1984; Brisson/Benzécri 1989. The theoretical basis is, among others, Muller 1973. According to Brisson [2]1977, 22 n. 1; Brisson 1978, 58 n. 1; Brisson 1984, 67 n. 3 the informatics of the first three papers was done by J. Meunier and S. Lusignan, while L. Brisson was responsible for the interpretation of the statistical results. According to Brisson/Benzécri 1989, 125 the work of Meunier/Lusignan in informatics partly formed the basis of the fourth article.

[39] Cf. Brisson [2]1977, 19; 22.

tion they deserved in major studies on the *Parmenides*.[40] The present approach – and its results as we shall see – differs from these studies in several crucial aspects. Of course, I do not thereby deny that both approaches are feasible. Firstly, my approach combines quantitative aspects with *qualitative* aspects, while L. BRISSON's approach remains solely quantitative. These qualitative evaluations cannot be done within the framework of a purely automatic and quantitative approach, but they will provide important results. Secondly, I evaluate the concepts with regard to their further *systematic usage* and especially their *ontological significance* in Plato, while L. BRISSON pays less attention to those aspects and makes little to no comparison to Plato's vocabulary in the other dialogues or the first part of the *Parmenides*. This is perfectly consistent with his purely quantitative approach and it ultimately also fits the fact that he regards the second part of the *Parmenides* as describing the position of the historical Parmenides in his later studies.[41] Thirdly, I concentrate primarily on a selected list of *nouns and verbs* with regard to their systematic significance, while particles, pronouns, and very common verbs (such as λέγω) play a much smaller role in my approach than they do in L. BRISSON's, where they actually form the focus. Fourthly, I do not confine myself to concepts that appear either in *all* sections or in *one* exclusively, as I. BRISSON does, but by investigating the characteristic distributions of certain concepts, I also pay particular attention to terms that occur in *some* of them, i.e. in certain *groups* of sections.[42] Fifthly, I pay greater attention to some nouns and expressions that occur *seldom or only once*. This is to analyse whether these terms fit or contradict the bigger picture of the conceptual patterns. Ultimately, I calculate the *exact p*-values of the multinomial distributions, which was virtually impossible forty years ago due to technical limitations. It will duly be noted, where my findings agree with or contradict L. BRISSON's statistical results or their interpretation. Besides his work, there have been, to the best of my knowledge, no similar approaches.

---

[40] If one takes a look at a range of monographs on the *Parmenides* since then – ALLEN [2]1997, HÄGLER 1983; MILLER 1986; MEINWALD 1991; HALFWASSEN [2]2006; DORTER 1994; VON KUTSCHERA 1995; GILL 1996; SAYRE 1996; SÉGUY-DUCLOT 1998; TURNBULL 1998; COXON 1999; SCHUDOMA 2001; GRAESER 2003; SCOLNICOV 2003; FERRARI [8]2019; RICKLESS 2007; SANDAY 2015; TABAK 2015; PRIOU 2018 –, none of them even mentions this approach and its method. Rare exceptions are e.g. MIGLIORI 1990 who refers to BRISSON 1978 (on the negations), PALMER 1999 (who IBID., 157 N. 24 refers to, among others, BRISSON/BENZÉCRI 1989, but as "detailed analys[is] of the plan of the dialectical exercise"), and FRONTEROTTA 1998 who refers to all four works mentioned above.

[41] Cf. e.g. BRISSON 2002. Cf. also O'BRIEN 2005B and BRISSON 2005.

[42] BRISSON/BENZÉCRI 1989 pay some attention to groups of sections, but again only with regard to those concepts that appear in all sections (IBID., 119; 123).

In general, there has been of course intensive research on the *Parmenides*, both with regard to the second part of the dialogue and the aporias in the first part, especially the so-called 'Third Man Arguments' (and among these especially the first one). Famously, the interpretations of the second part are more divergent than in the case of any other of Plato's dialogues. They range from regarding the second part as a mere joke or parody (e.g. BURNET 1914; TAYLOR 1934) to considering it the most valuable document of Plato's metaphysics, the most explicit exhibition of his Theory of Principles in the written corpus (e.g. HALFWASSEN ²2006). Between those, various intermediate positions propose different scopes and contents for the second part, including – to name just a few – a propaedeutic logical exercise in argumentation but without any positive doctrine (ROBINSON ²1953); an introduction of a powerful mereological logic (VON KUTSCHERA 1995); the differentiation of two types of predication (MEINWALD 1991); an exposition of Plato's ontology (CORNFORD 1939; SCOLNICOV 2003). This implies of course that combinations of different aspects and features are possible.[43] There is no need to recapitulate all this in detail since this has been done several times in the literature.[44]

In the outcome of the first and the second main step, the present study will share some features with those studies that see a positive systematic content in the second part of the dialogue, especially with regard to ontology and the Theory of Principles. However, my arguments are very different from theirs and I must confess that my sympathetic consent with some results as such and my assessment of the arguments that lead to them does not always coincide.[45] Hence, the present study does not presuppose any of those results or arguments. Neither does it presuppose any of the ancient approaches or arguments, as will be explained in greater detail in § 13. As has

---

[43] Cf. e.g. the mentioned approach by SCOLNICOV 2003, who locates a negative exposition of Eleatic ontology in S1, S4, S6, and S8, while locating a positive account of Plato's ontology in S2, S3, S5, and S7.

[44] Helpful overviews are provided, for instance, by RUNCIMAN 1959, 104–113; NIEWÖHNER 1971, 71–81; HALFWASSEN ²2006, 265–271; VON KUTSCHERA 1995, 4–12; FRONTEROTTA 1998, 106–122; CORRIGAN 2010, 29–35; FERRARI ⁸2019, 9–18; ERLER 2007, 227–229.

[45] Cf. e.g. WUNDT 1935. I ultimately agree, for instance, with his result (IBID., 53–55) that the sensible realm is discussed in S7. However, after only one and a half page of argument (which deal mainly with Plato's concept of αἴσθησις in general and provide a paraphrase of S7's text), I consider it anything but obvious that the sensible realm is "in diesem Abschnitt [S7] des Parmenides in einer höchst geistreichen *und nicht mißzudeutenden Weise* geschildert" (IBID., 54; emph. mine). Besides that, M. WUNDT is wrong in my eyes in supposing that S7 deals with the same subject as S3 (IBID., 53), though some of his observations on mereological aspects are helpful. Ultimately, M. WUNDT shares the main flaw of virtually all Neoplatonic approaches by trying to find a proper single subject for *every* section.

been outlined in the introduction, this study will advocate that Parmenides addresses multiple subjects throughout his exercise – in fact, this is one of the results that most strongly suggests itself based on the conceptual patterns. Of course, there have been approaches that contradict such a multiple-subject approach (ALLEN ²1997; MEINWALD 1991). I shall deal with these in § 10.

The concluding third main step of this study will exemplarily address two of Parmenides' objections in the first part of the dialogue, the 'Third Man Argument' and the 'Greatest Aporia'. As my interpretation in the third main step remains based on the conceptual patterns, my approach is quite different from what is to be found in the literature so far on these problems. With regard to the terminology employed in the 'Third Man Argument', my approach shares some features with observations made by PENNER (1987). It will duly be noted whenever I draw on previous research within the third main step of this study.

# 3. GENERAL EVIDENCE

In this chapter, I shall discuss evidence which I consider fairly uncontroversial with regard to the statistical results. Hence, I shall not give these results a further systematic, more specified interpretation. This will be done in chapter 5. The present chapter begins with a preliminary step, which discusses particles as a 'negative' control group for the approach as a whole (§ 4). I shall then provide an extensive analysis of three important patterns regarding Plato's general ontological distinction, i.e. being, becoming/passing away, and appearance (§ 5). This is supplemented by further remarks on the relation between S2C and S5 (§ 6) and on S7 (§ 7). Furthermore, I present a general observation on rare terms (§ 8) as well as one on the positive and negative distributions within the conceptual patterns (§ 9). Ultimately, the question of multiple subjects is discussed (§ 10) and some general remarks are given to conclude this chapter (§ 11). At the beginning of each paragraph, the first sentence (in italics) summarises its main claims and observations.

## § 4. Particles as a Control Group

*One can definitely state that there* are *conceptual patterns to be found in* S1–8 *and that the distribution of a range of particles forms a helpful control group for the present approach.* To state the most general result in the very beginning: as will be shown in detail in the next paragraphs of chapter 3 and in chapter 5, there is in fact a great number of conceptual patterns observable that show low or very low $p$-values, which means that in all likelihood these distributions are non-random. One good example of this are the patterns of motion and rest, which have very low $p$-values and which form clear, meaningful patterns that will be examined more closely in § 16. On the other hand, it is remarkable that a number of particles shows a very high or a comparably

| | S1 | S2 | S2C | S3 | S4 | S5 | S6 | S7 | S8 | p | DP |
|---|---|---|---|---|---|---|---|---|---|---|---|
| μέν | 15 | 44 | 4 | 6 | 4 | 7 | 1 | 5 | 1 | 0.985 | 0.054 |
| | 0.926 | 0.880 | 0.753 | 0.872 | 1.055 | 0.698 | 0.305 | 0.973 | 0.472 | | |
| δέ | 30 | 117 | 9 | 15 | 7 | 24 | 8 | 11 | 2 | 0.888 | 0.053 |
| | 1.853 | 2.341 | 1.695 | 2.180 | 1.847 | 2.393 | 2.439 | 2.140 | 0.943 | | |
| ἄν | 47 | 115 | 9 | 17 | 7 | 25 | 7 | 9 | 3 | 0.793 | 0.051 |
| | 2.903 | 2.301 | 1.695 | 2.471 | 1.847 | 2.493 | 2.134 | 1.751 | 1.415 | | |
| οὖν | 6 | 27 | 4 | 1 | 1 | 3 | 1 | 1 | 0 | 0.778 | 0.170 |
| | 0.371 | 0.540 | 0.753 | 0.145 | 0.264 | 0.299 | 0.305 | 0.195 | 0.000 | | |
| γε | 29 | 49 | 5 | 13 | 3 | 14 | 4 | 7 | 3 | 0.227 | 0.129 |
| | 1.791 | 0.980 | 0.942 | 1.890 | 0.792 | 1.396 | 1.220 | 1.362 | 1.415 | | |
| γάρ | 10 | 32 | 5 | 9 | 5 | 11 | 3 | 6 | 4 | 0.136 | 0.153 |
| | 0.618 | 0.640 | 0.942 | 1.308 | 1.319 | 1.097 | 0.915 | 1.167 | 1.887 | | |
| μήν | 22 | 26 | 2 | 5 | 1 | 10 | 3 | 2 | 2 | 0.0487 | 0.205 |
| | 1.359 | 0.520 | 0.377 | 0.727 | 0.264 | 0.997 | 0.915 | 0.389 | 0.943 | | |
| δή | 5 | 26 | 7 | 7 | 1 | 7 | 3 | 8 | 1 | 0.0242 | 0.198 |
| | 0.309 | 0.520 | 1.318 | 1.017 | 0.264 | 0.698 | 0.915 | 1.556 | 0.472 | | |

T.4.1 PARTICLES (PART I)

high $p$-value, such as μέν, δέ, ἄν, οὖν and γε, γάρ, μήν, δή respectively.[1] For each of them the absolute and relative count as well as the related $p$-value are given in T.4.1. This of course does not include a qualitative evaluation of these particles since they are neither affirmed nor negated, and hence their occurrences are only counted as such. The distributions of these particles are graphically displayed in D.4.1A–8A (pp. 34–35). Since for these balanced distributions the relative A-charts are much more informative than the absolute B-charts, only the former are provided here.

The high $p$-values of these particles are notable for two reasons. Firstly, these particles occur in great number and hence their distributions are very adequately addressable by statistical means. Secondly, these particles provide a negative countercheck since it can reasonably be assumed that Plato did not intentionally distribute these particles in some specific way throughout the sections, which would be detectable through meaningful patterns and low $p$-values. If we look, for instance, at D.4.1A and D.4.2A, we can see how the occurrences of the common particles μέν and δέ appear in a very

---

[1] The $p$-values of these distributions are calculated by using 'xmonte()' in ENGELS 2015 (run with 1e+08 trials). Further particles (and similar common words) with high or comparably high $p$-values are e.g. αὖ ($p$ = 0.970), ὅτι ($p$ = 0.990), κατά ($p$ = 0.346), οὐ ($p$ = 0.208), μήτε ($p$ = 0.189), and ἀλλά ($p$ = 0.017). Cf. also APPENDIX C.

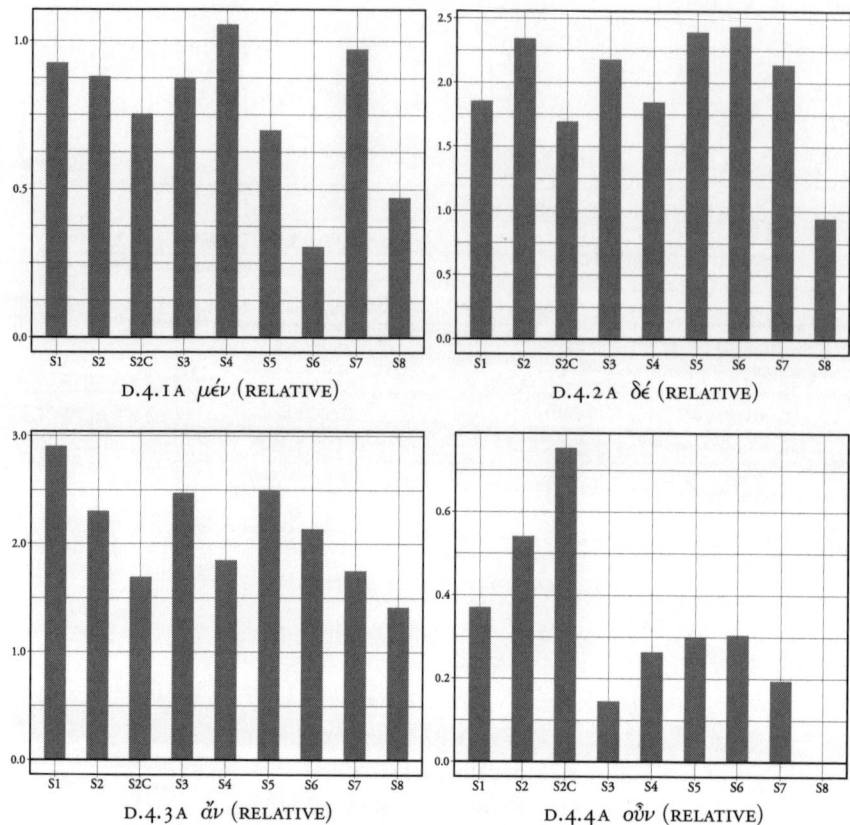

D.4.1A μέν (RELATIVE)

D.4.2A δέ (RELATIVE)

D.4.3A ἄν (RELATIVE)

D.4.4A οὖν (RELATIVE)

balanced manner throughout all sections. (In fact, once further conceptual patterns have been introduced in the subsequent paragraphs, it will become even more obvious *how* balanced and equalised these patterns are. Also note the very low DP-values in this respect.) Their very high *p*-values prove that these patterns are not in any way distinguishable from a random spreading. And since we do not suppose that Plato placed these particles intentionally with regard to the sections – they more or less simply 'come along' with writing a Greek text –, these *p*-values tie in quite perfectly with the present approach. For they prove that there *are* in fact some terms in the *Parmenides* that are distributed in ways undistinguishable from a random distribution and are so for quite plausible reasons. These patterns are clearly identifiable by their (high) *p*-values and by their characteristic A-charts. Since for that reason not every concept provides a significant, non-random pattern, there is a proven possibility of negative evidence and hence a concrete possibility of falsification. And this negative evidence occurs in those cases, i.e. the

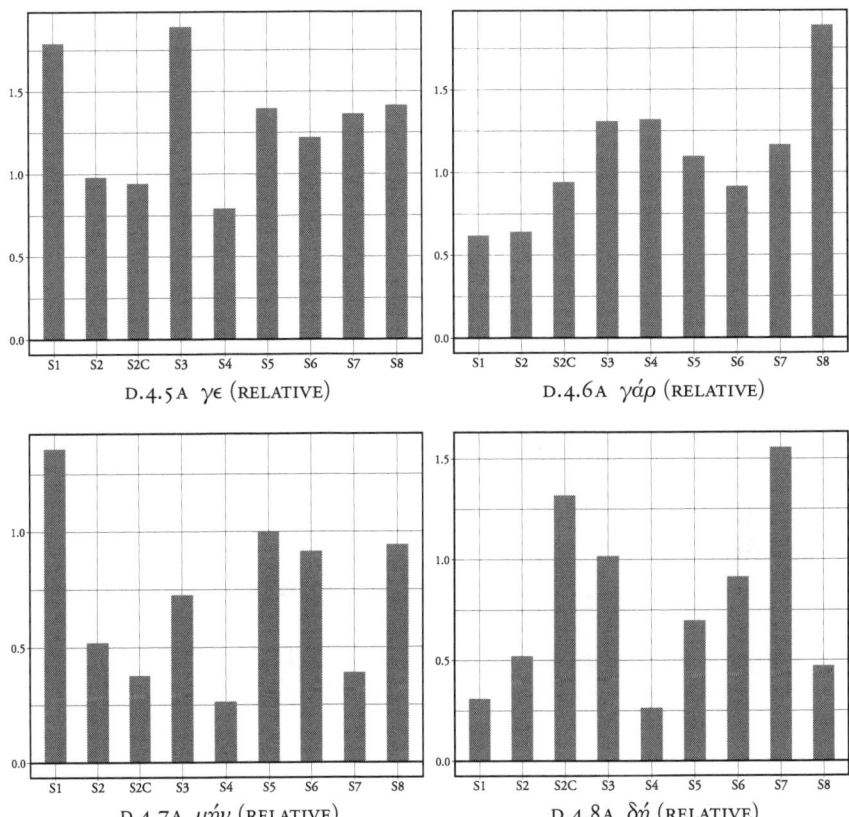

D.4.5A γε (RELATIVE)

D.4.6A γάρ (RELATIVE)

D.4.7A μήν (RELATIVE)

D.4.8A δή (RELATIVE)

particles, where it is plausible. The indicated particles thus form a valuable control group for the significant patterns to be discussed in the following paragraphs of chapter 3 and those in chapter 5.

There are however particles (and similar common words) with quite low or very low p-values, such as for instance οὔτε, μή, καί, and τε.[2] Their absolute and relative counts as well as the related p-values are given in T.4.2 (p. 36). Their relative A-charts are provided in D.4.9A–12A (p. 37). But since their non-random status is explainable, these patterns also lend additional support to the present approach. Οὔτε has significantly more occurrences in S1, S4, S6, and S8 and this fits the negative character of these sections perfectly.[3]

---

[2] Further examples of this would be e.g. ἄρα (p = 6.742e-04) and οὐδέ (p < 1.000e-08). Cf. also APPENDIX C.

[3] Cf. § 9 for a further and more detailed characterisation of the sections as such. In the case of the particles it is quite helpful to note how much the occurrences differ from the perfectly average share that would result from a perfectly random distribution. For οὔτε this is

|  | S1 | S2 | S2C | S3 | S4 | S5 | S6 | S7 | S8 | p | DP |
|---|---|---|---|---|---|---|---|---|---|---|---|
| οὔτε | 73 | 63 | 21 | 1 | 13 | 6 | 18 | 3 | 6 | < 1.0e–08 | 0.351 |
|  | 4.509 | 1.261 | 3.955 | 0.145 | 3.430 | 0.598 | 5.488 | 0.584 | 2.830 |  |  |
| μή | 11 | 45 | 6 | 4 | 1 | 54 | 13 | 10 | 11 | < 1.0e–08 | 0.375 |
|  | 0.679 | 0.900 | 1.130 | 0.581 | 0.264 | 5.384 | 3.963 | 1.946 | 5.189 |  |  |
| καί | 54 | 285 | 43 | 38 | 14 | 53 | 3 | 38 | 2 | 2.0e–08 | 0.112 |
|  | 3.335 | 5.702 | 8.098 | 5.523 | 3.694 | 5.284 | 0.915 | 7.393 | 0.943 |  |  |
| τε | 9 | 76 | 17 | 14 | 3 | 13 | 1 | 8 | 0 | 1.8e–04 | 0.164 |
|  | 0.556 | 1.521 | 3.202 | 2.035 | 0.792 | 1.296 | 0.305 | 1.556 | 0.000 |  |  |

T.4.2 PARTICLES (PART 2)

Besides that, the strong presence of οὔτε in the 'positive' section S2C is remarkable, though also in this case an explanation is probably available.[4] This means that we actually find a significant pattern with regard to οὔτε, which is proven to be non-random by the related $p$-value, and we can find a plausible explanation for this pattern. Of course, we might furthermore discuss whether Plato *directly* intended this pattern or whether it is a *mediate* consequence of the hypothesis and the arguments in the respective sections. The latter is definitely more likely, but then again, the pattern would in fact be non-random and, in any case, the given explanation ties in quite well with the negative character of the respective sections. The explanation of this non-random pattern of οὔτε is therefore coherent and plausible.

With regard to μή the A-chart D.4.10A immediately shows a remarkable density in the second half of the exercise (S5–8).[5] In this case, the strong and above-average presence of μή in S5–8 can also conveniently be explained through the inclusion of μή in the hypothesis itself (ἐν εἰ μὴ ἔστι). The pattern of καί ties in perfectly with the 'positive' sections S2, S2C, S3, S5, and S7, where an above-average occurrence of this conjunction is expectable and plausible – especially if we keep in mind that a negative conjunction in the sense of 'neither … nor …' can be formulated by e.g. οὔτε … οὔτε … and

(absolute/relative): +40.8/+2.518 (S1); –36.3/–0.727 (S2); +10.4/+1.957 (S2C); –12.7/–1.841 (S3); +5.7/+1.492 (S4); –14.0/–1.395 (S5); +11.5/+3.498 (S6); 7.2/ 1.401 (S7); +1.9/+0.906 (S8).

[4] This exception is explainable by the fact that S2C might ultimately be regarded as describing a kind of substratum, *in* which things like becoming and passing away happen, while neither becoming nor passing away apply to the substratum *itself*. However, this explanation presupposes a range of further arguments and will hence be touched again in §§ 19; 24–25.

[5] The divergence from a perfectly random distribution of μή is: –13.5/–0.833 (S1); –30.5/–0.610 (S2); –2.1/–0.388 (S2C); –6.4/–0.928 (S3); –4.6/–1.208 (S4); +38.8/+3.869 (S5); +8.0/+2.451 (S6); +2.3/+0.438 (S7); +7.9/+3.726 (S8).

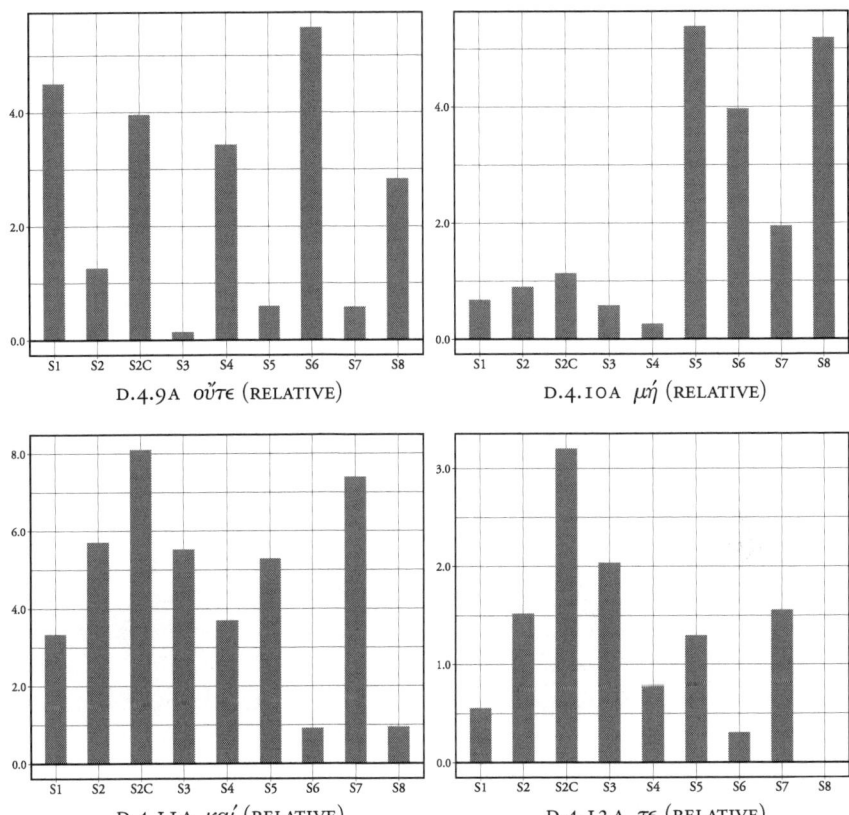

D.4.9A οὔτε (RELATIVE)

D.4.10A μή (RELATIVE)

D.4.11A καί (RELATIVE)

D.4.12A τε (RELATIVE)

hence without any positive conjunction.[6] The same applies to the particle τε, whose occurrences are again concentrated in the 'positive' sections S2, S2C, S3, S5, and S7.[7] Again, their $p$-values prove these patterns to be non-random. And again, we may well be able to find a plausible interpretation of their significance. The overall evidence of these four examples in T.4.2 thus lends further support to the present approach since their patterns are

[6] The divergence of καί is: −29.7/−1.837 (S1); +26.9/+0.538 (S2); +15.4/+2.908 (S2C); +2.5/+0.362 (S3); −5.1/−1.340 (S4); +1.1/0.106 (S5); −14.0/−4.256 (S6); +11.5/+2.237 (S7); −8.6/−4.057 (S8). In the graphical display D.4.11A, the bars of S1 and S4 might seem to be quite high with regard to this pattern − however, the absolute divergence proves that the occurrence of καί is clearly below average in these two sections.

[7] The divergence of τε is: −13.3/−0.820 (S1); +7.3/+0.147 (S2); +9.7/+1.821 (S2C); +4.6/+0.662 (S3); −2.1/−0.548 (S4); −0.8/−0.082 (S5); −3.5/−1.071 (S6); +0.9/+0.185 (S7); −2.8/−1.330 (S8). We may note that in S5 the number of occurrences of τε is slightly below average. However, this slight exception is not at all distinct (−0.8), especially since one has to note that the overall divergence of τε is less significant than in the cases of οὔτε, μή, and καί.

quite certainly non-random *and* a plausible explanation of their significant patterns is at hand.

So much for these rather technical and preliminary issues of the particles. I mainly introduced them to provide a control group since the evidence of these exemplary particles provides in total a valuable countercheck for the approach as a whole. However, since I am concerned with the more systematic concepts, I will not further deepen this investigation of the particles. Instead, I shall now turn to those patterns that provide more systematic insights.

## § 5. Being, Becoming, and Appearance

*There are very clear patterns in S1–8 with regard to the conceptual fields of being, becoming/passing away, and appearance. And, remarkably, their constellation is tripartite, but not bipartite.* There can be no doubt that Plato's general ontological distinction between the realm of forms and the realm of sensible particulars is at stakes in the dialogue's first half. Since the second half claims to somehow deal with these matters, it seems to be promising to look for this distinction first. For these purposes, let only the positive occurrences of the concepts mentioned below be taken into account for the time being.[8] For a general overview of possible patterns, let them be grouped with regard to being, becoming/passing away, and appearance.

Regarding the conceptual field of *being* (in the sense of the forms' eternal and intelligible being), the following concepts are taken into account: ἰδέα, εἶδος, and the famous formula of (αὐτὸ) καθ' αὐτό as well as Plato's well-known specific usage of αὐτός. All these can be found both in the *Parmenides* and in dialogues before and after it to designate the forms.[9]

---

[8] The positive *and* negative occurrences will be taken into account in §§ 6–7.

[9] Before and after the *Parmenides*, we find ἰδέα: PHDO. 104b9; 104d2; REP. 486d10; PHDR. 265d3; SOPH. 253d5; 254a8–9; 255e5; PHLB. 16d1; εἶδος: PHDO. 102b1; REP. 510b8; 511c1–2; SOPH. 255c5; 255d4; 255e1; (αὐτὸ) καθ' αὐτό: e.g. PHDO. 100b6; REP. 476b10; PHLB. 53d3; the specific usage of αὐτός: PHDO. 74a11–12; 74c4–5; 78d3–4; 100c4–5; 102d6; REP. 493e2–3; PLTC. 284d2. Within the *Parmenides* itself, we find ἰδέα: 132a3; 132c4; 133c8; 135a2; 135c1; εἶδος: 129a1; 130b8; 130d1; 131a8; (αὐτὸ) καθ' αὐτό: 128e6–129a1; 130b8; 133a9; 133c4; 135a8–b1; the specific usage of αὐτός: 129b1; 131c12; 132a6; 132a10–11; 134b14. In the present approach, I consider the *Phaedo* and the *Republic* prior to the *Parmenides*, and the *Timaeus*, the *Sophist*, and the *Philebus* posterior to it (the *Phaedrus* may be roughly from the same period as the *Parmenides*). I see definitely no reason for the proposal of OWEN 1953 and SAYRE 1983, 256–267 to date the *Timaeus* before the *Parmenides*. The identification of the late group rests on one of the few objective criteria that we actually have,

Next, οὐσία is included in this field since this concept is also clearly used to denote the realm of forms, both in the *Parmenides* and elsewhere.[10] Besides that, the nominalised forms of τὸ ὄν / τὰ ὄντα and τὸ εἶναι are included. Although Plato uses them in other dialogues to denote the being of the forms or the forms themselves,[11] one can doubt whether he does so in the *Parmenides*.[12] Still, one can heuristically include these terms in this field for two reasons: firstly, these concepts would clearly provide the respective patterns (or distort the results), in case they do *not* tie in with this conceptual field;[13] and secondly, there are some clear heuristic hints that Plato in the second part of the *Parmenides* uses these terms in the supposed sense.[14] For the field of *becoming and passing away*, as Plato introduces it for instance in the standard passages of the *Republic* and the *Phaedo*,[15] the terms γίγνομαι and ἀπόλλυμι are taken into account where they appear in pair.[16] For the

namely the stylometric results and statistics, especially with regard to the avoidance of hiatus in the late group (cf. the arguments by CHERNISS 1957; the overview in DORTER 1994, 7; and the very good remark by HÖSLE 2019, 333 N. 12).

[10] Cf. 133c4; 133c9; 135a8. For the other dialogues prior and after the *Parmenides* cf. e.g. PHDO. 101c3; REP. 479c7; 509b9; 524e1; 525c6; 534a3; PHDR. 247c7; SOPH. 248d2; TIM. 35a1–2; PHLB. 54a8.

[11] τὸ ὄν: PHDO. 78d4; REP. 477b10–11; 478a6–7; 479d5; 486d10; 490a8; 508d5; 511c5; 518c9; 521d4; 525a1; 526e4; 527b5; 537d6; 599a1; PHDR. 248b4; 249c4; TIM. 27d6; SOPH. 254a8; PHLB. 58a2; 59d4. τὰ ὄντα: PHDO. 100a2; PHDR. 247e3; 248a5; 249e5; SOPH. 258e1; PHLB. 59a7. τὸ εἶναι: REP. 478e2 (compare with 478d6–7; 479d4–5); REP. 509b7.

[12] The use of the plural τὰ ὄντα is ambiguous: it refers to the many particulars (135e6), but is also used to express that there are forms *of things* (135a2; 135b6; 135c1). Socrates obviously understands τὰ ὄντα (127e2) as possibly referring also to the forms (since he discusses the problem of being similar and unsimilar, 127e2–4, in this sense in 128e6–129b3 and thus transposes it to the level of forms, cf. 129e5–130a2). In 134a6–7, τὰ ὄντα clearly refers to the level of the forms (as compared to 'our' level in that aporia, 134a8–b1), the same applies to ὄντοιν (129a2). In 133b1, τῶν ὄντων is ambiguous, but, firstly, it could be regarded as a gen. part., and, secondly, 133a8–9 suggests that the forms are meant. For Plato's employment of gen. pl. τῶν ὄντων cf. also CRAT. 440b6. The singular τὸ ὄν is not to be found in the first part of the *Parmenides*. In 136b5–6, αὐτὸ τὸ εἶναι is contrasted with γένεσις καὶ φθορά and thus expresses the meaning of 'being itself' vs. 'becoming/passing away'.

[13] On could also compare the individual distribution of τὸ ὄν / τὰ ὄντα with that of οὐσία to get the same result.

[14] Cf. e.g. how 144e3–4 (τὸ ἓν ... αὐτὸ κεκερματισμένον ὑπὸ τῆς οὐσίας) is clearly parallel to 144e6 (αὐτὸ τὸ ἓν ὑπὸ τοῦ ὄντος διανενεμημένον) and how 142d2–3 (ἥ τε οὐσία καὶ τὸ ἕν) is parallel to 142d5 (τό τε ἓν καὶ τὸ εἶναι) and to 142e1 (τό τε ἓν καὶ τὸ ὄν); cf. also 163e7–164a1 (according to the text of MORESCHINI). For the apparently very close relation between τὰ ὄντα and οὐσία cf. 144a5–7; 144b1–2. The strong relation between τὸ εἶναι and οὐσία is suggested e.g. by 142b6 and a comparison between 142e2 (ἢ τὸ ἓν τοῦ εἶναι μορίου ἢ τὸ ὂν τοῦ ἑνὸς μορίου) and 142d2–3 (ἥ τε οὐσία καὶ τὸ ἕν).

[15] Cf. e.g. PHDO. 102e2; 102e7–103a1; 103a7; REP. 508d6; 527b4–5; TIM. 28a3.

[16] One could object that this decision to count them only where they are paired is arbitrary and one should employ *all* occurrences of γίγνομαι. This can be answered by an

|  | S1 | S2 | S2C | S3 | S4 | S5 | S6 | S7 | S8 | $p$ | DP |
|---|---|---|---|---|---|---|---|---|---|---|---|
| Being | 3 | 88 | 6 | 7 | 0 | 15 | 0 | 1 | 0 | 1.08e–08 | 0.280 |
|  | 0.185 | 1.761 | 1.130 | 1.017 | 0.000 | 1.496 | 0.000 | 0.195 | 0.000 |  |  |
| Bec. / Pass. | 0 | 0 | 12 | 0 | 0 | 6 | 0 | 2 | 0 | 9.70e–14 | 0.817 |
|  | 0.000 | 0.000 | 2.260 | 0.000 | 0.000 | 0.598 | 0.000 | 0.389 | 0.000 |  |  |
| App. | 0 | 2 | 0 | 0 | 0 | 1 | 0 | 18 | 0 | 2.66e–18 | 0.824 |
|  | 0.000 | 0.040 | 0.000 | 0.000 | 0.000 | 0.100 | 0.000 | 3.502 | 0.000 |  |  |

T.5.1  FIELDS OF BEING, BECOMING/PASSING AWAY, AND APPEARANCE

conceptual field of *appearance*, the concepts of φαίνω and δοκέω are included in those instances where they are used to describe the subject under consideration, but not the on-going argument as such and its results.[17] Again, these terms are clearly used elsewhere by Plato to denote the sensible appearance.[18] Counting only the positive occurrences of these three conceptual fields, we get the results that are shown in T.5.1 and D.5.1A–3B.

Unsurprisingly, these fields and their positive occurrences appear exclusively in the so-called 'positive' sections S2 (including S2C), S3, S5, and S7.[19] Yet, there are very significant patterns to be found by comparing these three conceptual fields to one another. The field of being is concentrated in S2, S2C, S3, and S5 (wherein its occurrences in S2C and S5 will differentiate significantly in § 6). If one takes into account T.A.1 (pp. 138–140) for the occurrences of each term in itself, one can see that τὸ ὄν / τὰ ὄντα and τὸ εἶναι clearly align with οὐσία, which is why it was correct to heuristically include the former in this first conceptual field. The field of becoming and passing away is predominantly found in S2C, and to a lesser extent also in S5 and S7. The field of appearance shows a very high, nearly exclusive concentration in S7. Very remarkably, even the occurrences of being and becoming/passing away in S7 happen in the mode of appearance, if one takes a closer look at the text.[20] The patterns thus become even more distinct since the occurrences of being and becoming/passing away in S7

intermediate step in the argument, in which one compares the pattern of γίγνομαι (in total) to the pattern of γίγνομαι/ἀπόλλυμι – to then conclude that the latter forms a significant pattern on its own (which is in turn used as described in the text). Cf. § 7 for more details.

[17] Cf. the remarks in APPENDIX B, s.v. φαίνω and δοκέω.

[18] For φαίνω, cf. e.g. REP. 476a7; 479b4; 479d7. For δοκέω (and the, in that sense, closely related expressions δοξάζω and δόξα), cf. e.g. REP. 478a8; 479d7; 479e4; 480a1; 508d7.

[19] Though this point will be differentiated significantly in §§ 6; 9. The remarkable positive instances in S1 will be discussed in greater detail in § 20.

[20] γιγνομένους καὶ ἀπολλυμένους (165d7) still implies the before-mentioned φαίνεσθαι (165d4). And also the splintered being (165b4–6) is somehow related to appearance (φαίνεσθαι 165c1; φανῆναι 165c2).

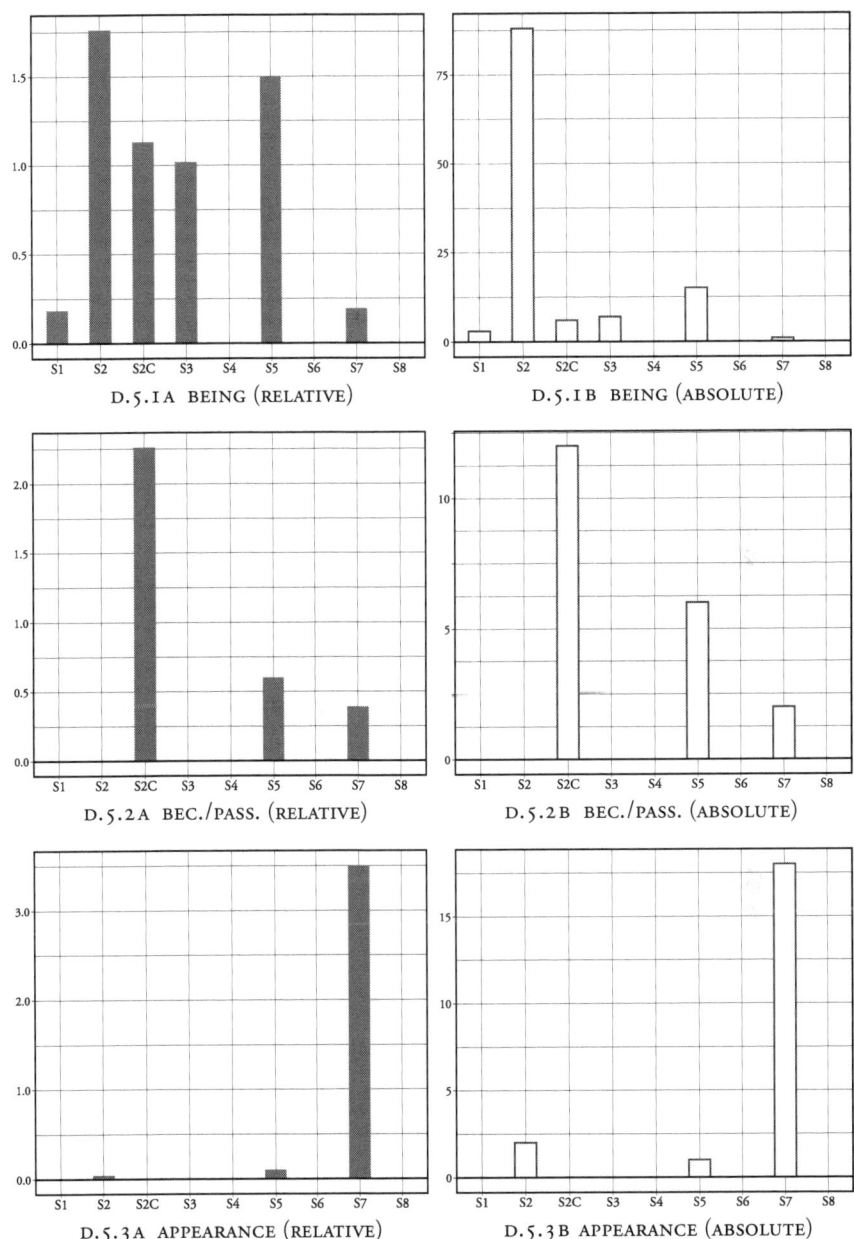

D.5.1A BEING (RELATIVE)

D.5.1B BEING (ABSOLUTE)

D.5.2A BEC./PASS. (RELATIVE)

D.5.2B BEC./PASS. (ABSOLUTE)

D.5.3A APPEARANCE (RELATIVE)

D.5.3B APPEARANCE (ABSOLUTE)

have to be put in parentheses to some extent. Each of these three patterns has a very low $p$-value, which is why we are allowed to regard them as non-random with certainty. Furthermore, the comparison of these three patterns allows us to get a better feel for DP's behaviour: as the fields of

becoming/passing away and appearance are concentrated in very few sections, their DP-value is very high, whereas for the field of being DP is moderately high since this field is a bit more dispersed and more concentrated in
S2, where the lion's share of occurrences is expected in any case.

With regard to the overall sequence of the sections, there is thus a clear
and significant shift from being to becoming/passing away and appearance,
which can be determined very safely. Even at this stage of the argument,[21] we
may furthermore state that there is obviously an incongruence of becoming/
passing away and appearance rather than a congruence of them, as one
might expect from the general ontological dichotomy Plato is known for.
Instead, one finds a clearly *tripartite* constellation with regard to these three
conceptual fields, which in a sense shifts through the sections in its emphasis
– though notably not in a simple linear succession.

With regard to these first conceptual patterns, one might object that a few
individual terms of the field of being, namely καθ' αὐτό, εἶδος, ἰδέα, and to
some extent τὸ εἶναι, have a higher *p*-value with regard to their individual
distribution (cf. Appendix A, T.a.1 and T.a.3). Yet, this does not refute the
present observation for four reasons. Firstly, one has to take into account
that there are only very few occurrences of esp. ἰδέα and εἶδος.[22] These terms
are therefore not suitable on their own for an individual statistical consideration. Secondly, one has to remark that the current claims are not made
specifically with regard to these concepts in particular, but with regard to the
conceptual field of being in total. As long as these concepts are consistent
with the pattern – with which they might very well interfere! – no problem
arises for the present argument. Thirdly, the given observations would show
absolutely no different result in its general outcome, if the first conceptual
field had been restricted to οὐσία and τὸ ὄν. And fourthly, such an objection
may not arise from some individual *p*-values, but would have to be directed
towards the criterion itself, according to which these terms were included in
the conceptual field of being – and with regard to this, there is no reason to
deny that Plato uses these terms to denote intelligible being and the forms.

---

[21] More on this topic in § 19.

[22] One could subsequently object that this evidence suggests that Plato/Parmenides is
in fact *not* talking about the forms and the realm of being in S2 and S3. But this objection
ignores that there are definitely *other* concepts of being – most of all the concept of οὐσία –
which all support the claim that he is. The small number of occurrences of εἶδος and ἰδέα may
thus only support the claim that Plato does not primarily use *these terms* in the second part
to describe being. And ultimately, one has to note that these few occurrences perfectly tie in
with the pattern of being (§ 21).

## § 6. Change and Alteration

*The conceptual pattern of becoming/passing away, concentrated in S2C and S5, is further confirmed by related patterns. Also, these two sections show some remarkable resemblances.* Let now also the negative occurrences of the field of being be taken into account. In order to do so, besides including the negative occurrences of the concepts from § 5, I shall also consider the negative nominalised forms τὸ μὴ εἶναι and τὸ μὴ ὄν / τὰ μὴ ὄντα in the conceptual field of being. For these terms a negated occurrence is counted as positive (in the sense of a double negation), and an affirmed one is counted as negative accordingly in order to ensure an adequate integration of these negative terms.[23] It has to be noted that S8 is not really to be evaluated in this way, since the text seemingly wishes to express that there is *not even* non-being and thus denies even τὸ μὴ ὄν (166a1–6). This is definitely to be understood as something negative rather than as resulting in something positive. Hence the method of double negation does not apply here adequately and the value of S8 has thus to be put in parentheses in the present context. For the conceptual field of being, we get the results in T.6.1 and D.6.1A–B (p. 44). Furthermore, one has to note that the many occurrences in S6 tend to distort this plot: the peaks of S2, S2C, S3, and S5 (in D.6.1A) are very much the same as those in D.5.1A (p. 41). To analyse things more adequately, D.6.1A–B (ALT.) adjusts the columns of S6 and S8 (according to the remarks above) in order to remove this distortion.

For both distributions, the positive and the negative one, the *p*-values are very low, which is why we are allowed to regard them as non-random. Again, this evaluation of the positive and negative occurrences shows a significant pattern. We can discern clearly between sections where being is affirmed,

---

[23] I also evaluated the inverse way (i.e. only according to negation or affirmation, regardless of whether the concept itself is positive or negative). The result becomes slightly more asymmetrical within S2C and S5 (but without changing the 'mixed' character of both sections), and a few (then) 'positive' occurrences of τὸ μὴ ὄν are to be noted in S6 (which definitely fits the character of these passages less well). There is no significant change in S1, S2, S3, S4, and S7. All occurrences in S8 are of course then inverted to negative tendencies. It is furthermore not very productive to evaluate the field of becoming/passing away by its positive and negative occurrences in this way. If one counts the negated occurrences of ἀπόλλυμι as positive and the negated occurrences of γίγνομαι as negative, the field remains concentrated in S2C and S5, whereas this approach of double negation is obviously not suited to characterise the way how S4 and especially S6 deal with becoming/passing away (this is very much the same problem as with S8 and being). S6 is obviously eager to deny *both* γίγνομαι and ἀπόλλυμι (cf. e.g. 163d7–8), as is S4, and hence the numerical results do not faithfully map how S4/S6 deal with these concepts. Counting the results this way gives: 0/0 (S1), 0/0 (S2), 7/–6 (S2C), 0/0 (S3), 1/–1 (S4), 6/–6 (S5), 5/–3 (S6), 1/–1 (S7), 0/0 (S8).

|   | S1 | S2 | S2C | S3 | S4 | S5 | S6 | S7 | S8 | $p$ | DP |
|---|----|----|-----|----|----|----|----|----|----|-----|-----|
| + | 3 | 88 | 6 | 7 | 0 | 18 | 0 | 1 | [5] | 5.77e-09 | 0.268 |
| - | -6 | -4 | -5 | 0 | -2 | -18 | -16 | 0 | [0] | 4.52e-20 | 0.598 |
| + | 0.185 | 1.761 | 1.130 | 1.017 | 0.000 | 1.795 | 0.000 | 0.195 | [2.358] | | |
| - | -0.371 | -0.080 | -0.942 | 0.000 | -0.528 | -1.795 | -4.878 | 0.000 | [0.000] | | |

T.6.1 FIELD OF BEING (INCL. NEGATIVE OCCURRENCES)

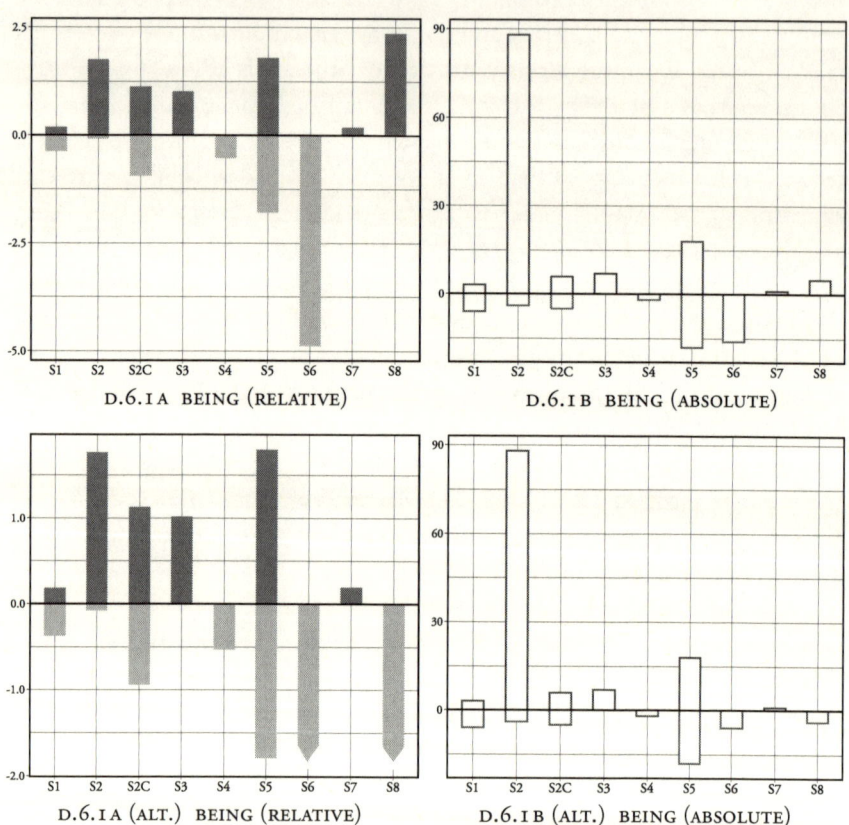

D.6.1A BEING (RELATIVE)     D.6.1B BEING (ABSOLUTE)

D.6.1A (ALT.) BEING (RELATIVE)     D.6.1B (ALT.) BEING (ABSOLUTE)

where it is negated and where both apply. In S2 and S3, being is (virtually) exclusively affirmed (on S8 see above). In S4, there is exclusive negation of being, though in only very few occurrences. S6 shows an exclusive and extremely emphasised negation of being.[24] In S1, we find very few occurrences of both negation and affirmation, while the former is dominant. S2C and S5 exhibit a remarkable similarity since both show many occurrences of both affirmation *and* negation and this is perfectly consistent with the two peaks

---

[24] For further systematic interpretation of this evidence, cf. §§ 14–15.

of S2C and S5 in the field of becoming/passing away in D.5.2A (p. 41). Hence, this allows to understand S2C's and S5's peaks of being in D.5.1A more precisely. In both cases, these peaks were only 'half of the story', whereas in S2 and S3 the respective peaks were already the full characterisation of these sections with regard to being. We may thus conclude cautiously that S2 and S3 seem to be concerned with being, whereas S2C and S5 seem to somehow deal with becoming/passing away and with being only in the sense as it is involved in this process. Even if one does not wish to go much further at this point, it has to be stated in any case that S2C and S5 show a remarkable resemblance. This is a finding which is easily overlooked if one follows a close reading of the arguments instead of getting the bigger picture. A resemblance between S2C and S5 has, in a very brief remark, already been noted by L. BRISSON, but for different reasons.[25] We may thus state with some certainty that S2C and S5 have some closer connection to one another, regardless of how one further interprets this evidence.[26]

Besides these observations there is a further conceptual pattern that may be taken into account with regard to the present context of change and alteration, as it is found in S2C and S5. Among the concepts of the second part, one can reasonably pick the following ones to heuristically investigate a conceptual field of *change*: μεταβάλλω, μεταβολή; ἀλλοιόω, ἀλλοίωσις, ἀλλοῖος; μεταβαίνω; μεθίστημι; ἀπαλλάττω, ἀφίημι; αὐξάνω; φθίω. T.6.2 and D.6.2A–B show the results with regard to positive and negative occurrences of the field of change (p. 46).

Again, the *p*-values allow us to regard this pattern as non-random with certainty. Its high DP-values confirm this pattern as a very distinct and marked one. We also find two clear and remarkable peaks in the conceptual field of change in S2C and S5. Again we see the characteristic pattern of both affirmation *and* negation related to a concentration of these concepts in both sections. In S2C affirmation dominates, whereas in S5 affirmation and negation are more equally balanced. This pattern confirms two observations made before: on the one hand, it further underlines that S2C and S5 are somehow dealing with *change and alteration* in the sense of becoming and passing away. And on the other hand, this pattern strengthens the claim that S2C and S5 are in some sense *connected* to one another by showing remarkable similarities between various conceptual patterns. This connection will furthermore be supported by the pattern of motion and rest (cf. § 16).

---

[25] Cf. BRISSON ²1977, 22. For more details on this, cf. § 17.
[26] In § 16 a possible systematic explanation of this similarity will be provided.

|  | S1 | S2 | S2C | S3 | S4 | S5 | S6 | S7 | S8 | $p$ | DP |
|---|---|---|---|---|---|---|---|---|---|---|---|
| + | 0 | 4 | 21 | 0 | 0 | 12 | 0 | 1 | 0 | 6.65e–21 | 0.734 |
| – | –4 | –3 | –4 | 0 | 0 | –11 | –2 | 0 | 0 | 3.60e–06 | 0.547 |
| + | 0.000 | 0.080 | 3.955 | 0.000 | 0.000 | 1.196 | 0.000 | 0.195 | 0.000 | | |
| – | –0.247 | –0.060 | –0.753 | 0.000 | 0.000 | –1.097 | –0.610 | 0.000 | 0.000 | | |

T.6.2 FIELD OF CHANGE

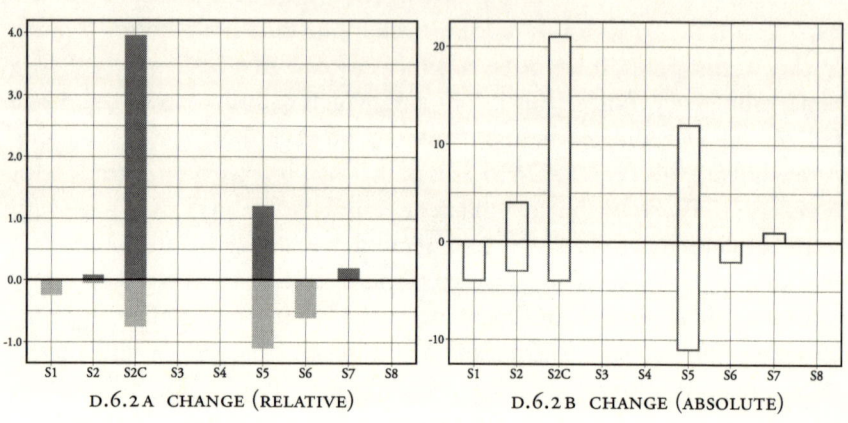

D.6.2A CHANGE (RELATIVE)     D.6.2B CHANGE (ABSOLUTE)

As can be seen from T.A.1–4 (APPENDIX A), in the field of change μεταβάλλω and μεταβολή are quite dominantly used in S2C, whereas the concept of ἀλλοιόω most dominantly characterises S5. One may note that in S6 the complete negation of being (D.6.1A–B, p. 44) also applies to the field of change (though this is only caused by two occurrences in this short section).

## § 7. Appearance

*The concentration of appearance in S7 is emphasised by further evidence.* One finding of § 5 was that the positive occurrences of the conceptual field of appearance are almost exclusively concentrated in S7. In the following, two aspects will be included. Firstly, the negative occurrences of this field and, secondly, further concepts that support this evidence. For the latter, we may have a look at the concepts in T.7.1 and the absolute numbers of their occurrences (at first without further qualification). It has to be remarked that except in the case of ὄγκος we are dealing here with very few occurrences, whose $p$-values are thus in themselves not informative; they are neither sufficient to confirm nor to dismiss any claim, as remarked before in § 5 with

| | S1 | S2 | S2C | S3 | S4 | S5 | S6 | S7 | S8 | $p$ | DP |
|---|---|---|---|---|---|---|---|---|---|---|---|
| ὄγκος | 0 | 0 | 0 | 0 | 0 | 0 | 0 | 7 | 0 | 1.40e-08 | 0.970 |
| ὄναρ. ὕπνος | 0 | 0 | 0 | 0 | 0 | 0 | 0 | 2 | 0 | 0.015 | 0.970 |
| φάντασμα | 0 | 0 | 0 | 0 | 0 | 0 | 0 | 2 | 1 | 1.65e-03 | 0.949 |
| σκιαγραφέω | 0 | 0 | 0 | 0 | 0 | 0 | 0 | 1 | 0 | 0.140 | 0.970 |

T.7.1 SPECIFIC CONCEPTS

regard to εἶδος and ἰδέα.[27] However, their few occurrences are perfectly consistent with the conceptual pattern of appearance. And Plato indeed employs all these terms for the sensible world of appearance in dialogues before and after the *Parmenides*.[28] If we thus include these terms in the field of appearance and evaluate this field now with regard to the positive and negative occurrences, we get the results presented in T.7.2 and D.7.1A–B (p. 48).

These results completely confirm the findings of § 5 with regard to the conceptual field of appearance. Both distributions, positive and negative, have very low $p$-values and we are therefore entitled to regard them as non-random for certain. With regard to the positive and negative occurrences, we find the very high concentration of appearance in S7 to be exclusively positive, whereas S8 presents a quite strong and exclusively negative concentration. Given these very clear results, it seems fairly uncontroversial to assume that the discussion in S7 is in some way concerned with the sensible world of appearance, regardless of how one interprets or further develops this evidence.

The positive and dense concentration of terms pointing to the sensible world in S7 has already been remarked by scholars[29] – yet, as far as I can see,

[27] More or less the same applies to the DP-values which are, of course, very high.

[28] For ὄναρ (and related verbs), see REP. 476c4–5; TIM. 52b3; 52b7–c1. For ὕπνος, cf. REP. 476c5; *ex negativo* TIM. 52b7. For σκιαγραφέω/σκιαγρφία, cf. REP. 365c3–4; 586b7–c5 (cf. PROT. 356c4–e4); 602c10–d4; PHDO. 69b5–8. For φάντασμα, cf. REP. 510a1; 598b3; TIM. 52c3. For ὄγκος (referring to the physical, sensible body), cf. PHDO. 96d4; THT. 155b8; 155c3; TIM. 54d1; 56d3; 58e6; 59a3; 60c3; 61b3; 62c7; 81b8; 83d3; LEG. 959c4–5.

[29] BRISSON/BENZÉCRI 1989, 122–123 briefly state the concentration of esp. φαίνω as well as δόξα, φάντασμα, δοκέω, δοξάξω in S7–8 and refer to some unnamed "interprètes ne pratiquant pas la statistique lexicale" (IBID., 122), who remarked this before. Their explanation ("Il est tellement paradoxal d'imaginer quelles conséquences positives et négatives on peut tirer pour les autres de la formule 'l'un, s'il n'est pas' qu'on est renvoyé à un monde d'apparences où tout n'est que reflets se répercutant dans un miroir." IBID., 123) concentrates on the contradictory character of what follows from the hypothesis of S5–8. Yet, there seems to be no consideration of whether this might in fact refer to the sensible world itself (whose intrinsically contradictory character is clearly present in Plato and also in the *Parmenides* itself, cf. 129a6–8; 129b3–6; 129c4–d6). Neither is there any indication that this finding in S7–8 should be compared to the distribution of the concepts of being etc.

|   | S1 | S2 | S2C | S3 | S4 | S5 | S6 | S7 | S8 | *p* | DP |
|---|----|----|-----|----|----|----|----|----|----|-----|-----|
| + | 0 | 2 | 0 | 0 | 0 | 1 | 0 | 30 | 0 | 4.90e–33 | 0.877 |
| – | 0 | 0 | 0 | 0 | 0 | 0 | 0 | 0 | –4 | 1.93e–07 | 1.000 |
| + | 0.000 | 0.040 | 0.000 | 0.000 | 0.000 | 0.100 | 0.000 | 5.837 | 0.000 |  |  |
| – | 0.000 | 0.000 | 0.000 | 0.000 | 0.000 | 0.000 | 0.000 | 0.000 | –1.887 |  |  |

T.7.2 FIELD OF APPEARANCE (INCL. T.7.1)

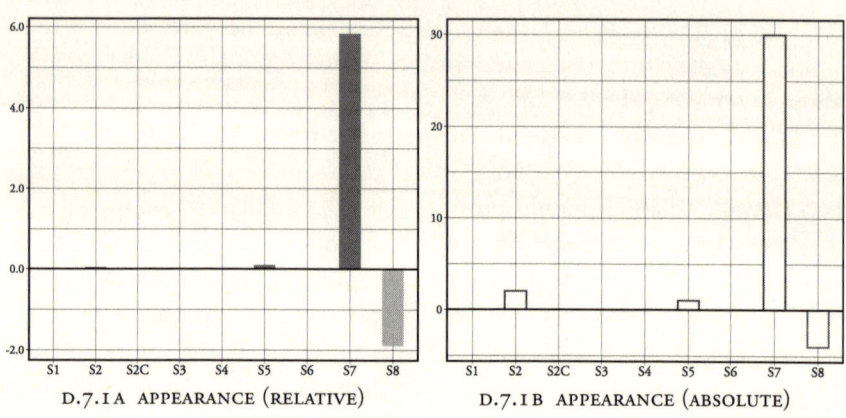

D.7.1A APPEARANCE (RELATIVE)   D.7.1B APPEARANCE (ABSOLUTE)

this observation has remained quite isolated and has never been integrated in a more extended comparison with other conceptual fields, as is given here. I shall deal with these conceptual patterns with regard to S7, especially with the difficult term ὄγκος, in more detail in § 15. This will also provide a possible interpretation of the many negative occurrences in S8.

Besides these findings, there is one more general conclusion to be drawn from the findings so far, which seems hardly controversial to me and which is almost completely independent of how one further interprets the evidence systematically. It is clear that S1 and S2, as a first pair of sections, do *not*, as some scholars have stated, provide the *whole* conceptual framework (which is then only reeled off according to the different hypotheses).[30] Instead, especially the pattern of appearance proves that the later sections introduce *new* concepts to the overall argument. To some extent, this also applies to the

---

Besides these, cf. furthermore WUNDT 1935, 55; SPEISER [2]1959, 69; MILLER 1986, 162–165; SCOLNICOV 2003, 38; FERRARI [8]2019, 118.

[30] Cf. e.g. SAYRE 2005, 131 ("Each of the remaining six hypotheses [S3–8] is concerned with basically the same list [of properties and relations, in S1–2], albeit in truncated form"). In a similar sense SCOLNICOV 2003, 29. It is of course true that *some* concepts – such as ταὐτόν and ἕτερον – are taken up again and again throughout the sections. For relations and connections between the sections with regard to the definitions of some of these fundamental concepts cf. WALTER (forthcoming).

pattern of becoming/passing away, which is first introduced in full in S2C and S5, though in this case this hinges on how one interprets the relation between S2 and S2C in more detail. Similarly, the complex chiasm of being and non-being in S5 (162a4–b8) can be regarded as an unprecedented novelty, at least to some extent.[31] Likewise, one can state without too much controversy that there are in fact concepts that Parmenides ceases to consider at some point during the exercise, such as the concepts of mereology (§ 18) and the concept of measure (§ 20). In total, this evidence underlines and objectively supports an impression which in my view suggests itself if one reads the second part of the *Parmenides* impartially: time and again, it seems that Parmenides is not only drawing conclusions, but that he deliberately introduces new concepts, subjects, and perspectives or ceases to consider certain concepts.[32] And these decisions cannot be explained solely on the grounds of logical deduction. One may therefore at least surmise that Parmenides uses his overall argument not only to draw conclusions, but also to circumscribe in some sense a certain structure (or structures) which he has in his mind and before his inner eye while going through the sections.

The second half of the sections (S5–8) introduces something essentially new and this novelty is first and foremost the conceptual field of appearance. This claim is furthermore strongly supported by another piece of textual evidence. Regardless of how one interprets the two dense and perplexing summaries after S4 and S8 in detail, one clearly remarkable difference between PS and FS is that PS only mentions being, while FS also features the concept of appearance.[33] This strongly suggests that Parmenides himself – whatever it is precisely that he does in S5–8 – regards the concept of appearance as something crucial and typical which he has introduced in these sections. In consequence, one could justifiably infer that S1–4 is in some way concerned

[31] Though there is admittedly the possibility to explain this by the introduction of non-being in the hypothesis of S5 and the chiasm as a consequence of it. However, it has to be noted that, firstly, there is in principle little necessity that non-being inevitably *needs* such a chiasm (as a δεσμός; cf. 162a4), while being (in the former sections) does *not*; hence the chiasm is something new and might thus be regarded as significant. And secondly, the way in which Parmenides draws exactly the opposite conclusion from the same hypothesis at the beginning of S6 (e.g. 163c4–d1) suggests that he has *something specific* in mind, which he wants to introduce in S5 (cf. also 162d8: he does talk περὶ ἄλλου τινός, i.e. 'a specific other thing'; already before 161a1: τό ... ἓν ἐκεῖνο and 161a3–4: εἰ δὲ τὸ ἓν ἐκεῖνο καὶ μὴ ἄλλο ὑπόκειται μὴ εἶναι).

[32] Cf. e.g. the introduction of τὰ μὴ ἕν in S2 (146e5–147a8); or the beginnings of S5 and S6 respectively (cf. also § 13).

[33] Cf. πάντα τέ ἐστι τὸ ἓν καὶ οὐδὲ ἕν ἐστι καὶ πρὸς ἑαυτὸ καὶ πρὸς τὰ ἄλλα ὡσαύτως (160b2–3) and πάντα πάντως ἐστί τε καὶ οὐκ ἔστι καὶ φαίνεταί τε καὶ οὐ φαίνεται (166c4–5).

with being, while S5–8 is somehow – additionally or dominantly – concerned with appearance.[34] This fits the respective patterns perfectly, while the pattern of becoming/passing away seems to adopt an intermediate position.

## § 8. Some Rare Terms

*There are several concepts which may be systematically significant and which appear only once or very rarely.* If one takes a look at S1–8, it is doubtlessly remarkable and fairly uncontroversial that several concepts potentially bear systematic weight, but appear only a few times or even only once. Unique occurrences are to be found for ἀλλοίωσις (S1), διαφορότης (S1), ὅρος (S2), δύναμις (S2), συζυγία (S2), ἕδρα (S2), προαίρεσις (S2), τέλος (S2), γένεσις (S2), τὸ ἄτοπον (S2C), ἰδέα (S3), ἀπειρία (S3), δεσμός (S5), ἡσυχία (S5), and ἀπουσία (S6).[35] Besides these, the following terms occur only very rarely[36] and may be assumed to be systematically significant: μηχανή (S1, S2), σχῆμα (S1, S2), πάθημα (S1, S2C), μέθεξις (S1, S2, S3), τρόπος (S1, S4), ἀνισότης (S1, S5), δυάς (S2), κοινωνία (S2, S8),[37] στάσις (S2C), ἕξις (S5), ἑτεροιότης (S5, S6), ὄναρ (S7), ὕπνος (S7), and φάντασμα (S7, S8). Taken on their own, they may, of course, not be evaluated statistically. But since there is some tendency in Plato to name central terms seldom or even only once,[38] one might surmise that these terms perhaps contribute to understanding the single sections and thus further support the conceptual patterns in S1–8. For now, this is only to be stated. I shall ask again in § 21 how these rare terms can be integrated in a more specified interpretation.

## § 9. Characterisation of the Sections

*The evidence strongly suggests that a binary categorisation of the sections as either negative or positive is too simple.* If one takes a close look at the distribution of positive and negative occurrences of several concepts, one finds – as has been

---

[34] One may remark that the second part of the *Parmenides* would thus align quite well to the two parts of the poem of the historical Parmenides.

[35] I confine myself to nouns here. Again, APPENDIX C provides full transparency with regard to all rare terms.

[36] By 'rare' I mean occurring less than four times in the present context.

[37] Along with one occurrence of κοινωνέω (S3).

[38] Cf., for instance, αὐτὸ τἀκριβές in the *Politicus* (284d2), which is doubtlessly of great importance; however, it appears only once.

remarked, for instance, with regard to the field of being (§ 6) – not two, but *three* ways in which affirmation and negation appear. There are sections that exclusively, or with a very strong tendency, affirm *or* negate a certain concept, while others characteristically affirm *and* negate it. This was the result with regard to the field of being (§ 6), for instance, and will be shown for further patterns, such as motion and rest (§ 16). Given these patterns, it seems too simple to just categorise the sections as positive or negative ones, as has been done in the literature,[39] though these binary classifications are of course of heuristic value in structuring the huge number of arguments in the second part. However, a binary characterisation decisively blurs the difference in character, especially among the so-called 'positive' sections S2 (including S2C), S3, S5, and S7. This is not at all to deny that these sections have a positive tendency in general (cf. also § 4), but it allows us to further differentiate them – especially as it yields results such as the specific resemblance between S2C and S5. All this calls for a more cautious and differentiated procedure when characterising each single section as a whole and for implementing, at least heuristically, a trichotomic characterisation of them (positive, negative, as well as positive and negative).

## § 10. Multiple Subjects

*The conceptual patterns prompt a multiple-subject approach and this approach is defendable.* Given the conceptual patterns so far, I think it can be stated without much controversy that the results at least encourage a point of view according to which Plato has his Parmenides speak of *different subjects* throughout the sections. This is, however, not motivated by explaining the apparent contradictions and tensions between the results of the single sections, but primarily a result of looking impartially at the statistical distribution of different concepts. According to C. C. Meinwald, solving the apparent contradictions is one of the main motivations for what she calls the "multiple-subject type of interpretation".[40] There are two main objections against a multi-subject approach according to her: a) it "gives different interpretations to the hypothesis If The One is" and b) it fails "to explain Parmenides' demand to keep repeating the exercise with different subjects".[41] With regard

---

[39] Cf. e.g. Robinson ²1953, 241–242; Gill 1996, 58; Coxon 1999, 120; Sayre 2005, 131; Rickless 2007, 110–111; Gill 2014, 500.
[40] Meinwald 1991, 24.
[41] Meinwald 1991, 25.

to a) it has to be remarked that C. C. MEINWALD likewise fails to adequately identify the, in fact, *four* hypotheses of Parmenides (cf. § 13); these different hypotheses to some extent even *demand* different interpretations of the sections, if one closely follows the exact text of the exercise. This will be discussed in detail later on (§§ 13; 19). b) is doubtlessly challenging. But it has to be noted that Zeno clearly states that the one following exercise will go through everything (ταύτης τῆς διὰ πάντων διεξόδου 136e1–2). This of course primarily refers back to the programme in 135e8–136c5, whose goal is to reach the truth.[42] But it also forms an obvious parallel to REP. 534c1–3[43] and hence not only strengthens the parallel of REP. 534b8–c1 to what is done in S1, but also calls up dialectics, which deals with the overall structure of being and reality as a whole. One can thus counter b) in the following manner: choosing a different starting point does not *a priori* exclude discussing the very *same* overall systematic constellation (i.e. one proposed by a multiple-subject approach) from a different perspective and potentially with regard to only some of its aspects. The full dialectician – who is the only one able to execute the exercise (136d4–5) – may thus be able to describe this overall constellation in its outline regardless of which concept or subject forms the actual starting point. That means: just as, say, ἀνόμοιον occurs if τὸ ἕν is hypothesised, likewise (τὸ) ἕν may occur if τὸ ἀνόμοιον is hypothesised. This rejoinder is furthermore supported by the fact that Parmenides can obviously follow specific intentions when deriving different conclusions from the same hypothesis, as becomes especially obvious at the beginning of S5 and S6 (§ 13). In total, a multiple-subject approach like the present one is thus able to integrate Parmenides' demand to repeat the exercise.

Likewise, every approach that holds that there are *no* different subjects[44] has to provide an explanation of the conceptual patterns and how they can be integrated into a single-subject approach or a no-specific-subject approach. On the other hand, it has to be noted that the conceptual patterns so far do *not* suggest that there is a single subject for *each* section, as is characteristic for some ancient and some modern approaches.[45] Instead, the patterns sug-

---

[42] Cf. εἰ μέλλεις τελέως γυμνασάμενος κυρίως διόψεσθαι τὸ ἀληθές (136c4–5) – τῷ ἀληθεῖ νοῦν σχεῖν (136e2–3). The two statements are made by Zeno and Parmenides respectively, however, they may fairly reasonable be read together.

[43] τῆς διὰ πάντων διεξόδου (136e2–3) – διὰ πάντων ἐλέγχων διεξιών (REP. 534c1–2); cf. already ADAM ²1963, II 142.

[44] As e.g. ALLEN ²1997, 211–215 and MEINWALD 1991.

[45] WAHL ²1951; WUNDT 1935; SPEISER ²1959; LYNCH 1959; WYLLER ²2006; SCHUDOMA 2001 may be regarded as examples of this interpretation (though, of course, with differences amongst them). In antiquity, this intention to find a one-on-one correspond-

gest that *several* sections may in fact deal with the *same* subject, as especially the remarkable similarity between S2C and S5 suggests. One is thus not well advised to simply look for nine, eight, five or four particular subjects that fit the single sections.[46]

## § 11. Concluding Remarks

*A general, though complex ontological movement downwards may quite safely be assumed. The patterns furthermore suggest not two, but three ontological levels.* In total, I think, it can be stated without too much controversy that the patterns at least suggest a general tendency of an ontological 'downward movement' throughout S1–8.[47] Though it is quite important that the patterns do not point to a simple linear succession with nine, eight, five, or four discrete steps, but a somehow more complicated structure. This downward direction will receive further support from other patterns, such as the field of measure (§ 20).

Given the results in §§ 5–7, it is furthermore definitely remarkable that becoming/passing away and appearance do *not* coincide, but are clearly separated by their respective patterns. At first sight, they both seem characteristic of the same realm in Plato, i.e. the sensible world of physical particulars. Accordingly, one would expect their patterns to overlap and coincide. However, the statistical evidence of their divergence is clear and obvious. Therefore, if one is willing to attribute some general systematic significance to the conceptual patterns and if the general concentration of being (in S2–3) and appearance (in S7) – that was further supported by IS and FS (§ 7) – is significant, one is thus confronted not with a bipartite, but with a general *tripartite* structure regarding the ontological patterns. I shall furthermore discuss a possible explanation of this with quite far-reaching systematic consequences in § 19.

ence between section and subject is the main characteristic of the Neoplatonic interpretations, e.g. of Amelius or Iamblichus (cf. SAFFREY/WESTERINK 1968, LXXX–LXXXIII). For the Neoplatonic interpretations, cf. furthermore § 13.

[46] Nine or five if one considers S2C to be a section in its own right, eight or four if not. Nine or eight if one considers S5–8 to contain positive systematic information, whereas five or four if not.

[47] This implies that claims such as those by SCOLNICOV 2003, 27; SZLEZÁK 2021, 255 and others, according to which there is no mentioning of the forms and the sensible particulars in the second part, have to be discussed further with regard to a possible *indirect* allusion to them, which is revealed by the conceptual patterns.

All in all, these are the results and consequences that I consider fairly uncontroversial with regard to the statistical evidence. In the second main step of this study, I shall now turn to further conceptual patterns as well as to a more specific interpretation of all these patterns. In this second main step, I shall first outline my interpretation as such (chapter 4), in order to then connect it to the conceptual patterns (chapter 5).

# 4. AN INTERPRETATIVE PATTERN

In this chapter, I put forward an interpretative pattern (IP) which in my eyes provides a coherent interpretation of the statistical evidence and the sections in the *Parmenides*. IP thus forms a scheme which permits of a concise explanation and a more systematic understanding of the results given in chapter 3 as well as those to be discussed in chapter 5. I do not claim that IP is the *only* possible interpretative scheme consistent with these results. But I do have the strong impression that the coherence of the conceptual patterns in total demands such a general, holistic interpretation of the dialogue's second part and that IP does this job quite well. Furthermore, it has to be noted that what will be done in chapters 4 and 5 is no final proof of IP; this conclusion would demand a line-by-line analysis of the whole text of the *Parmenides* and each single argument in the light of IP, which is beyond the scope of the present study. But what is shown in greater detail is that IP ties in with the conceptual patterns in question remarkably well. In the following, I shall first name the core thoughts of IP, in order to then give it a further possible – though not necessary – foundation in a passage of the *Republic* (§ 12). After that, I shall justify the core features of IP in greater detail, thereby also dealing with possible objections to IP in general (§ 13).

## § 12. A Geometric Analogy

If we take Parmenides' methodological programme (135e8–136c5) in a very general sense, it tells us the following: take one thing A and another (opposed?) thing B, suppose that A *is*[1] and then consider the consequences

---

[1] There has been some discussion how this 'is' has to be understood and whether it is meant, for instance, as existential, 'A exists', or as an incomplete predication, such as 'A is [F]' or '[x] is A'; cf. e.g. SCOLNICOV 2003, 16–17; O'BRIEN 2005A on this issue. I agree

for A itself, for B itself, for B in relation to A, and for A in relation to B.[2] Then examine the same chiastic combination under the supposition that A *is not*. This results in eight sections.[3] With regard to this programme, IP consists of five core thoughts:

i)    that we can subdivide the sections in two types according to the difference πρὸς αὐτό vs. πρὸς ἄλλο: those that deal with one subject *in itself* (call them 'subject section', 'SuS') and those that deal with the *relation* between two subjects (call them 'relation section', 'ReS'). Thus, according to the programme, there are four SuS and four ReS.

ii)    that each half of the exercise (i.e. S1–4 and S5–8) first deals with two SuS and then with two ReS.

iii)    that the subject that 'is not' in the exercise's second half (S5–8) is not the A of the first half, but a newly introduced subject C, and that this new subject consequently also has a new correlate D. The second half of the exercise thus considers the consequences for C itself, for D itself, for D in relation to C, and for C in relation to D.

iv)    that this eight-fold structure is overlain by a second structure which in a certain sense sets off the very first and the very last of the sections (i.e. S1 and S8) from the rest.

v)    that the two subjects in each half of the exercise form a relation between principle (A; C) and principiate (B; D).[4] The relation between SuS and ReS as well as the relation between principle and principiate is therefore the same in both halves of the exercise and we can thus equate both analogously as shown in the following equation.[5]

with O'BRIEN 2005A (who argues mainly against SÉGUY-DUCLOT 1998) that the position of εἰ does not constrain εστιν to a copulative or an existential meaning. However, I think it is obvious that the position of εἰ gives a *decisive emphasis* to what is especially under consideration in the hypothetical expression: it emphasises the element(s) which come(s) *after* it (especially since Plato had no diacritics). Thus, EI EN EΣTIN clearly emphasises that (the) EN is under consideration, while HEN EI EΣTIN emphasises that the focus is now on EΣTIN (regardless of how that is to be understood further). In that sense the apparent exception of ἀλλ' εἰ ἓν ἔστιν (142c3) in S2 is directly opposed to εἰ ἓν ἕν (142c3) and hence does not violate the idea that what is emphasised comes after the conditional εἰ. (An even clearer way would have been νῦν δὲ οὐχ αὕτη ἐστὶν ἡ ὑπόθεσις, ἕν εἰ ἕν, τί χρὴ συμβαίνειν, ἀλλ' ἕν εἰ ἔστιν, but this seems to be a quite odd word order in the dependent clauses to me; the difference and emphasis in 142c3 would have been clear to every Greek reader.)

  [2] The order of these combinations will be discussed in the following.

  [3] I thus side with e.g. WUNDT 1935, 29; 57; MEINWALD 1991, 38 and SAYRE 2005, 129–132 that the programme in its general impetus provides a good argument in favour of counting eight main sections instead of nine; on the status of S2C, see below.

  [4] By 'principiate' I mean that which is directly governed and caused by the principle.

  [5] S1 (as a SuS) thus deals with A, S2 with B, S5 with C, and S6 with D, while S3 (as a ReS) deals with the relation of B to A, S4 with the relation of A to B, S7 with the relation of

$$\frac{A}{B} = \frac{C}{D} \qquad S3\left(\frac{S1}{S2}\right)S4$$

$$S2C$$

$$S3\left(\frac{S1}{S2}\right)S4 = S7\left(\frac{S5}{S6}\right)[S8] \qquad S7\left(\frac{S5}{S6}\right)[S8]$$

The basic pattern behind the eight main sections would thus be a concise analogy – a figure of thought that Plato employs commonly.[6] IP furthermore proposes to identify the four subjects A–D with the following systematic elements: A is the One as a principle of the forms (as is the Good to the forms, s. below); B is the realm of forms; C is the World Soul; and D is the physical cosmos. In each relation, A and C thus form the direct principles of B and D respectively. In each case this relation is hence a relation of 'One governing Many',[7] since in both cases it is a single principle that governs a specific multitude: the One governing the multitude of forms, and the World Soul governing the manifold particulars.

In this constellation, IP furthermore proposes a very specific function for the notorious section S2C. This section describes the *same subject* as S5. The function of S2C is thus to systematically *link* B with C (and D) in the sense that it remains, on the one hand, closely connected to S2 (i.e. B) by following it directly, while on the other hand it deals with the same subject that is taken up again in S5 (i.e. C). This means that S2C establishes an 'anchor point' after the two subject sections S1 and S2, before S3–4 discuss the relation between these two subjects. S5 with its third subject then takes up this 'anchor point' of S2C afterwards and goes on from there. According to IP, S2C is thus not a ninth main section in its own right, but an anticipation

D to C, and S8 with the relation of C to D (though S8 has to be understood a bit differently; cf. § 13 on core thought iv). The vertical alignment on the right, which furthermore includes S2C, will be explained in the following.

[6] Cf. PHDO. 111a7–b1; REP. 509d6–8 (cf. POETSCH 2019, 89–98); REP. 534a3–7; TIM. 31b8–32a7. In total, cf. the important contributions of AUBENQUE 1992, 39–44; DÖRRIE/ BALTES 1996, 324; DESJARDINS 2004, 121–126; GERLACH 2008 and FRONTEROTTA 2016 on this issue.

[7] This, of course, is not to be confused with the 'One-over-Many'-constellation that Aristotle discusses with regard to the forms (cf. e.g. META. A 9, 990b7–8 and *apud* Alexander, IN META. 67,13 GOLITSIS = Περὶ ἰδεῶν frg. 3 ROSS; on this cf. FINE 1980; FERRARI 2000, 370–371; cf. also 131b9 within the *Parmenides*) – even though this may be regarded to some extent as an analogous case of the two relations described above.

of the second half in the first, which permits to connect both halves of the exercise. However, by τὸ τρίτον (155e4) it introduces a third subject which then forms the subject of S5.[8]

In its overall structure, this constellation receives further support from the *Republic*. As I have argued extensively elsewhere,[9] the same constellation of A | B and C | D can in fact be found in the Analogy of the Sun. For within this analogy the sun is ultimately to be considered as the visible representation of that entity which grounds and causes the vital genesis of the physical realm (REP. 509b3–4), i.e. that entity later to be called the "Soul of the All" (cf. τὴν τοῦ παντὸς ψυχὴν TIM. 41d4–5) or, more commonly, the 'World Soul'.[10] Within the *Republic* we therefore find – according to that argument – a very similar constellation: as the Good is to the forms, such is the World Soul to the physical cosmos. Now, one could at least surmise that it is relevant for the One of the *Parmenides* that Plato ultimately identified the Good and the One,[11] which he did according to Aristotle's and others' reports.[12]

---

[8] There might be an echo of this threefold succession A, B, C in CRAT. 396a4–c3 and also in the (spurious) EPIS. II 312e1–313a3; cf. more in detail POETSCH 2021A, 265–268. On the connection between the Second Letter and the *Parmenides*, cf. TARRANT 1983, 90 ("I have no doubt that [EPIS. II] 312e is referring to the discussion of the One in the five positive hypotheses [sc. S1–4] of Plato's *Parmenides*."); TARRANT 1993, 170–173. For an overview of the different approaches to 155e4 cf. GILL 2014, 499 N. 9; GONZALES 2022, 379–383.

[9] Cf. POETSCH 2021A (A–D in the present study coincide with $A_1$, $B_1$, $C_1$, and $D_1$ in that article).

[10] One might object that there is no such thing as a World Soul in Plato's philosophy prior to the *Timaeus*. For the present argument it is sufficient that nothing forbids the view that Plato might have found this theorem while writing the *Parmenides*. This theorem would then be one innovation in the attempt to solve the difficulties of the Theory of Forms. I think, however, that we have good reasons to suppose that Plato actually held this theorem even before (or simultaneously to) the *Parmenides*, in the *Phaedrus* (cf. SZLEZÁK 2021, 313–315), the *Symposium*, and also the *Republic* (cf. POETSCH 2019, 69–98; 242–253; POETSCH 2021A, 246–250; 260). Further arguments with regard to this theorem will be provided in § 25.

[11] Cf. HORN 1995, 96.

[12] Cf. Aristotle, META. A 6, 988a14–15; A 7, 988b12–13 (with b9; b15); Δ 6, 1016b20–21; M 8, 1083a24; N 4, 1091b13–15; esp. EE A 8, 1218a20–21; 1218a25; PHYS. A 9, 192a14–19. Cf. on these issues very instructively HALFWASSEN ²2006, 236–245; GERSON 2020, 120–162. Even passages within the dialogues – such as REP. 443d7–e2, PHDO. 99c5–6, and esp. REP. 462a2–b2 – render it in fact inevitable that the Good and Unity are very closely connected (CORNFORD 1932, 178; GADAMER 1978, 82; BURNYEAT ²2022, 252–253; cf. also FERRARI 2000, 389 in the context of the fifth book of the *Republic*, as well as the remarks by DESJARDINS 2004, 110–111). With regard to the present task, it is in any case crucial in my eyes to remark that we have, on the one hand, historical evidence of the equivalence of the Good and the One (e.g. EE A 8, 1218a20–25; cf. BRUNSCHWIG ²2018) and of the systematic importance of the One in Plato (e.g. META. A 6, 987b18–25); while we have, one the other hand, a dialogue in which a person that Plato obviously held in the highest esteem

To those who agree that this is the case, the systematic parallel of the Analogy of the Sun mentioned before can thus provide additional support to IP since it finds IP anticipated to some extent in the *Republic*. To those who deny this relevance, IP remains an interpretative pattern in its own right that has to prove its validity against the text of the *Parmenides* itself (as will be examined in chapter 5).

To those who follow the mentioned parallel between the *Republic* and the *Parmenides*, there are two more arguments to support the present approach. Firstly, it has to be remarked that the parallel between these two dialogues might receive even further support from the *Republic* since one may suspect that a passage in the Line (REP. 511b5–c2) could be regarded as some kind of abbreviated programme of S1–2 (with τῶν ἐκείνης ἐχομένων REP. 511a8 as the general categories that are successively derived in S2). There is further-more a passage in the *Sophist* that is of potential relevance here.[13] In addition to that, in the *Republic*, the change from the plural ἐξ ὑποθέσεων to the singular ἐξ ὑποθέσεως in the Line (REP. 510b5–7) might furthermore be significant – a change which occurs precisely at the time when the approach to the first principle of everything is described.[14] This change might hence be interpreted in the sense that there is actually only *one* hypothesis that ultimately leads to the ἀνυπόθετος ἀρχή, namely εἰ ἕν ἐστιν.

Secondly, one may support the analogy of IP not only by the Analogy of the Sun, but also by a very similar statement in the *Timaeus*. There, the World Soul is said to be "created by the best of the intelligibles and eter-nal beings as the best of all generated things", τῶν νοητῶν ἀεί τε ὄντων

(cf. THT. 183e5–184a1; SOPH. 217c4–7; both passages refer not only to Parmenides but also to the *Parmenides*) speaks about the One itself, τὸ ἓν αὐτό. This – to say the very least – suggests that there may be some connection, both between the Good and the One and between the *Republic* (esp. the Analogy of the Sun) and the *Parmenides*.

[13] The passage I have in mind is SOPH. 244d14–245e2. The way how the Eleatic Visi-tor discusses, criticises, and modifies Parmenides within these arguments shares several sim-ilarities with what happens in the sections of the *Parmenides*, especially in S1–2 and S3. Cf. e.g. how the ἀληθῶς ἕν in SOPH. 245a1–10, strictly without any parts at all, resembles the One of S1 (cf. also 159c5–7 in S4), while the description of the ἓν ὄν (cf. SOPH. 244d12; 244d14) closely resembles the being One in S2 (cf. e.g. 145a2–b5 with SOPH. 244e2–245a3 and 142d1–e7 with SOPH. 245b7–9). Furthermore, there are apparent similarities between how, on the one hand, the One itself is split up by being in S2 (144e3–7) and something very similar is described in S3 (157c8–158d6), while, on the other hand, a certain depriva-tion, which is linked to being (SOPH. 245c1–6), seems to be involved in splitting up the ἀληθῶς ἕν itself (SOPH. 245a5–c9). The present aim is not to analyse in every detail this very dense passage of the *Sophist* in comparison to the *Parmenides*, but there are for sure further important connections between both. Cf. also the valuable remarks by GERSON 2013, 140 N. 23 on these links.

[14] Cf. τὴν τοῦ παντὸς ἀρχὴν (REP. 511b7; cf. 516c1–2; 517c1–4).

ὑπὸ τοῦ ἀρίστου ἀρίστη γενομένη τῶν γεννηθέντων (TIM. 37a1–2).
This ties in strikingly well with the Analogy of the Sun, where Socrates states
that the Good – which is later explicitly called the ἄριστον ἐν τοῖς οὖσι
(cf. REP. 532c5–6) – has created its offspring, the sun, as an analogue of
itself, τὸν τοῦ ἀγαθοῦ ἔκγονον, ὃν τἀγαθὸν ἐγέννησεν ἀνάλογον ἑαυτῷ
(REP. 508b12–13). In the *Republic* as well as in the *Timaeus* we thus find
two principles at the top of their respective realms, and hence the very same
ἀναλογία.[15] In both cases the first of these principles is called the creator
of the second. Of course, this prompts subsequent questions,[16] but if this
line of reasoning is in principle correct, then the general analogy of IP finds
further support since its core analogy is to be found both prior to *and* after
the *Parmenides*.


## § 13. Interpretative Core Thoughts

Let me explain in greater detail the five core thoughts I)–v) of IP. This also
allows us to deal with some possible general objections. Although it will go
into greater detail, this preparatory step primarily secures the possibility and
internal consistency of IP, while its factual productivity will be demonstrated
mainly in chapter 5.

Against IP one could object on a very general level that it does not exactly
correspond to Parmenides' methodological remarks in 135e8–136c5. For
instance, one could argue that the proposal of core thought III), to regard
the subject of S5 as a *new* subject C and not as the same subject A (but
now as non-being), is not consistent with Parmenides' programme. I agree
that the programme does not suggest the view expounded here.[17] However,

---

[15] In fact, I should have included TIM. 37a1–2 more extensively in POETSCH 2021A, 250
in order to strengthen the argument there.

[16] There are – at least – two subsequent questions. Firstly, whether this does not imply
that the demiurge is in fact to be identified with the topmost position of Plato's system. On
this issue, cf. the helpful remarks and observations by SZLEZÁK 2021, 453–456. Secondly, one
may ask if the quotations from the *Timaeus* and the *Repulic* do not locate the first principle
*within* the realm of being (i.e. at its topmost position) and hence contradict the theorem
that the Good is ultimately *beyond* the realm of being (cf. REP. 509b9). As I have argued
extensively in POETSCH 2021A, 235–259, I think one can solve this apparent contradiction
by positing a transcendent principle and its immanent representation at the topmost position in the direct principiate (this then applies also to the World Soul and the sun for
the realm of becoming). However, this is not within the scope of the present study. Hence,
I would like to refer those interested in these matters to the article mentioned above.

[17] Cf. especially the expression τὸ αὐτὸ τοῦτο (136a1–2) and RICKLESS 2007, 100–101
with N. 4–5 on that.

I think it is provable that Parmenides' factual execution in S1–8 differs in *numerous* and *significant* aspects from what he proposed in the programme (I shall provide some important examples in the following). Discrepancies between the programme and its implementation have been remarked time and again by interpreters.[18] In other words: had we only the text of S1–8 and were asked to reconstruct the programme from its implementation only, we would never end up exactly with the programme that Parmenides establishes. This means that since the actual execution and the programme differ *de facto*, one *inevitably* has to decide to which part one assigns priority in case of a discrepancy. As the present approach is primarily based on the actual execution and its conceptual patterns, it tends to cling to this execution. Besides that, this decision is based on the argument that the actual implementation is ultimately our main interpretandum, while the programme has only a preparatory function; I consequently give preference to the former. Putting it more colourfully, I think the programme resembles to some extent a blues scheme or the chord pattern of a jazz piece: it provides a framework and thus orientation, but the virtuoso (that Parmenides definitely is) will not stick to it slavishly.

Considering the relation between the programme and its implementation, we have to furthermore keep in mind that we possess too little genuine verbatim material from the Eleatic context, especially from Zeno. It is thus impossible to adequately judge in what sense Plato might in fact provide a – perhaps creative – adaptation of some Eleatic method that would have been familiar to his contemporary readers.[19] In the strange etymological section of the *Cratylus*, for instance, Plato employs a method that he for sure regarded as inadequate, but that seemingly had serious proponents as we know e.g. from the Derveni Papyrus. However, Plato can still use and adapt this method to provide a veritable florilegium of some of his positions.[20] Hence, it cannot be excluded that something similar applies to the exercise of the *Parmenides* as well. In fact, it appears quite likely to me if we look at

---

[18] Cf. WUNDT 1935, 5–6; CORNFORD 1939, 107; MEINWALD 1991, 29; DORTER 1994, 51–51; GILL 1996, 56–57; GRAESER 2003, 34; RICKLESS 2007, 107–108 – though, of course, with different observations. GRAESER 2003, 34 suspects that "Platon bei der Gestaltung der Übung im zweiten Teil die Dinge sehr viel weniger genau nimmt als noch bei der Formulierung des *modus procedendi* im Mittelteil" – given the fact that several aspects of the implementation are more detailed than the programme, one should, in my eyes, sooner advocate the opposite view.

[19] Speaking very tentatively, we might also suppose that only S1–4 resembled an actual Eleatic method, while adding the negative sections might be an addition of Plato to suit his needs and to have the results resemble the poem of Parmenides (cf. p. 50 n. 34).

[20] Cf. SCHADEWALDT ²1970, 630; GAISER 1974.

the few fragments of Zeno.[21] If this line of thought is correct, it could help us to understand why Plato has Parmenides' execution differ from the programme in the way he does.[22]

i) The first core thought states that we can characterise the main sections as either subject sections (SuS) or relation sections (ReS) according to the distinction πρὸς αὐτό vs. πρὸς ἄλλο. This aspect of IP implies that the qualification πρὸς αὐτό does not primarily mean some kind of *relation*, but the consideration of something *in itself*.[23] Accordingly, the SuS each consider one subject in itself (the One or the Others), while the ReS deal with the relation between these subjects from two different perspectives. I do not claim that this is the only way to understand the distinction πρὸς αὐτό vs. πρὸς ἄλλο. But it is a reasonable one, and may hence be assumed for IP.

ii) The second core thought states that we should regard S1–2, S5–6 as SuS and S3–4, S7–8 as ReS. This may seem doubtful at first glance since usually S2/3 are regarded as dealing with the *relation* between the One and the Others, while S1/4 are considered as SuS, dealing with the One and the Others in themselves respectively, hence SuS–ReS–ReS–SuS.[24] S5–8 are normally understood as following the scheme ReS–SuS–ReS–SuS.[25] There are, however, several arguments in support of the second core thought.

First of all, one has to admit that in executing his exercise Parmenides does not explicitly classify each section as one of the two types. The text thus leaves a certain margin to categorise the single sections with regard to the distinction πρὸς αὐτό vs. πρὸς ἄλλο, as esp. F. VON KUTSCHERA, A. GRAESER, and F. KARFÍK rightly emphasised.[26]

Secondly, it has to be noted that one crucial suggestion of IP consists exactly in the following: the very same thing that is called τὸ ἕν ὄν in its *overall* structure in S2 is addressed as τὰ ἄλλα in S3 (now with greater emphasis on

---

[21] Esp. DK 29 B 3; cf. also ALLEN ²1997, 217.

[22] I would like to thank B. STROBEL for emphasising this aspect of the Eleatic context in our discussions on the *Parmenides*.

[23] Cf. the valuable remarks of KARFÍK 2005, esp. 148; 153 on this point.

[24] Cf. e.g. HALFWASSEN ²2006, 299–300; GRAESER 2003, 60 N. 97; SCOLINCOV 2003, 28; KARFÍK 2005, 151–156; SAYRE 2005, 131. One quite often finds the idea that the sections are regarded as (contradictory) *pairs* (e.g. ALLEN ²1997, 216; MILLER 1986, 79; GILL 1996, 56). CURD 1989, 349 rightly emphasises that this results in a remarkable inversion in S1–2: the only pair where the negative section precedes the positive (cf. also GILL 1996, 57).

[25] Cf. e.g. HALFWASSEN ²2006, 300; SCOLINCOV 2003, 28; KARFÍK 2005, 156–161 (though with S7 as a special ReS: the Others in relation to the Others); SAYRE 2005, 131. DORTER 1994, 52 differs from this by having SuS–ReS–SuS–ReS for S1–4 and ReS–SuS–SuS–ReS for S5–8, though – as far as I can see – without further explanation.

[26] Cf. VON KUTSCHERA 1995, 46–47; GRAESER 2003, 36; KARFÍK 2005, 150–151.

the single *parts* forming this holistic structure)[27] and hence S2 already refers implicitly to τὰ ἄλλα. The appearance of τὰ ἄλλα in S2 (which suggests regarding S2 as ReS) is thus regarded as describing the internal structure of τὸ ἓν ὄν in itself, but not as qualifying S2 as ReS.

Thirdly, one has to recognise that the standard view also comes with certain inconsistencies or, at least, oddities. According to this view, we get the two sequences SuS–ReS–ReS–SuS / ReS–SuS–ReS–SuS. One therefore has to admit an "ordre [...] inverse"[28] at the beginning of the second half and the two halves obviously become unbalanced in this regard (which is at least not suggested by the programme). This imbalance is avoided by IP, which proposes two perfectly analogous sequences: SuS–SuS–ReS–ReS / SuS–SuS–ReS–ReS. This is, of course, no knock-down argument against the standard view, but it is an advantage of IP that has to be recognised. Furthermore, one has to note that S2 proposes at its very beginning to investigate the being One and the consequences περὶ αὐτοῦ (142b4) without any further qualification; this rather suggests that S2 is a SuS, but no ReS.[29]

Besides that, one has to take into account that S4 also definitely talks about the Others *and* the One (159b6; 159c2–4; 159c5–7). It does so admittedly with greater emphasis on the former, but it is not as exclusively concentrated on the Others as S1 is on the One. The standard view, to regard S4 as a SuS (dealing with the Others *solely in themselves* as did S1 for the One itself), is thus neither in complete and perfect accordance with the text.

Ultimately, there is one further indication to categorise exactly S3–4 (and S7–8) as ReS. It is the fact that in these sections, but not in S1–2 (and S5–6 respectively), Parmenides says that he will skip further categories for the sake of brevity (165d7–e1) or discusses them very briefly and summarily (159a6–b1; 160a4–7; 166b5–7). This ties in better with the present categorisation than with the standard view since S3 and S4 are thus understood as telling roughly the same story as S2 and S1 respectively, but now under the perspective of their *relation* to one another.[30] Since Parmenides had discussed these things in detail before, he can now shortcut the deductions. On the contrary, if S4 were again a SuS (as the standard view suggests), there would be significantly less sense in the shortcut that Parmenides takes here since S4 should then

---

[27] SCOLNICOV 2003, 35–36; 139–140 and KARFÍK 2005, 156 see to some extent a similar connection between S2 and S3.

[28] KARFÍK 2005, 157. Cf. in some sense also DORTER 1994, 51–52.

[29] Cf. περὶ αὐτοῦ (163c1) in S6, which is unanimously considered to be a SuS.

[30] Ultimately, this relation between A (S1) and B (S2) is decisively asymmetrical. In fact, S4 discusses this relation very much in the sense that there is *no* such relation at all (cf. esp. 159b6–7; 159d1–e1).

– at least to some extent – provide *new* information on the Others *in them-selves*, which could not be abridged.

iii) The third core thought consisted in regarding the subject of S5 as a *newly introduced* subject C (and not as taking up A, now as non-being). As I said, I admit that the programme does not suggest such a new subject. However, if we take an impartial look at the text of S5 itself, there is evidence which at least suggests that Parmenides *does* in fact introduce a new sub-ject and thus deviates from his programme. He seems to have some specific subject in mind, when he points to τό ... ἓν ἐκεῖνο καὶ μὴ ἄλλο (161a1; cf. also 161b5–7). *That* One he is now pointing to is the non-being One, but not the being One from the first half of the sections (160e7–161a3; cf. also 162d5–8). Parmenides clearly emphasises that he now investigates *that* specific One and nothing else as non-being.[31] This is especially sup-ported by 162d8, where Parmenides says explicitly that he is talking about "a specific other thing" (περὶ ἄλλου τινός). Moreover, Parmenides already says in the transitional passage TP that he now talks of a ἕτερον τῶν ἄλλων (160c5; 160c7–8), which he then takes up in S5 (160d7; 160e1–2). All this evidence allows in my eyes to at least *suppose* that Parmenides introduces a new subject C, instead of taking up A again.

In a certain sense, IP proposes to regard τὸ μὴ ὂν ἕν in S5 as something like τὸ γιγνόμενον ἕν.[32] This would correspond remarkably well to the later text of the *Timaeus*, where the World Soul is explicitly called the ἀρίστη γενομένη τῶν γεννηθέντων (Tim. 37a2; cf. also Leg. 892a4–5; 896a6–7). In that sense, S1–4 and S5–8 would thus be perfectly consistent in their main focus with the realms of being and becoming respectively. We shall produce further evidence for this in § 16.

iv) The fourth core thought proposes to overlay the basic analogical struc-ture with a second layer that to a certain extent separates S1 and S8 from the overall arrangement. This is motivated by the fact that the hypotheses[33] of these sections differ significantly from those of S2–4 and S5–7 respectively. It is true that the programme suggests only two hypotheses: 'if (the) One is' and 'if (the) One is not'. However, it is also true that Parmenides again

---

[31] εἰ δὲ τὸ ἓν ἐκεῖνο καὶ μὴ ἄλλο ὑπόκειται μὴ εἶναι (161a3–4).

[32] Or also: τὸ ἓν γιγνόμενον in analogy to τὸ ἓν ὄν. There is even a motivation at hand why τὸ μὴ ὂν ἕν is used instead of τὸ γιγνόμενον ἕν: if we think of the very strict dicho-tomy between being and non-being in Parmenides' poem, which leaves virtually no place for becoming (as a mixture of being and non-being), the usage of τὸ μὴ ὂν ἕν becomes quite plausible.

[33] By 'hypothesis' I mean the antecedental εἰ-clause which Parmenides uses within the different sections.

does *not* cling to his programme in the actual implementation. In fact, he uses *four* hypotheses: one in S1, a second one in S2–4, another one in S5–7, and again a different one in S8. In the Greek text there can be little to no doubt that the hypothesis of S1 (εἰ ἕν ἐστιν 137c4) differs significantly in its emphasis from S2–4 (ἓν εἰ ἔστιν 142b3).[34] This difference is clearly upheld throughout S1 and S2–4 respectively[35] and it is in fact mirrored statistically in some sense.[36] It is even more emphasised by the remarks at the beginning of S2, where εἰ ἓν ἕν (142c3) refers most naturally back to S1;[37] firstly, since it tallies with εἰ ἓν ἔσται τὸ ἕν (137d3) in S1 quite well, and secondly, since νῦν (142c2) emphasises that S2 (as well as S3–4) *now* implements another hypothesis. There would have been no necessity to implement this change from S1 to S2. Parmenides could have started with ἓν εἰ ἔστιν right away, had he wished to perfectly fulfil his programme, since this programme asks to assume its main subject to be (and not to emphasise this subject's very own character, as εἰ ἕν ἐστιν does by by prioritising unity over being).[38] The fact that he did not do so can be regarded as significant, and allows us at least to implement it in an interpretative pattern as the one proposed here.[39] An exemplary review of the research literature shows that only some

---

[34] Cf. p. 55 n. 1.

[35] In S1 we find: εἰ ἓν ἔσται τὸ ἕν (137d3); cf. also οὕτως εἴη ὅπερ ἔστιν, ἕν (139c1); ἕως ἂν ᾖ ἕν (139c4); εἰ τοιοῦτον εἴη (141a6). In S2–4 we find: [S2] ἓν εἰ ἔστιν (142b5); ἓν εἰ ἔστιν (142c8); εἰ ἄρα ἔστιν ἕν (144a4); εἴπερ ἓν ἔστιν (151e7; O'BRIEN 2005A, 241 rightly emphasises that in the case of εἴπερ this word order is inevitable; hence this does not contradict the general impetus of S2–4); [S2C] τὸ ἓν εἰ ἔστιν (155e4); τὸ ἕν, εἰ ἔστιν (157b4); [S3] ἓν εἰ ἔστιν (157b6); ἓν εἰ ἔστιν (157b7); [S4] ἓν εἰ ἔστιν (159b3); ἓν εἰ ἔστι (159b5); [IS] ἓν εἰ ἔστιν (160b2). Cf. also [S2] τοῦ αὐτοῦ δὲ ἐκείνου οὗ ὑπεθέμεθα, τοῦ ἑνὸς ὄντος (142d3–4); [S3] ἐπείπερ ἄλλα τοῦ ἑνός ἐστιν (157b9); εἴπερ ἕκαστον ἔσται (158a3). The only exception in S2–4 is ἀλλ᾽ εἰ ἓν ἔστιν (142c3), which is directly opposed to εἰ ἓν ἕν (142c3); hence ROBINSON ²1953, 245 is wrong in claiming that 142c3 proves the word order to be irrelevant; cf. also p. 55 n 1. In S2, εἰ δέ γε ἓν μόνον ἐστίν, δυὰς δὲ μὴ ἔστιν, ἅψις οὐκ ἂν εἴη (149c4–5) is either counterfactual or again pointing to S1.

[36] Cf. BRISSON/BENZÉCRI 1989, 123 (with regard to their "classe 14").

[37] Cf. CORNFORD 1939, 136 N. 1.

[38] Parmenides could even have kept on clinging, in some sense, to εἰ ἕν ἐστιν in S2 since the beginnings of S5 and S6 prove that he can (quite arbitrarily as it seems) deduce more or less whatever he wants from one and the same hypothesis by emphasising different aspects of it: compare 160d3–e2; 161e3; 162b6–7 (partial presence of οὐσία in S5) with 163c1–d1 (complete absence of οὐσία in S6). Cf. the good remarks by ŠPINKA 2005, 185.

[39] One could even argue that the very controversial sentence περὶ τοῦ ἑνὸς αὐτοῦ ὑπο-θέμενος, εἴτε ἕν ἐστιν εἴτε μὴ ἕν (137b3–4) points to this specific difference and hence sup-ports the partial detachment of S1 from the scheme as core thought IV) proposes. If we take the transmitted text to be sound, 137b3–4 could in fact emphasise the difference between S1 (i.e. 'if the One itself is one', in a strict sense) and all other sections ('if the One itself is not one', in that strict sense – but something else); cf. HALFWASSEN ²2006, 299 N. 98; 304 N. 113.

interpreters have taken into account this change in the hypothesis between S1 and S2–4,[40] while others have silently[41] or explicitly[42] ignored this change. So much for the difference of the hypothesis in S1 and S2–4.

To the best of my knowledge, however, no one has ever noted that the hypothesis of S8 also differs significantly from all the other hypotheses: ἓν εἰ μὴ ἔστι, τἆλλα δὲ τοῦ ἑνός, τί χρὴ εἶναι (165e2–3).[43] The obvious difference lies in the fact that this is the only case where the Others are actually included in the antecedent. It is obviously two different things to ask '¬p → …?' or to ask '¬p ∧ q → …?'. The new hypothesis thus says something like 'If the One is not, but the Others are – what needs to be?'. Again there was no need to implement this change. Again this differs significantly from the programme. And again this change seems to be neither an inaccuracy nor caused by inattention, for it is instead carefully prepared and anticipated twice towards the end of S7.[44] It is thus again justified to integrate this evidence into IP. We shall see that that which 'needs to be' or 'needs to be given' may be regarded as fulfilling a similar medial role as the χώρα in the *Timaeus* (§ 15). S1 thus deviates from the programme by emphasising the first principle as such, while S8 deviates by not being a proper ReS, but in some sense introducing yet another quasi-subject.

v) The fifth core thought, according to which we find an analogous relation between principle and principiate in S1–4 and S5–8, needs no specific justification. It either finds its motivation in the parallel to the *Republic* (to those who regard this as significant; cf. pp. 58–59) or could simply be understood as an interpretative proposal following from the other core thoughts. The relation of the World Soul and the physical cosmos in S5–8 could be motivated, for instance, with reference to the *Timaeus*; while the constella-

Perhaps, this view might to some extent receive further support from 160b2–3: πάντα τέ ἐστι τὸ ἓν καὶ οὐδὲ ἕν ἐστι – however this is to be understood, it suggests that the text in 137b3–4 is sound. GILL 1996, 67 provides another explanation of 137b4.

[40] Cf. e.g. HARDIE 1936, 101–102; CORNFORD 1939, 136; MILLER 1986, 237 N. 6; HALFWASSEN ²2006, 304; GILL 1996, 57; 65–69.

[41] Cf. e.g. BRISSON/BENZÉCRI 1989, 123; FRANCES 1996, 54 N. 5; GRAESER 2003, 40–42; KARFÍK 2005, 151–155; ERLER 2007, 228.

[42] Cf. e.g. ROBINSON ²1953, 245–246; ALLEN ²1997, 214 N. 43; SCOLNICOV 2003, 95; RICKLESS 2007, 107–108.

[43] Cf. e.g. RUNCIMAN 1959, 100 (who summarises the hypothesis of S8 solely by "If unity does not exist"); ALLEN ²1997, 213–214 N. 43 (who leaves out τἆλλα δὲ τοῦ ἑνός when referring to 165e2–3); DORTER 1994, 66; GILL 1996, 58; GRAESER 2003, 66–68; SCOLNICOV 2003, 163; KARFÍK 2005, 149–150; 159 ("la même protase négative" for S7–8); RICKLESS 2007, 107. SCHUDOMA 2001, 102 quotes the full antecedent as conditional clause, but considers it to be the "Gegenbetrachtung" to S7.

[44] ἓν εἰ μὴ ἔστιν, τἆλλα δὲ τοῦ ἑνός (164c5); εἰ ἑνὸς μὴ ὄντος πολλὰ ἔστιν (165d8–e1).

tion in S1–4 could then be regarded as a possible second constellation in analogy to the former. In total, IP thus uses four elements that are known to be part of Plato's philosophy from other dialogues: the physical cosmos, the World Soul, the realm of forms, and a principle of the forms.[45] IP then proposes to arrange these four elements in a discrete geometrical analogy – a figure of thought that is again well-known in Plato. This concise constellation forms the nucleus of IP as explained.

Note that IP takes its four elements from the dialogues and thus remains restricted to them. The present argument does therefore not depend on any understanding of Plato's inner-academic teachings. However, I see in principle no contradiction to these teachings and I think the interpretation of the *Parmenides* could benefit from them. But my argument does not depend on them. In the same vein, my argument does not take into account the arguments the Neoplatonists used to establish their interpretations of the *Parmenides*. I do not make use of them, but I do not regard an argument as discredited only because its outcome resembles in some aspect the Neoplatonists' interpretations either. In fact, there is enough evidence that an interpretation that seeks for certain systematic subjects of the sections existed already before the Neoplatonists, probably dating back as far as the Old Academy.[46] The main flaw of virtually all Neoplatonic interpretations is in my eyes to be found in the aim to find a proper subject for *every* section (be it in the first five or in all nine sections according to their most common way of counting). This fails to properly recognise the role of the ReS in the second part and thus tends to go decisively wrong from S3 (their fourth section) onwards. In some sense, the interpretation of Damascius comes perhaps closest to mine, especially with regard to S7 (his eighth section), but again my arguments remain independent of his.[47]

So far, IP remains of course mainly an interpretative assumption. It thus has to prove its validity with regard to the exercise itself and its conceptual patterns. Let us therefore return to these patterns.

---

[45] It has to be remarked that my argument is not constrained to a specific understanding of this principle of the forms (e.g. the question of how to understand REP. 509b8–10 exactly). Note furthermore that a principle (or principles) of the forms is still present in the *Timaeus* since the ἀρχή or ἀρχαί περὶ ἁπάντων are left out explicitly (TIM. 48c2–4; cf. also τὴν τοῦ παντὸς ἀρχὴν REP. 511b7). This deliberate omission is not caused by uncertainty about those principles; it remains withheld solely due to the mode of investigation employed by Timaeus (TIM. 48c4–d4).

[46] Cf. DODDS 1928; HALFWASSEN 1993; DILLON 2005.

[47] For helpful surveys of the Neoplatonic interpretations, cf. SAFFREY/WESTERINK 1968, LXXV–LXXXIX; COMBÈS 1997, XII–XVII; GLEEDE 2008.

# 5. SYSTEMATIC INTERPRETATIONS

The aim of the present chapter is to further analyse the statistical evidence, this time with regard to a more specific interpretation and especially to IP. Accordingly, the following conclusions are more far-reaching and may thus be considered more controversial. However, some of the present conclusions are fairly descriptive in part and may hence be considered by some to rightfully belong to chapter 3. The present chapter will discuss to what extent IP is generally consistent with the ontological patterns (§ 14), especially the field of appearance (§ 15). It will then investigate the special relation of S2C and S5 (§ 16) and produce some evidence regarding the relation between S2 and S3 (§ 18). During this analysis, previous statistical evidence is also taken into account (§ 17). Subsequently, further systematic conclusions will be drawn, especially with regard to the concept of participation (§ 19). I shall then discuss the difficult status of S1 with regard to IP (§ 20) and the occurrences of several rare terms (§ 21). Ultimately, some general considerations will conclude the second main step of this study (§ 22).

## § 14. A Constellation of
## Being, Becoming, and Appearance

*IP permits a concise understanding of the conceptual patterns in general, especially the patterns of being, becoming/passing away, and appearance.* According to IP, we are to expect strong similarities between S2 and S3, since they both are expected to deal with the same subject. This resemblance is already to be found in the conceptual pattern of being (§§ 5–6) and we shall find further evidence in § 18. Since this pattern includes the key terms of the Platonic forms, it generally matches the proposal of IP in locating the realm of forms in S2 and S3.

With regard to the special position of S2C and the subject this section shares with S5, the patterns of becoming/passing away and change provided some evidence of their resemblance (§ 6). We shall discover further patterns that support this, as well as the identification of S2C and S5 with the realm of the (World) Soul (§ 16). This will ultimately imply consequences for how we understand Plato's concept of participation and the precise way in which he integrates change and alteration in his system (§ 19).

According to IP, S1 describes a first principle that lies in some way beyond the forms by being their principle. This matches the first results in the pattern of being to some extent (§ 5), though we shall find some more evidence for this identification of S1 later (§ 20).

Furthermore, IP is very helpful to interpret in detail the immensely negative account of being in S6 (§ 6) and the positive account of appearance in S7. Since S6 is a subject section according to IP, it deals with the physical realm solely *in itself*. Thus isolated, this realm remains nothing and is characterised only by the absence of being (cf. esp. οὐσίας ἀπουσίαν 163c3). However, in S7 this very same subject is considered in a relation section, now *in relation* to its direct principle, i.e. the subject of S5 (just as, exactly analogously, S3 described the relation of the principiate in S2 to its principle in S1). And this relation perfectly explains why there is now positive evidence to be found in S7. The appearance of being emerges at the very moment the physical realm gets in contact with the realm of forms via the World Soul as its direct, and at the same time mediating principle. Again, we shall find further and more specific evidence for this constellation of S6–7 (along with S8) in the subsequent paragraph (§ 15).

In total, one can state a very good accordance of what is expected according to IP and what is provided by the conceptual patterns so far. More detailed confirmation will follow in the subsequent considerations.

## § 15. The Sensible Realm

*The concepts in S7 tie in with Plato's account of the sensible world quite well, especially with regard to the Timaeus, and this dialogue may also serve to explain the negative account in S8.* Let us consider in greater detail those concepts besides φαίνω and δοκέω which we found to support the conceptual field of appearance in § 7. Among these, the concepts of ὄναρ/ὕπνος are remarkable since Plato uses them both in the *Republic* (476c2–d4) and the *Timaeus* (52b3–c2; cf. also below) to describe our (premature) attitude towards the sensible world.[1] Even if Parmenides uses this concept only twice (§ 7, T.7.1), its occurrence in S7 is perfectly consistent with the present interpretation (§ 21). The same goes for σκιαγραφέω, which is used several times by Plato to allude to the, at times, potentially illusory and deceptive character of sensual appearance.[2]

Another concept, which is to be found exclusively and quite dominantly in S7, is ὄγκος. The term normally means bodily 'mass' or 'bulk'. This concept is remarkable for two reasons. First of all, Plato uses this term several times in other dialogues to refer to the bodily mass and hence to physical bodies.[3] Especially remarkable is an occurrence in the *Timaeus* again, where ὄγκος is used to specifically describe three-dimensionality as such (Tim. 31c4). While the present mode of investigation may of course not provide a definitive argument of how to translate ὄγκος in S7, it strongly encourages us to understand this term in relation to the sensible world of three-dimensional physical particulars. The conceptual pattern of ὄγκος in any case strongly supports the present interpretation and IP.

Secondly, ὄγκος is remarkable for another reason. This term might have been used already by Zeno to describe the mass of physical bodies.[4] My reason for supposing this runs as follows. Directly before quoting Zeno verbatim, Simplicius explains that Zeno is dealing with μέγεθος, πάχος and ὄγκος (In Phys. 1 139, 10 Diels). Although we only find μέγεθος and πάχος in the transmitted verbatim quotes,[5] I think it is quite plausible to assume that the third of these three terms, ὄγκος, was also used by Zeno to describe the physical, bodily mass in some other argument – especially since Simplicius explains that he selects only a few exemplary of many arguments (In Phys. 1 139, 5–7 Diels). This is furthermore supported by the fact that Aristotle also uses the term ὄγκος in his description of Zeno's

---

[1] Szaif 2022 makes some detailed observations on S7, but takes the allusion to dreaming as "a first indication that this deduction [sc. S7] will take us to an ontological exploration of illusory entities" (ibid., 442) and, in general, sees S7 as an investigation of purely illusionary "pseudo-objects". However, this dismisses too easily, in my eyes, the possibility of an approach to the sensible world in S7 (cf. also Miller 1986, 163–165). J. Szaif's argumentation too readily takes appearances as *mere* appearances without considering that Plato often uses the term to refer to the physical world as such.

[2] Rep. 365c3–4; 586b7–c5 (cf. also Prot. 356c4–e4); 602c10–d4; Phdo. 69b5–8. Schudoma 2001, 99–100 rightly emphasises this term, but takes it too literal in my eyes.

[3] Cf. Tht. 155b8; 155c3; Phdo. 96d4; Tim. 54d1; 56d3; 58e6; 59a3; 60c3; 61b3; 62c7; 81b8; 83d3; Leg. 959c4–5. In Soph. 244e3, ὄγκῳ is quoted from the comparison in Parmenides' poem (DK 28 B 8, 43).

[4] Cf. also Graeser 1996, 163, who furthermore points to the fact that Heraclides Ponticus used this term in a comparable sense.

[5] Cf. In Phys. 1 139, 12–13; 141, 1–4; 8 Diels.

'stadium paradox' (PHYS. Z 9, 239b34).[6] Since the second half of the *Parmenides* enacts a method similar to that of Zeno (135d7–8), it may indeed seem plausible that Plato has his Parmenides allude to this Eleatic concept to describe the sensible world, with whose plurality Zeno was primarily concerned (albeit with quite diametrically opposed intentions). Though we cannot be definitely sure of whether Zeno employed ὄγκος, its occurrence in S7 thus ties in quite well with the bigger picture and might hence support the view that ὄγκος in S7 refers to the physical particulars in the sensible world.

Besides this, and especially with regard to the concept of φάντασμα (the positive occurrences of which are to be found exclusively in S7[7]), there is a passage in the *Timaeus* that strikingly matches the position of S7 in the overall constellation of S6–8. The passage runs as follows: "an image – since it does not have as its own that towards which[8] it has come to be, but always bears the appearance of something else – is therefore obliged to arise in something else, clinging to being somehow or otherwise is itself nothing at all".[9] This ties in with the present approach in several aspects. Firstly, this passage states that the image – which stands also *pars pro toto* for the whole physical world as an image (cf. e.g. TIM. 92c7) – is *in itself* nothing at all (μηδὲν τὸ παράπαν αὐτὴν εἶναι). It can only be if it clings to οὐσία in some way (οὐσίας ἀμωσγέπως ἀντεχομένην). This is exactly what is described by S6–7 according to IP: the physical world, regarded solely in itself, is nothing at all (S6),[10] but it becomes the image and appearance of οὐσία the very moment it comes, via the World Soul, in contact with οὐσία (S7; § 16). Secondly, it is stated in the *Timaeus* that a physical particular only bears in itself[11] a φάντασμα of something else (ἑτέρου ... τινος ἀεὶ φέρεται φάντασμα), which again perfectly and even literally fits the presence of this term in S7. The sensible world is itself an image and a world full of images – a claim which is hardly surprising in Plato. And thirdly, TIM. 52c2–5 tells

---

[6] In this context, it might be quite noteworthy that Aristotle (PHYS. Δ 1, 209a23–27; Δ 3, 210b22–24; cf. DK 29 A 24), in his report of one of Zeno's paradoxes, implies the very same premise (i.e. that everything that is must occupy a place), which we find alluded to in TIM. 52b3–5, again with regard to the sensible world.

[7] The only other occurrence (in S8; 166a5) is negative.

[8] There has been a lot of discussion concerning ἐφ' ᾧ γέγονεν (cf. e.g. CHERNISS 1956). I have dealt with this expression in greater detail in POETSCH 2019, 214–218, but it is of secondary importance to the present argument.

[9] ὡς εἰκόνι μέν, ἐπείπερ οὐδ' αὐτὸ τοῦτο ἐφ' ᾧ γέγονεν ἑαυτῆς ἐστιν, ἑτέρου δέ τινος ἀεὶ φέρεται φάντασμα, διὰ ταῦτα ἐν ἑτέρῳ προσήκει τινὶ γίγνεσθαι, οὐσίας ἀμωσγέπως ἀντεχομένην, ἢ μηδὲν τὸ παράπαν αὐτὴν εἶναι (TIM. 52c2–5; my trans.).

[10] This is the explanation of the many negative occurrences of being in S6 (§ 6).

[11] As MILLER 2003, 142 n. 100, I understand φέρεται as a middle.

us that in order to establish the relation between image and archetype "something else", a third thing is required as a medium in which the image arises
(διὰ ταῦτα ἐν ἑτέρῳ προσήκει τινὶ γίγνεσθαι). This ties in remarkably well
with the way in which the wording of the hypothesis is altered decisively during the course of S7 and at the beginning of S8. It is now asked what (else)
is needed, if the One is not, but the Other are.[12] If one is willing to understand by this the relation between the World Soul (the non-being One in S5;
cf. §§ 12; 16) and the physical particulars (the Others as direct principiates
of the non-being One in S7), this altered hypothesis in S8 and Tim. 52c2–5
are indeed concerned with the very same thing: the medium which consti-
tutes a necessary condition for establishing the constellation and in which
the principiate emerges.[13] The way S8 describes something in purely negative
terms and denies even non-being may thus in its impetus be understood as a
close parallel to the way in which the *Timaeus* talks in negative terms of the
χώρα.[14] In a certain sense, S8 thus talks again of another quasi-subject: the
space-matter χώρα that forms the substratum of the sensible world. This is
the precise sense in which S8 is detached from the constellation of subject
and relations sections.[15]

In total, Tim. 52c2–5 thus seems to be a very dense and quite general,
but nevertheless remarkably coherent description of what happens in S6–8
of the *Parmenides* according to IP.[16] Regardless of how the *Parmenides* relates
to the dialogues prior to it, this accordance with the *Timaeus* may therefore
count as a supporting, supplementary argument for the present interpretation and IP. For it is doubtlessly plausible that a systematic constellation
Plato uses to respond to challenges against his Theory of Forms in the *Parmenides* is also to be found in the dialogues after it.

---

[12] Cf. § 13 for these formulations in S7–8.

[13] Cf. also the second beginning in the *Timaeus* (esp. 47e4–48b3), which is in a similar
sense concerned with a necessary medium.

[14] Cf. esp. μορφὴν οὐδεμίαν ποτὲ οὐδενὶ τῶν εἰσιόντων ὁμοίαν εἴληφεν οὐδαμῇ
οὐδαμῶς (Tim. 50c1–2) with τἆλλα τῶν μὴ ὄντων οὐδενὶ οὐδαμῇ οὐδαμῶς οὐδεμίαν κοινωνίαν ἔχει (166a1–2). If τὰ μὴ ὄντα are understood as τὰ γιγνόμενα (as IP
proposes to understand τὸ μὴ ὂν ἕν as τὸ γιγνόμενον ἕν; cf. § 13), then τὰ μὴ ὄντα occupy
a very similar position as τὰ εἰσιόντα in the *Timaeus* (cf. also Tim. 50d2). Cf. furthermore
Tim. 50d7–e1; 50e4–5; 51a1–3; 51a7–b2; 52b1–2 for negative descriptions of the χώρα.

[15] Cf. the fourth core thought in § 13.

[16] There is even one further argument to connect this passage of the *Timaeus* to the *Parmenides*. The immediate subsequent passage Tim. 52c6–d1 takes up a problem that is also
stated, in a very similar way, in 131b1–2 (how can one form remain one and in itself while
appearing as a whole in many instances?) and that appears again in Phlb. 15b7–8 in relation
to the Theory of Forms. Cf. also Poetsch 2019, 218–222.

## § 16. The Realm of the Soul

*Conceptual patterns indicate that the resemblance between S2C and S5 points to the intermediate realm of the World Soul. S5 furthermore seems to deal with a single entity in a specific sense.* In its interpretation of S2C's position and function in the scheme of the sections, IP has us expect a strong resemblance between S2C and S5 since it supposes that both deal with the same subject. This resemblance was already found in § 6, but it has not yet been interpreted systematically. One therefore has to ask whether it is possible to find further support of this resemblance and whether one can find indicators that allow us to interpret S2C and S5 as a description of the soul's ontological level – an ontological level which on a macroscopic scale is formed by the World Soul.

Two conceptual patterns that fulfil both tasks are the fields of rest and motion. κίνησις, κινέω, and ἀκίνητος (as negative) are included in the latter, while, among the terms of S1–8, στάσις, ἡσυχία, ἡσυχάζω, and ἵστημι belong in the former. Among the terms employed in the exercise, Parmenides furthermore uses φέρω, περιφέρω, ἀλλάττω, μεταλλάττω, ἀμείβω, and στρέφω in the sense of motion. In this case it is most expedient to evaluate both fields separately, so there is no need to consider whether one might count, for instance, a negative account of motion as a positive count for rest. The results of the fields of motion and rest are given in T.16.1 and D.16.1A–2B (p. 74).

All *p*-values are quite low and we are thus entitled to regard the patterns as non-random. The DP-values are quite high and prove that those patterns are marked ones. There is little surprise with regard to S1, S4, and S6, which all show exclusively negative results. A few positive results in S2/3 could perhaps be explained by help of the greatest kinds of motion and rest in the *Sophist*,[17] though I do not think that one can establish this relation solely based on the present evidence. In that sense, the two negative occurrences of rest in S2 (146a5) obviously serve the primary need to quickly establish a positive account of motion besides rest, which is dominant in that passage and in S2. Nevertheless, it is undeniably obvious that Parmenides pays very little attention to motion and rest in S2. As is the case with other terms, the exclusively positive occurrences in S7 are found in the mode of φαίνεσθαι (165d4). This in turn confirms the idea that essential change somehow happens on another level, and is only mirrored in the phenomenal world (§ 19).

---

[17] Cf. SOPH. 249b2–c1; 250b8–c4 et passim.

| | | S1 | S2 | S2C | S3 | S4 | S5 | S6 | S7 | S8 | $p$ | DP |
|---|---|---|---|---|---|---|---|---|---|---|---|---|
| Motion | + | 0 | 3 | 9 | 1 | 0 | 6 | 0 | 2 | 0 | 1.60e-07 | 0.62 |
| | − | −19 | 0 | −5 | 0 | −1 | −9 | −2 | 0 | 0 | 1.29e-12 | 0.65 |
| | + | 0.000 | 0.060 | 1.695 | 0.145 | 0.000 | 0.598 | 0.000 | 0.389 | 0.000 | | |
| | − | −1.174 | 0.000 | −0.942 | 0.000 | −0.264 | −0.897 | −0.610 | 0.000 | 0.000 | | |
| Rest | + | 0 | 4 | 9 | 1 | 0 | 4 | 0 | 1 | 0 | 3.23e-06 | 0.55 |
| | − | −4 | −2 | −5 | 0 | −1 | 0 | −3 | 0 | 0 | 7.88e-05 | 0.60 |
| | + | 0.000 | 0.080 | 1.695 | 0.145 | 0.000 | 0.399 | 0.000 | 0.195 | 0.000 | | |
| | − | −0.247 | −0.040 | −0.942 | 0.000 | −0.264 | 0.000 | −0.915 | 0.000 | 0.000 | | |

T.16.1 FIELDS OF MOTION AND REST

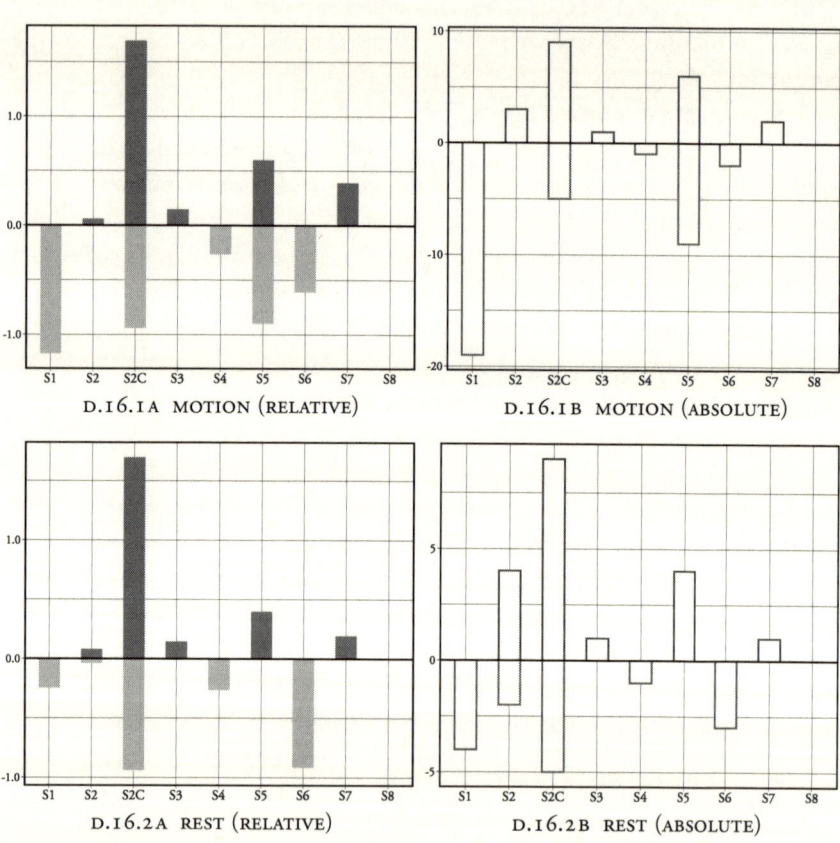

D.16.1A MOTION (RELATIVE)  D.16.1B MOTION (ABSOLUTE)

D.16.2A REST (RELATIVE)  D.16.2B REST (ABSOLUTE)

Most prominent are of course the relatively numerous occurrences in S2C and S5, which are most distinct in S2C, but recognisable also in S5. Again, this not only supports the resemblance between these two sections; it may also help in their further interpretation. Since for Plato soul is the principle of motion,[18] that which is able to spontaneously and autonomously perform the transition between motion and rest, it is hardly controversial to regard these patterns as supporting IP's location of the soul in S2C and S5. In a similar sense, J. DILLON emphasised with regard to S2C that the concepts of motion, rest and others therein fit Plato's concept of the soul quite well.[19] Although J. DILLON does not discuss that section explicitly, I see no reason why this should not also apply to S5, since the patterns of these concepts are quite clear in that respect. One could argue that the pattern is less strongly marked in S5 than in S2C. This, however, is only a matter of relative tendency, while the patterns in general are definitely similar. In both cases the characteristic alternation of motion and rest is doubtlessly present. We should therefore not overemphasise the fact that rest is only affirmed, but not negated in S5, since there is still a clear alternation between both concepts due to the positive instances of both motion and rest in S5.

Some of the results of § 6 may serve to further support the claim that the psychic realm is to be found in S2C and S5.[20] There we found a characteristic pattern of positive *and* negative accounts of being as well as a strong concentration of becoming/passing away and change in S2C and S5 (D.6.1A–2B). If one takes a look at the Platonic hierarchy of reality downwards, the level of the soul is definitely the first one in which change and alteration happen in an eminent sense.[21] Soul's decisive involvement in these processes is even stated quite explicitly in the *Laws*, where the Athenian claims that it is "soul more than anything else that takes the lead in every change and reorganisation of the bodies."[22] Very remarkably, we find separation and combination, increase and decrease, as well as becoming and passing away very densely grouped together in the *Laws*, while precisely the very same pairs are to be

[18] Cf. e.g. PHDR. 245c5–246a2; 246c3–4; LEG. 895e10–896c3.

[19] "This [sc. S2C], it will be recalled, concerns an entity which is both one and many, exists in time, and is subject to (at least spiritual) motion and change – a description which fits the Platonic soul passably well." (DILLON 2005, 310 N. 31).

[20] By 'psychic realm' I heuristically mean an intermediate ontological level, in the sense that the soul is neither ontologically identical with the physical nor with the forms (though it is more akin to the latter; cf. PHDO. 78b4–80b5). This intermediate level of the soul is already to be found in REP. 508d4–9; 584d3–586b4 (cf. POETSCH 2019, 96–98; 233; POETSCH 2021A, 246–250); 587b11–588a10 (cf. POETSCH 2022); SYMP. 208e5–209b4; 210b6–c6.

[21] Regarding the position of κίνησις among the μέγιστα γένη in the *Sophist*, one has to note that, firstly, κίνησις primarily means primarily 'knowability' in this context (cf. SOPH. 249b5–6) and that, secondly, this form of κίνησις does obviously not cause any substantial change or alteration within the forms.

[22] καὶ μεταβολῆς τε αὐτῶν [sc. τῶν σωμάτων cf. 892a5] καὶ μετακοσμήσεως ἀπάσης ἄρχει [sc. ψυχή cf. 892a2] παντὸς μᾶλλον (LEG. 892a5–7; my trans.).

found in direct neighbourhood in S2C.[23] In the *Laws*, these pairs are explicitly linked to the soul (Leg. 894b1–6). Furthermore, one has to note that all these types of change in Leg. 894b10–11 are not linked to the ninth form of motion (which moves only other things, but not itself),[24] but to the most fundamental, tenth form of motion, which moves itself *and* others.[25] As is well-known, this tenth form is most closely related to the soul. In fact, soul *is* this form of motion.[26] Moving 'itself and others' then means that something being in motion according to this tenth form moves – or better: changes in a broad sense of the term – others, while or by changing (also) itself.[27] This is of course not to say that the soul *as such* changes (in the sense that it is not soul anymore), but to state that there is change *within* the soul. Besides that, this tenth form of motion in the *Laws* is called the "true change and motion of all beings."[28] Hence, this emphasises again that μεταβολή is – to say the least – very closely related to the soul, if not primarily located there. It is of course not possible in the present context to provide a full discussion of these complicated issues in the *Laws*,[29] but these passages surely provide some crucial evidence for the claim that S2C/S5 both deal with the soul. With regard

---

[23] Cf. τε συγκρίσεις ἔν τε διακρίσεσιν αὔξαις τε καὶ τῷ ἐναντίῳ καὶ γενέσεσι καὶ φθοραῖς (Leg. 894b10–11) with διακρίνεσθαί τε καὶ συγκρίνεσθαι (156b5; only here within the whole exercise); αὐξάνεσθαί τε καὶ φθίνειν (156b8; again, only here in the exercise); and γιγνόμενον καὶ ἀπολλύμενον (156b2).

[24] It is, more precisely, moved/changed by something else to then (actively) move something else (Leg. 894c3–4; 895b6–7). This ninth form is quite explicitly linked to the soul in Leg. 894b1–6. Hence, it is in some sense a psychic motion, but an inferior one compared to the tenth form. To some extent, this may remind one of the intermediate position of πνεῦμα in Aristotle (cf. Mot. An. 703a4–23, esp. 703a5), though, of course, in Aristotle's account this intermedium is corporeal (later on, of course, the ninth form is also associated with the body; Leg. 896b7–8).

[25] Moving itself *and* others is emphasised by τε καί in Leg. 894b9, cf. also Leg. 894c4–9. In Leg. 894d3–4, this aspect of moving others is omitted. But the latter is, firstly, a statement not by the Athenian, but by Clinias and, secondly, 'self-motion' may very well, from then on, be a kind of short title for the tenth form of motion, which moves itself and others (cf. also 894e8 with 895a2–3).

[26] Cf. Leg. 894a8–b6; 894c10–d1; 895e10–896a2.

[27] Cf. αὐτὸ αὑτὸ κινῆσαν ἕτερον ἀλλοιώσῃ (Leg. 894e8). Cf. Leg. 893e7; §§ 24–25.

[28] ὄντως τῶν ὄντων πάντων μεταβολὴν καὶ κίνησιν (Leg. 894c6–7; cf. also 896b1). Besides relating ὄντως to καλουμένην (and thereby to μεταβολὴν καὶ κίνησιν), it might also be related to τῶν ὄντων πάντων (perhaps it could even stand ἀπὸ κοινοῦ). If one relates it to τῶν ὄντων πάντων, this would to some extent tie in with the ὄντως ὄν mentioned earlier in Leg. 894a6. This in turn would support an interpretation of Leg. 894a1–5 according to which the World Soul mediates – in terms of motion and in a dimensional succession – between the forms as ὄντως ὄντα and the perceptible, three-dimensional bodies.

[29] For a recent analysis of self-motion in *Laws* x and a valuable survey of prior studies cf. Marinescu 2021.

to the fact that μεταβολή is concentrated in S2C, while ἀλλοίωσις is more prominent in S5 (p. 46), it is furthermore very helpful to note how these two terms are apparently used quite interchangeably within this passage in the *Laws*.[30]

The soul's content and its internal constitution may change (in time)[31], for instance during the process of education. But during that process, soul itself remains the underlying permanent substratum of concrete change.[32] In that sense the alternation in the conceptual patterns between positive *and* negative accounts of motion, rest, and change may be interpreted as pointing to a systematic constellation within which the soul *as such* remains the same unaltered substratum of change, while *within* the soul change does indeed happen. I shall return to this constellation in § 24.

One could object that if S2C and S5 deal with the realm of the (World) Soul, one would expect a strong concentration of numerals in these passages, since numerical ratios are definitely characteristic of the World Soul in the *Timaeus*. Yet, numerals are almost exclusively concentrated in S2. To this, there are two rejoinders. The first one is to point out that Aristotle repeatedly reports that Plato advocated two kinds of numbers, eidetic and mathematical ones.[33] It may thus be the case that in the *Parmenides* we only find the former but not the latter, and there is indeed some evidence for that.[34] Since the intermediate realm of the soul is surely linked to the latter kind of numbers, the lack of numerals in S2C and S5 is no ultimate refutation of IP. Similarly, a second rejoinder may reply that especially the sections after S2 definitely do not give the impression of being *exhaustive* accounts of what they are concerned with. (And for all we know S2 might not be exhaustive either.) On the contrary, Parmenides mentions abridgments several times.[35] The objection based on the missing occurrence of numerals thus remains largely an argument *ex silentio*.

---

[30] LEG. 894c3–4 with 895b6–7; and 894e4–895a3.

[31] Within the scope of the present study it is not possible to adequately discuss in detail the very complex passages on time in S2 and S2C. But I suspect that – as regards time (cf. also Aristotle, META. Δ 11, 1019a1–4) – these passages describe precisely the constellation of S1, S2, S2C, and S3. Compare, for instance, how the passage on time describes the emergence of the One as a perfect whole (153c5–d3; 153e3) with the description in S3 (157c8–e2); or how number is treated in the context of time (153a4–b7) with the emergence of number at the beginning of S2 (143d1–144a9).

[32] Cf. e.g. the allusion SYMP. 207d4–e1.

[33] Cf. esp. Aristotle, META. M 8, 1083a31–b1 (with context); M 9, 1086a11–13; N 3, 1090b20–27; 32–1091a5 (= TEST. PLAT. 28b; 56–57 GAISER).

[34] Cf. DILLON 2005, esp. 301–303 on this question.

[35] Cf. 159a6–b1; 160a4–7; 165d7–e1; 166b5–7.

Regarding the specificity of S5 in relation to the other 'positive' sections (S2, S3, S7), three other conceptual patterns are of importance. They all show a similar peculiarity which very much underscores IP's specific claim that in S5 a *single* entity is described, whereas S2, S3, S7 are concerned with a *manifold* structure. This becomes especially obvious if one takes into account the conceptual field of 'multitude', in which the lemmata πόλυς, ἄπειρος, and πλῆθος belong above all.[36] The pattern is given in T.16.2 and D.16.3A–B.

The *p*-values of the positive as well as of the negative distribution allow us to regard these distributions as definitely non-random. The DP-values are moderately high, though lower than those of the most distinctive patterns. The strong negative accounts in S1, S4, and S8 are very unsurprising – especially with regard to S1. Of greater interest are the positive occurrences of multitude. It is quite remarkable that these occurrences are not simply distributed equally among all 'positive' sections. There is a significant gap in S5 since this section shows significantly fewer occurrences of this conceptual field. This becomes even clearer if one takes into account that the only two occurrences of πόλυς in S5 (160e8; 161a5) denote something that the subject of S5, τὸ μὴ ὂν ἕν, may *participate in* (160e7–161a2; 161a4–5). The manifold in question may hence indeed be something different from the specific subject of S5. It might in fact be the multitude of forms in S2/3,[37] in which the subject of S5 participates according to IP. In any case, the exception of S5 in the conceptual field of multitude may count as a quite remarkable hint that S5 deals in some sense with one single entity. This in turn ties in quite well with the claim of IP that in S1 and S5 we have a specific 'One-over-Many'-hierarchy with regard to S2/3 and S7 respectively (though the present pattern supports of course only the claim with regard to S5).

However, it also has to be stated that the pattern of multitude does not support the resemblance between S2C and S5 in this respect since the former shows greater similarity to S2 and S3 regarding this pattern. With all due precaution, this might on the one hand be considered as a hint to the connection that according to IP S2C *also* bears to the subject of S2/3 in order to ultimately support the connection between the forms and the sensible world. On the other hand, one could suspect that S2C might be describing

---

[36] Where πόλυς is employed in the formula πολλὴ ἀνάγκη, it is not counted. The field includes the few cognates ἀπειρία, ἀπέραντος as well as πλεονάκις, πλεονεκτέω of ἄπειρος and πλῆθος respectively. Cf. APPENDIX B.

[37] Cf. in this context the valuable remarks by GERSON 2013, 140–142 on the multitude of the forms and the Theory of Principles in the context of the Old Academy.

|   | S1 | S2 | S2C | S3 | S4 | S5 | S6 | S7 | S8 | $p$ | DP |
|---|---|---|---|---|---|---|---|---|---|---|---|
| + | 1 | 46 | 6 | 14 | 0 | 2 | 0 | 15 | 0 | 1.88e-10 | 0.316 |
| − | −13 | −8 | −3 | −4 | −3 | 0 | 0 | 0 | −8 | 9.40e-09 | 0.471 |
| + | 0.062 | 0.920 | 1.130 | 2.035 | 0.000 | 0.199 | 0.000 | 2.918 | 0.000 |  |  |
| − | −0.803 | −0.160 | −0.565 | −0.581 | −0.792 | 0.000 | 0.000 | 0.000 | −3.774 |  |  |

T.16.2 FIELD OF MULTITUDE

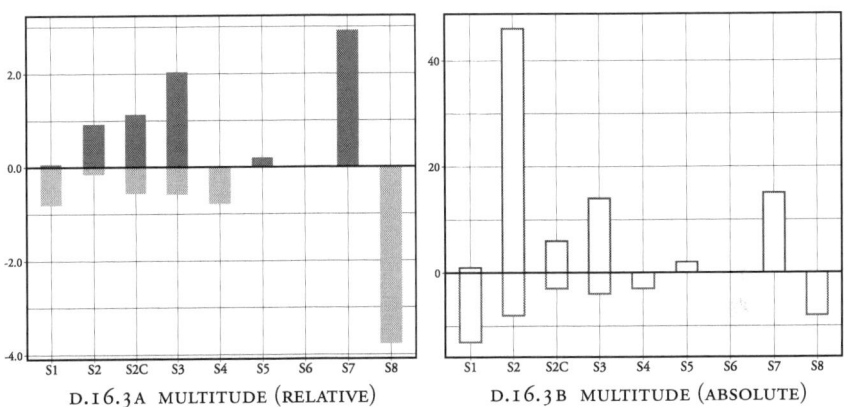

D.16.3A MULTITUDE (RELATIVE)    D.16.3B MULTITUDE (ABSOLUTE)

the immanent plurality within the soul, while S5 is primarily concerned with the soul *as a whole*. There is thus, in my eyes, no need to regard this as a decisive counter-argument against the strong resemblance between S2C and S5, which is to be found in numerous patterns (§§ 5–6).

Besides the field of multitude, two other patterns provide very similar evidence by again leaving out S5 among the 'positive' sections: the conceptual pattern of πέρας, which is given in T.16.3 and D.16.4A–B (p. 80). And to some lesser degree the 'holistic' conceptual field of ἀρχή-μέσον-τελευτή (including ἔσχατος),[38] a structure that appears several times in the second part of the *Parmenides*. Its results are given in T.16.4 and D.16.5A–B (p. 80).

Within the pattern of πέρας, the two negative occurrences seem to be of little interest, both due to their high *p*-value and due to their small number (the same applies to the DP-value). But the positive accounts of that concept again show the remarkable gap in S5, which is the only one among the 'positive' sections where this concept is not mentioned even once. Here, this applies also to S2C, so that S2C and S5 again resemble each other – in this case on account of being the only 'positive' sections *without* the concept of

---

[38] ἀρχή is not counted where it is part of the formula ἐξ ἀρχῆς. ἔσχατος is included since it is used in the same sense as τελευτή (cf. 137e2; 137e4 in the context of 137d4–138a1).

|   | S1 | S2 | S2C | S3 | S4 | S5 | S6 | S7 | S8 | *p* | DP |
|---|---|---|---|---|---|---|---|---|---|---|---|
| + | 0 | 4 | 0 | 5 | 0 | 0 | 0 | 2 | 0 | 6.32e−03 | 0.530 |
| − | −1 | 0 | 0 | 0 | 0 | 0 | 0 | −1 | 0 | 0.17 | 0.809 |
| + | 0.000 | 0.080 | 0.000 | 0.727 | 0.000 | 0.000 | 0.000 | 0.389 | 0.000 | | |
| − | −0.062 | 0.000 | 0.000 | 0.000 | 0.000 | 0.000 | 0.000 | −0.195 | 0.000 | | |

T.16.3  *πέρας*

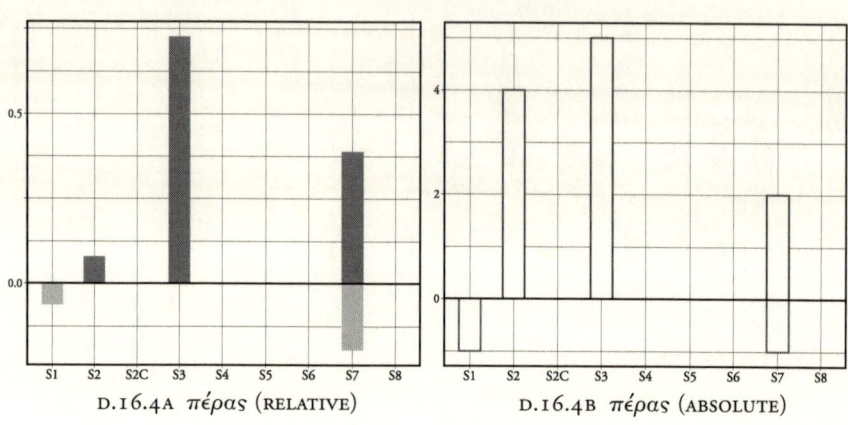

D.16.4A *πέρας* (RELATIVE)          D.16.4B *πέρας* (ABSOLUTE)

|   | S1 | S2 | S2C | S3 | S4 | S5 | S6 | S7 | S8 | *p* | DP |
|---|---|---|---|---|---|---|---|---|---|---|---|
| + | 0 | 23 | 0 | 2 | 0 | 3 | 0 | 7 | 0 | 1.62e−03 | 0.327 |
| − | −15 | −1 | 0 | 0 | 0 | 0 | 0 | −2 | 0 | 2.32e−07 | 0.752 |
| + | 0.000 | 0.460 | 0.000 | 0.291 | 0.000 | 0.299 | 0.000 | 1.362 | 0.000 | | |
| − | −0.926 | −0.020 | 0.000 | 0.000 | 0.000 | 0.000 | 0.000 | −0.389 | 0.000 | | |

T.16.4  FIELD OF *ἀρχή-μέσον-τελευτή*

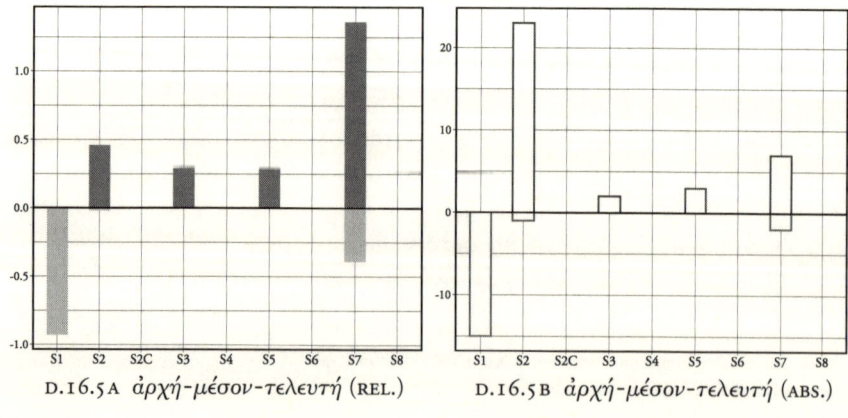

D.16.5A *ἀρχή-μέσον-τελευτή* (REL.)          D.16.5B *ἀρχή-μέσον-τελευτή* (ABS.)

πέρας. If one is willing to further interpret this pattern in the sense of IP, one could argue that S2/3 describe the boundaries between the individual forms, while S7 – where πέρας occurs only in the mode of appearance – describes the apparent distinctions between individual entities (which are not as strict and clear as the demarcations among the forms).

The 'holistic' field is non-random in both its negative and its positive occurrences; its DP-values are moderate and high respectively. However, it is only of interest with regard to the present observation concerning S5 if one is willing to take into account that the three occurrences of this pattern in S5 are all used within the complex chiasm (162a4–b8) to give a definition of being and non-being respectively. These occurrences thus do not (directly) relate to the subject of S5 itself (which seems to be a mixture of both), whereas the few occurrences of the same concept in S3 describe the very subject of that section as a perfect whole (ἓν τέλειον 157e1; ἓν ... ὅλον τέλειον 157e4). If one is willing to concede this, then also the holistic pattern shows the significant gap in S5. However, even then this is admittedly not very distinct, especially in comparison to the patterns of multitude and πέρας considered before.

So far, the conceptual patterns provided evidence of the resemblance between S2C and S5. And it has been argued that both sections are dealing with the World Soul. In fact, there has been previous statistical evidence that has to be discussed with regard to the resemblance of these two sections.

## § 17. Previous Statistical Evidence

In his first paper on statistics in the *Parmenides* L. BRISSON also very briefly remarked that there seems to be some connection and resemblance between S2C and S5–6. He notes that becoming and passing away form a "parallélisme entre 2b [sc. S2C] et les hypothèses 5 et 6"[39]. According to his purely quantitative approach (§ 3), this equally includes the exclusively negative occurrences of these concepts in S6 and hence does not distinguish between S5 and S6 in the qualitative respect. But obliquely this still hints to the resemblance in question. Furthermore, a certain relation between S2C and S5 is implicitly present in the data of this paper. If one takes a closer look at Annexe 1b,[40] one finds that S2C and S5 show by far the highest $\chi^2$-values

---

[39] BRISSON ²1977, 22. BRISSON/BENZÉCRI 1989, 124 remark the "caractère atypique de l'hypothèse 5" based on the high frequency of λέγω and μή in this section.

[40] Cf. BRISSON ²1977, 25 with R = 9 (i.e. considering nine sections).

of part 3.1 of the paper.[41] This investigation considers all terms that occur in *all* sections, i.e. the as it were 'common vocabulary', and the data shows that S2C/S5 both deviate significantly from what one would expect under the null hypothesis of random distribution. In fact, S2C is significant in using far *less* of the common vocabulary than one would expect under the null, while S5 uses significantly far *more* of it. There is thus a *common* – and statistically highly significant – stylistic feature of S2C and S5. They both stand out within S1–8 by deviating significantly from the average use of the common vocabulary, although in different directions.[42] It is therefore remarkable that the resemblance between S2C and S5, which is found in several conceptual patterns, is also mirrored in their uncommon usage of the common vocabulary.

In fact, some of the evidence in L. BRISSON's first paper may be interpreted to some extent in the light of the present interpretation. To support the claim that S2C cannot be separated from S2, L. BRISSON considers S2C a) with regard to the common vocabulary in *all* sections and b) with regard to the unique vocabulary to be found in *one* section only.[43] The former is considered to signify the "degré d'indépendance" of each section, while the latter indicates the "[degré] d'originalité" of each section.[44] Thus, 'independence' is implicitly defined as using less[45] of the common vocabulary in a statistically significant way, while 'originality' is defined as using unique vocabulary (i.e. vocabulary that appears in no other section) to a statistically significant extent. Since the expected distribution of the null hypothesis is calculated by relating the sum of all 325 occurrences of all these unique

[41] 15.64 (S2C) and 26.96 (S5) respectively; the corresponding exact *p*-values are 7.66e–05 (S2C) and 2.08e–07 (S5).

[42] It is, notabene, no objection to the present approach that these different directions suggest no common ground but a difference of S2C and S5, for the very reason that the present argument is based on key concepts such as becoming/passing away – whose occurrence is also admitted by L. BRISSON as quoted above –, while L. BRISSON's analysis and the mentioned $\chi^2$-values are based on very common verbs such as εἰμί, articles, and particles.

[43] Cf. BRISSON ²1977, 16–19. I shall concentrate on the statistical arguments in part 3.1 and 3.2 of that paper. Part 3.3 (IBID., 19–21; 28–29) makes an interesting approach to characterise each single section, but it does so by only concentrating on the twenty most common terms in each section. Since these terms include all kinds of common verbs, articles, particles and so on, this approach and its results are dominated by these parts of speech, while the vocabulary of (potentially) greater systematic significance remains almost completely out of sight.

[44] BRISSON ²1977, 19.

[45] But not: to deviate *uncommonly* from the average and expected usage of the common vocabulary. Cf. the remarks above in the main text. If 'independence' were defined as using the common vocabulary *uncommonly*, then S2C and S5 would be the two (most) independent sections among S1–8.

terms to the word counts of S1–8,[46] 'originality' in this definition consists in using unique vocabulary significantly *more often* than the general share of these 325 would have one expect. One could ask whether this definition thereby overrates quantity (i.e. the occurrences) over diversity of unique terms. If, say, S4 would use *two* unique terms twelve times each, it would thus be 'more original' according to that definition than if it used *eleven* unique terms, but only two times each. Likewise, one could object that simple particles are considered equally weighty as, say, specific nouns. Thus, for instance, the single occurrence of τοίνυν in S8 supports the originality of this section as much as the single occurrence of δεσμός in S5 does for S5.[47] It is, however, an admittedly difficult task to implement features like independence or originality in a statistically feasible way.

Given these definitions, the results are as follows: the first result, with regard to independence, is that, if S2 and S2C are considered separately, S2C is the only section in the dialogue's second part that is independent (in a statistically very significant way).[48] S2C "apparaît comme le passage de la seconde partie [...] le moins bien intégré, c'est-à-dire celui présente le degré le plus bas d'interdépendance par rapport à toutes les autres hypothèses."[49] The second result, with regard to originality, is that only S2 and S7 show a significant originality in the given sense.[50] While L. Brisson decides that this second finding overrules the first and S2C is thus no section in its own right,[51] both results in fact tie in remarkably well with the present observations regarding IP and the conceptual patterns. On the one hand, the

---

[46] Cf. Brisson ²1977, 26–27.

[47] In fact, it supports it even more, since S5 is much larger than S8 and hence a single occurrence in S8 has relatively more statistical weight. Note that in L. Brisson's approach FS is part of S8 and hence τοίνυν counts for S8.

[48] Cf. Brisson ²1977, 17–18. The $\chi^2$-value is 15.64, its (very low) corresponding exact $p$-value is 7.66e–05.

[49] Brisson ²1977, 18.

[50] Cf. Brisson ²1977, 18–19.

[51] "Force est donc de conclure que, puisque l'excédent de l'effectif réel de l'ensemble des vocables de R = 1 [sc. terms that appear only in one section] sur l'effectif théorétique attendu ne constitue pas, en 2b [sc. S2C], un fait stylistique significatif, ce passage du *Pàrmenide* [sc. S2C] [...] ne présente pas un degré d'originalité particulièrement élevé, même si, par ailleurs, son degré d'indépendance par rapport aux hypothèses de la seconde partie du *Parménide* de Platon s'avère tout à fait significatif." (Brisson ²1977, 19). I must confess that I personally see no internal necessity within this argument why the second finding (regarding originality) should so easily overrule the first finding (regarding independence), especially since the latter has a much higher $\chi^2$-value and the independence of S2C is thus, roughly speaking, more significant than its lack of originality (compared to S2 and S7). Secondly, the statistical implementation of independence seems to be sounder than the implementation of originality (cf. the considerations above).

fact that S2C is highly independent may be interpreted as consistent with IP's proposal that S2C is independent of S2 and actually introduces a new subject. With regard to the definition of originality, it becomes obvious, on the other hand, why there is no need for S2C to be original in this specific sense. According to IP, it shares a common subject with S5 and thus is not even expected to be original in the sense defined by L. Brisson. Instead, the decision to concentrate on vocabulary that is either common to all sections or unique to a single one actually prevents, right from the beginning, observations like the resemblance between S2C and S5 (or S2 and S3) with regard to vocabulary used only (or mainly) in *these two* sections.[52]

## § 18. The Realm of the Forms

*The close relation between* S2 *and* S3 *is supported by further conceptual patterns.* According to IP, S2 and S3 share the same subject, once in regard to itself and once in regard to the subject of S1. We should thus expect similarities between S2 and S3. Besides those already mentioned in § 14, there is one more conceptual field that supports IP in claiming the same subject for S2 and S3: the field of mereology. Among the terms that Parmenides uses in S1–8, one may include into this field the concepts ὅλος, μέρος, and μόριον as well as the very few occurences of μερίζω, μεριστός, and ἀμέρης (as negative).[53] A separate consideration of each term can be found in T.A.1–4 and Appendix C. A comprehensive view is provided in T.18.1 and D.18.1A–B.

Again, the *p*-values are very low and confirm that these patterns are non-random. Yet, the DP-values are not as high as one would expect. This is mainly caused by the fact that a great deal of this pattern is concentrated in the large section S2. Except for one single negative mentioning in S8, the conceptual field of mereology is exclusively concentrated in S1–4. We find exclusively negative occurrences in S1 and S4. The former is hardly surprising since S1 strictly follows the premise to discuss the One as an absolute unity without any parts at all (137c4–d3). The latter is consistent with IP since S4 is again, in a sense, a description of the same subject (now in relation to the subject of S2).[54] Besides that, the large number of positive

---

[52] Furthermore, the originality of S7 fits of course very well to the results of §§ 7; 15.

[53] One could argue with regard to Appendix C that also ὅρος and ἀφορίζω might be related to mereology in a wider sense. However, this would only slightly further emphasise the pattern since each term occurs only once, in S2 and S3 respectively.

[54] On the asymmetry of this relation, cf. p. 63 n. 30.

|   | S1 | S2 | S2C | S3 | S4 | S5 | S6 | S7 | S8 | $p$ | DP |
|---|----|----|-----|----|----|----|----|----|----|-----|----|
| + | 0 | 78 | 0 | 45 | 0 | 0 | 0 | 0 | 0 | 6.60e-34 | 0.456 |
| − | −29 | −34 | 0 | 0 | −10 | 0 | 0 | 0 | −1 | 9.64e-11 | 0.340 |
| + | 0.000 | 1.561 | 0.000 | 6.541 | 0.000 | 0.000 | 0.000 | 0.000 | 0.000 | | |
| − | −1.791 | −0.680 | 0.000 | 0.000 | −2.639 | 0.000 | 0.000 | 0.000 | −0.472 | | |

T.18.1 FIELD OF MEREOLOGY

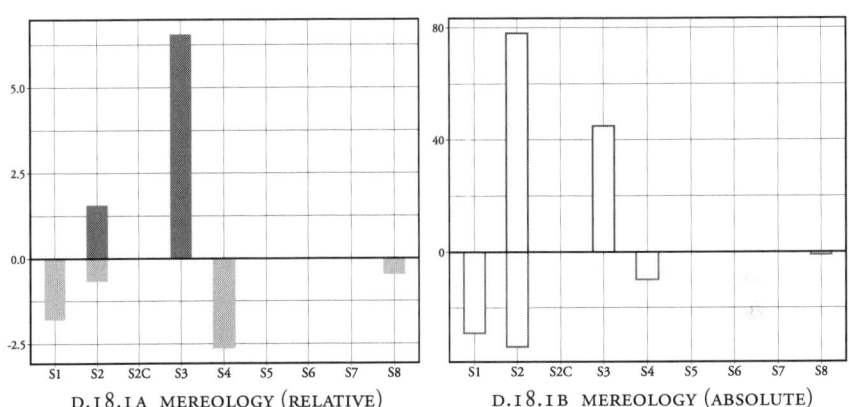

D.18.1A MEREOLOGY (RELATIVE)          D.18.1B MEREOLOGY (ABSOLUTE)

occurrences, concentrated only in S2 and S3, is the most remarkable feature of this pattern, which therefore supports the claim that both sections have something in common. This is furthermore supported by the fact that S2 and S3 are the *only* ones among the 'positive' sections where these concepts occur, while neither S5 nor S7 show any traces of this conceptual field. And S2C forms a clear and remarkable gap between S2 and S3. This may thus count as another indicator that S2 and S3 are concerned with the same structure. In fact, guided by these statistical heuristics a closer look at the text of S3 could indicate further how this section describes the same perfect and limitless (ἄπειρος) whole, which is also to be found in S2, as emerging dependent on the One as pure unity (S1).[55] S3 may thus be understood as a description of how the first principiate (S2) emerges in relation to its direct principle (S1) – perfectly analogous to S7 with regard to the second principle (S5). Using the field of mereology in paricular to compare S2 and S3 is thus no arbitrary choice, but may in fact be regarded as pointing to a key feature of the realm of forms: being a unified and perfect whole of perfectly well-defined parts which are in perfect and harmonious order (cf. especially REP. 500c2–5).

---

[55] Cf. esp. 158d3–6. Cf. also the remark p. 63 n. 27.

However, one has to remark that S2 also provides a considerable number of negative occurrences of the mereological field, while S3 remains exclusively positive. At first sight, this suggests a difference between S2 and S3 (just as S2C and S5 differed from these two in the field of being). Yet, if one takes a closer look at these negative occurrences in S2, one finds them concentrated in four dense passages: 145c7–e1, 146b2–c4, 147a6–b5, and 150a1–b7. In the first and the second passage the mereological concepts serve the need to ascribe different attributes to the One as the principal subject of S2.[56] In both cases, this terminology is affirmed and denied simultaneously to approach the subject in different aspects and thus to conclude that contrary attributes apply to the ἓν ὄν in different respects. In principle, I do not regard this as a contradiction, but rather as a resemblance to the way in which S3 deals with the mereological concepts, though S3 does not imply negation.[57] The greater part of these negative occurrences (20 of 32) is concentrated in the two latter passages that are, in all probability, not dealing with the main subject of S2. The very difficult passage 147a6–b5 is concerned with something that Parmenides calls τὰ μὴ ἕν (146e6) and it seems quite likely that these have to be considered in some sense as a different subject than the principal subject of S2, τὸ ἓν ὄν. In 150a1–b7, Parmenides is specifically concerned with σμικρότης (150a2) and the overall impetus of the passage is to argue that neither a τι σμικρόν nor σμικρότης is among τὰ ὄντα (neither in parts nor in the whole of them), but only ἡ σμικρότης αὐτή (150b5–7). Given the other evidence regarding τὰ ὄντα and the use of αὐτή, these negative mereological accounts could be said to be concerned with the subject of a concrete small thing or smallness as a property instantiated in an individual thing. The negated mereological terms might hence be regarded as serving the need to exclude *both these* from τὰ ὄντα, while Smallness itself is explicitly among them.

The absolute majority of the negative accounts in S2 thus occurs in those passages where presumably something else than the main subject of S2 is primarily under consideration. It may therefore seem reasonable to not consider the negative accounts in S2 as a decisive difference between S2 and S3 and thus as contradicting their overall resemblance. However, this difference nevertheless remains doubtlessly remarkable and ultimately would have to

---

[56] In 145c7–e1, the aim is to reach the conclusion that the One is 'in itself' as well as 'in something different' (145e5). In 146b2–c4, the aim is to show that the One is identical with itself (146c4), though via 146d4 this is already indirectly connected to τὰ μὴ ἕν (cf. the remarks on the next passage 147a6–b5).

[57] Cf. e.g. the twofold, dialectical perspective in 158a7–b1.

|   | S1 | S2 | S2C | S3 | S4 | S5 | S6 | S7 | S8 | p | DP |
|---|----|----|-----|----|----|----|----|----|----|----|-----|
| + | 2 | 8 | 1 | 3 | 0 | 0 | 0 | 0 | 0 | 0.57 | 0.257 |
| − | 0 | 0 | 0 | 0 | 0 | 0 | 0 | 0 | 0 | — | — |
| + | 0.124 | 0.160 | 0.188 | 0.436 | 0.000 | 0.000 | 0.000 | 0.000 | 0.000 | | |
| − | 0.000 | 0.000 | 0.000 | 0.000 | 0.000 | 0.000 | 0.000 | 0.000 | 0.000 | | |

T.18.2 FIELD OF φύσις

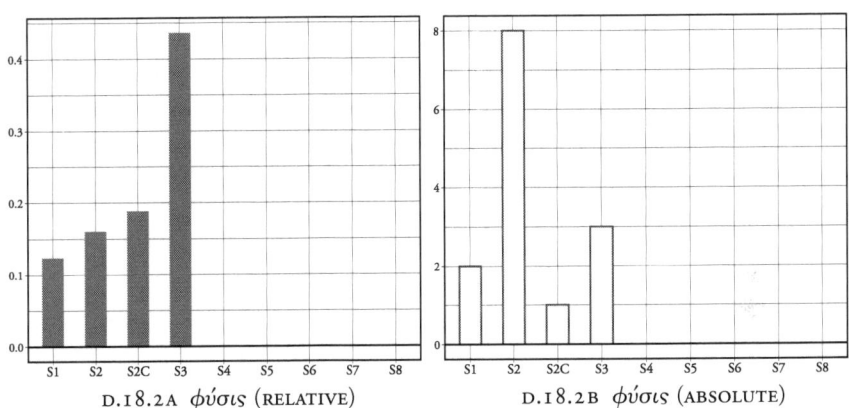

D.18.2A φύσις (RELATIVE)　　　　D.18.2B φύσις (ABSOLUTE)

be taken into account and explained in a line-by-line analysis, especially regarding the status and the difficult interpretation of τὰ μὴ ἕν.

Besides that, it is peculiar and thus at least noteworthy that μόριον is the only term used in S3 to designate parts, while in S2 it is both μόριον and μέρος. I can see no decisive significance in this fact.[58] One might suspect that μόριον emphasises more specifically the 'aspects' of an integral whole and S3 would in this respect stress the wholeness, unity, and coherence of the intelligible being as a totality of forms.[59] However one may integrate this fact in a line-by-line analysis, it does not in any case distort the clear mereological pattern with regard to S2 and S3.

There is another conceptual field which has to be taken into account with regard to the realm of being in S2/3: the field of φύσις (in which the verb φύω may also be included). Plato does indeed use the term φύσις to refer to the realm of forms in other dialogues.[60] Also, in the first half of the *Par-*

---

[58] As von KUTSCHERA 1995, e.g. 82; 108–113 seems to implicitly presuppose when discussing S2/3.

[59] Cf. esp. μιᾶς τινὸς ἰδέας (157d8; cf. SOPH. 254a8–9, where the totality of being is also described as one single ἰδέα, and TIM. 39e8, which addresses the totality of forms as the form 'Life': ὃ ἔστιν ζῷον; cf. also Aristotle, DE ANM. A 2, 404b19–20); ἐξ ἁπάντων ἓν τέλειον (157e1); ἓν ... ὅλον τέλειον μόρια ἔχον (157e4); ἓν ὅλον (158a7).

[60] Cf. especially PHDR. 254b6; REP. 476b7; 597c2; 597e4; PHDO. 103b5; SOPH. 250c6.

*menides* there is an instance where φύσις is obviously intended to refer to the realm of forms (132d2). This field is shown in T.18.2 and D.18.2A–B (p. 87). The distribution of φύσις is roughly equal to the conceptual field of being. Hence, one might be tempted to suspect that Plato uses the terms φύσις/ φύω in the second part of the *Parmenides* to denote the intelligible realm of being; for the distribution of φύσις is doubtlessly consistent with the overall picture in its remarkable exclusive concentration on S1–3.[61] However, with regard to this conceptual pattern one has to conclude that solely in itself this pattern may not be regarded as non-random with sufficient certainty since its *p*-value is too high.[62] This of course is not proof positive of the contrary, i.e. that this specific distribution is in fact *not* intended by Plato in some sense; but it does not allow us to regard it as non-random based on the statistical evidence.

## § 19. A Tripartite Ontology and the Concept of Participation

*The given evidence suggests a different approach to Plato's systematic ontology and his concept of participation.*[63] If the interpretation given so far is correct and if it in principle represents Plato's position that he puts forward in the second part of the *Parmenides*, it calls to some extent for a novel approach to Plato's systematic ontology. This approach is principally tripartite instead of bipartite. It furthermore implies a different conception of becoming/passing away and especially of the crucial relation between forms and sensible particulars. According to what one might call the 'standard interpretation' of Plato's position in the so-called 'middle dialogues' (i.e. mainly *Phaedo*, *Symposium*, *Republic*) his Theory of Forms is basically *bipartite*, in the sense that there are, on the one hand, transcendent forms and, on the other hand, physical, sensible particulars, which participate in the former. These physical

---

On Plato's concept of φύσις, cf. in detail the contributions in KOCH/MÄNNLEIN-ROBERT/ WEIDTMANN 2019.

[61] For the positive accounts in S1 (139d2; 139e9), cf. § 20.

[62] If one included this field into the conceptual field of being (§ 5) – based, for instance, on the evidence of 132d2 in the first part of the dialogue –, it would not distort, but in fact emphasise that pattern, and at the same time not change the very low *p*-value of that field in any decisive way.

[63] By 'participation' I am not referring to a specific term (nor am I dealing with the question whether systematic change is entailed by changes in terminology, as FUJISAWA 1974 has argued), but the *general systematic* question of how forms and physical particulars relate to each other.

particulars come to be and pass away, and they are themselves the sensible perceptible appearance of the forms. However, the conceptual patterns of the *Parmenides* paint quite a different picture. Becoming and passing away occur elsewhere than sensible appearance does (§ 5), and – provided that IP is correct in its outlines – the former happens primarily on the level of the soul, while the latter is to be found on the level of physical particulars.[64] As mentioned already before in § 16, one finds the idea that becoming/passing away happens first and foremost in the soul quite explicitly in the *Laws*. There, the Athenian states that one has proven sufficiently that the "soul is identical to the first becoming and motion of those that are, those that have been, and those that will be, and also of everything that is opposite to these [i.e. all processes of passing away] since we have seen that it is for all things the principle of all change and motion."[65] One may note in addition that even for Aristotle – whose position is without any doubt more 'down-to-earth' and closer to the material body in this respect – the soul is the principle of becoming and passing away.[66]

While in the standard bipartite view participation consists in a physical particular's direct participation in a certain form, the present conclusions suggest that in the *Parmenides* Plato puts forward another view. According to this view, the process of becoming and passing away consists in a temporary presence of some οὐσία inside the soul, whose content is then in turn displayed on the perceptible physical level if the latter is in contact with the former (§§ 14–15). The eidetic structures thus enter and leave the soul (cf. 162b5–c6; 162e2–163b5)[67] – which is the real process of becoming and passing away – and this current status is then mirrored in the sensible world, where becoming and passing away *appear* to happen (cf. 165d4 with 165d7). An understanding of the relation of participation thus inevitably has to

---

[64] As stated already in § 16: this is of course not to state that the soul changes *itself and as such*. But it differs from the view according to which soul is the principle of becoming/passing away only in the sense that it causes becoming/passing away *in something different* (i.e. in the physical bodies). The position I propose is an intermediate one: the soul is the principle of becoming/passing away in the sense that these processes happen primarily *inside* the soul (as their constant substratum; cf. also § 24) and are only then 'displayed' in the sensible realm of physical particulars.

[65] ψυχὴν ταὐτὸν ὂν καὶ τὴν πρώτην γένεσιν καὶ κίνησιν τῶν τε ὄντων καὶ γεγονότων καὶ ἐσομένων καὶ πάντων αὖ τῶν ἐναντίων τούτοις, ἐπειδή γε ἀνεφάνη μεταβολῆς τε καὶ κινήσεως ἁπάσης αἰτία ἅπασιν (LEG. 896a6–b1; my trans.). Cf. also LEG. 892a5–7, quoted above in § 16, p. 75.

[66] Cf. Aristotle, DE ANM. B 4, 415b25–28; 416a8–9; 416b9–11.

[67] 162d7–8; 163a7–b5 might then point to the fact that change only happens within the soul, while the soul *as such* remains unchanged (cf. also § 24). It might also be noteworthy that S5 ends at the very moment that it has introduced becoming and passing away.

take the soul into account.[68] If this is correct, it implies several subsequent questions. Firstly, what are the consequences for the *Parmenides* as a whole? Secondly, is this tripartite view plausible with regard to the dialogues *after* it? And thirdly, how does it relate to the middle dialogues *prior* to it? The first question will be addressed in the third main step of this study (§§ 25; 28). However, already at this stage of the argument, it is obvious that such a 'tripartite' result potentially has far-reaching effects on how the second part of the *Parmenides* may help to solve the problems of the first part. For the way to exactly understand the relation between forms and particulars is doubtlessly at the centre of these problems. With regard to the second question, I think that there is some prima facie plausibility to the tripartite view since it appears consistent with the position Plato proposes in the *Timaeus*. It is true that the explanation of the exact process of participation is deliberately omitted (TIM. 50c5–6). However, there is little doubt that in the *Timaeus* the soul – in whose mixture a τρίτον ... οὐσίας εἶδος (TIM. 35a3–4) plays a very prominent part – clearly forms an intermediate and interconnecting level between the transcendent forms and the physical cosmos (esp. TIM. 30b3–5; 31b8–c1). Hence, one can fairly reasonably state that there is at least some plausibility that a tripartite view in the *Parmenides* would be in general accordance with the position in the later dialogues, especially since such an accordance was also suggested by TIM. 52c2–5 (§ 15). Regarding the third question, the answer is more complicated since the tripartite view obviously seems to contradict Plato's position in the middle dialogues. If the present interpretation based on the conceptual patterns is sound, it would hence suggest a fundamental change in Plato's ontology in the *Parmenides*. However, I think that the tripartite view in fact already applies to the middle dialogues, though this is subject to further detailed argumentation with regard to the middle dialogues.[69] Again, I shall return to this question in some depth in the third main step (§ 25).

[68] For very useful remarks on this systematic position of the soul in Plato, cf. DILLON 2003, 22–24.

[69] To sketch only one argument in the present context: in the *Phaedo*, Socrates famously distinguishes αὐτὸ τὸ μέγεθος (PHDO. 102d6), τὸ ἐν ἡμῖν μέγεθος (102d7) and the πράγ-ματα, whose largeness is οὔτε τὸ ἐν ἡμῖν οὔτε τὸ ἐν τῇ φύσει (103b5). The intermediate largeness is thus said to be 'in us' (ἐν ἡμῖν 102d7) or 'in Socrates' (cf. ἐγὼ 102e3). Since one of Socrates' principal goals in the *Phaedo* is doubtlessly to proof that 'he' is not his body, but his soul (115c4–5), τὸ ἐν ἡμῖν μέγεθος can only mean the presence of the εἶδος *in our souls* – otherwise Socrates would have forgotten his main claim when he introduces the Theory of Forms (which is explicitly introduced for the sake of this argument, cf. 100b7–9). This suggests a tripartite view in the *Phaedo*, which resembles the one in the conceptual patterns of the *Parmenides* quite closely.

| | S1 | S2 | S2C | S3 | S4 | S5 | S6 | S7 | S8 | $p$ | DP |
|---|---|---|---|---|---|---|---|---|---|---|---|
| + | 0 | 20 | 6 | 11 | 0 | 5 | 0 | 0 | 0 | 1.07e-05 | 0.314 |
| − | -14 | -3 | -5 | -2 | -8 | 0 | -5 | 0 | 0 | 1.89e-11 | 0.599 |
| + | 0.000 | 0.400 | 1.130 | 1.599 | 0.000 | 0.499 | 0.000 | 0.000 | 0.000 | | |
| − | -0.865 | -0.060 | -0.942 | -0.291 | -2.111 | 0.000 | -1.524 | 0.000 | 0.000 | | |

T.19.1 FIELD OF μέθεξις

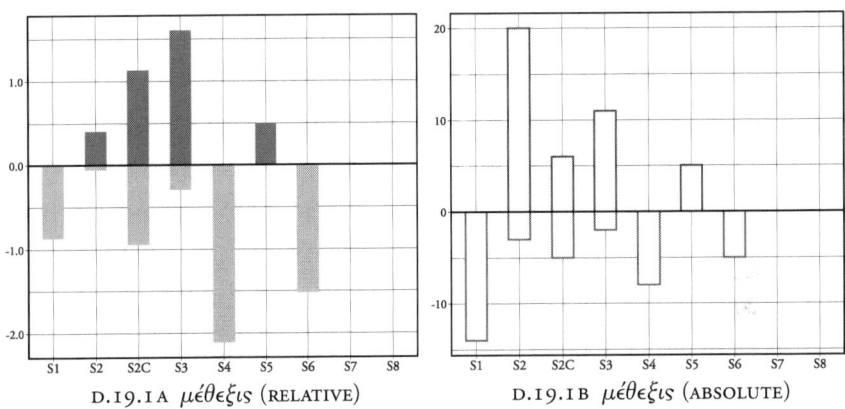

D.19.1A μέθεξις (RELATIVE)　　　　D.19.1B μέθεξις (ABSOLUTE)

In fact, there is one more important observation with regard to the conceptual patterns that quite perfectly ties in with the present considerations: the field of μέθεξις.[70] The positive and negative distributions of this field are given in T.19.1 and D.19.1A–B. This pattern, which again has sufficiently low $p$-values in both respects (and moderate to high DP-values), is remarkable for several reasons. First of all, hardly surprisingly and in perfect accordance with IP, there are exclusively negative accounts of this field in S1, S4, and S6. In the first case, this may be interpreted as the absolute position of the first principle (cf. § 20 below for more details), which in S4 is expressed as an asymmetrical relation, wherein the forms do participate in the first principle (cf. S3 and § 20), while the latter does not participate in them. And in S6, the physical cosmos *solely in itself* (§ 14) does not participate either. The clear dominance of positive accounts in S2 might be regarded as pointing to the internal, horizontal participation *within* the realm of

---

[70] Besides μέθεξις and μετέχω, μεταλαμβάνω and λαμβάνω are included where they are used in that sense, but not as the subjective ability to grasp something (cf. APPENDIX B). One could argue that among the terms of the exercise the very few instances of ἑκτέος, μεταληπτέος, and perhaps – in a negative sense – ἀπαλλακτέος should also be included in this field since Parmenides uses them in this sense (163d5–6). However, this would not alter the picture decisively, but only slightly further emphasise the negative account in S6.

forms, that Plato alludes to prior and after the *Parmenides*.[71] The very strong dominance in S3 and its many occurrences may furthermore support the claim that was made above, according to which S3 describes the internal relations among the forms as a result of the forms' participation in the first principle (§§ 18; 20). The nearly perfectly balanced positive and negative accounts in S2C fit the observations in § 6 very well. However, it is remarkable that S5 does not mirror this balance, but remains solely positive with regard to the concept of μέθεξις. This might indicate the intention to establish primarily the *connection* between the forms and the soul, which would then underline S5's position according to IP. In any case, the exclusively positive account in S5 in my eyes does not overrule the clearly balanced, positive *and* negative occurrences found in §§ 5–6; 16. Ultimately, it is most remarkable that there is not a single occurrence of μέθεξις in S7 and S8. The positive occurrences end in S5, i.e. on the level of the soul according to IP. This might count as a further indication of the tripartite view insofar as the proper concept of vertical μέθεξις only reaches down to the level of the soul, while appearance in the sensible world seems to happen in a different mode, which Plato describes time and again in terms of images.[72]

The last observation regarding S7–8 is noteworthy for yet another reason. As E. R. DODDS proposed in a famous article, we grasp the traces and outlines of a Neopythagorean interpretation of the *Parmenides* by Moderatus of Gades in Simplicius who reports and quotes Moderatus from a treatise on matter by Porphyry.[73] The text doubtlessly contains many challenges to the interpreter, yet a majority of scholars seem to agree that Moderatus is at least somehow concerned with the *Parmenides* in this passage.[74] What is remarkable in the context of the present conceptual pattern is the fact that Moderatus seems to describe exactly the above-mentioned position with regard to μέθεξις. Underneath three hierarchical Ones – among which the first is the primary principle, the second is the totality of forms, and the third is the soul – Moderatus[75] locates the physical world (IN PHYS. 1 230, 36–231, 4 DIELS).

---

[71] Cf. REP. 476a6–7; SOPH. 250b9; 254c4–5; 257a8–9.

[72] Cf. more extensively on that topic POETSCH 2019.

[73] Simplicius, IN PHYS. 1 230, 34–231, 24 DIELS. Cf. DODDS 1928, 136–140.

[74] Cf. TARRANT 1993, 150–177, esp. 161–162; HALFWASSEN 1993, 343–349; TORNAU 2000, 204–205; 219; KAHN 2001, 109–110. Cf. LAKMAN 2017, 185 for further literature.

[75] I am not concerned here with the question whether this is primarily a) the position which Moderatus ascribes to Plato, or b) Moderatus' own position (which he considers as derived from Plato and especially from the *Parmenides*). This depends on whether one reads οὗτος (IN PHYS. 1 230, 36) as referring to Plato (HALFWASSEN 1993, 343) or to Moderatus (DODDS 1928, 137–138). Though grammar is in favour of E. R. DODD's solution, I suspect that οὗτος must refer to Plato. For in 230, 34–36 it is said that *Plato* followed the Pythagoreans

And with regard to the latter two it is said that "the third (One)[76], which is the psychic (realm), participates in the (second) One and the forms, whereas the final nature (originating) from this – which is the nature of the sensible particulars – does not participate (in them, i.e. the forms), but has been arranged by being reflections of them."[77] Also to Moderatus the psychic level thus forms an intermediate step, where μέθεξις in the forms properly takes place and which is then in turn mirrored in the sensible world of physical particulars.[78] Of course, I do not claim that Moderatus arrived at this view via an approach like the present one based on conceptual patterns, and I think it remains doubtful whether he arrived at this systematic constellation solely through an interpretation of the *Parmenides*. However, it seems hardly controversial that the present pattern and its conception of μέθεξις as well as the general accordance of IP's core elements with the sections tie in strikingly well with this crucial text from the first century CE.[79]

## § 20. A First Principle

*There is some indication that* S1 *is to be understood in the sense of IP, i.e. as dealing with a first principle in the hierarchy.* The question of how to understand S1 and its subject has been suspended so far. According to IP, S1 is supposed to describe the principle of the forms (as the Good is in the *Republic*) and, since the forms in turn are the principles of everything else, the principle of everything.[80] There are several indications in the conceptual patterns that S1

in some concept of matter and that Moderatus only *reports* this; since the οὗτος is κατὰ τοὺς Πυθαγορείους, it is most naturally Plato; though of course still in Moderatus' report and interpretation. What is important with regard to the present argument is that there *is* a position – be it Moderatus', be it Plato in Moderatus' eyes, be it ultimately Plato himself (if Moderatus refers to him in an adequate way) – which describes a differentiated view on participation that resembles the one we find in the conceptual patterns of the *Parmenides*.

[76] As HALFWASSEN 1993, 343; TARRANT 1993, 150, I assume that it is most natural to understand this as a third *One*.

[77] τὸ δὲ τρίτον, ὅπερ ἐστὶ τὸ ψυχικόν, μετέχειν τοῦ ἑνὸς καὶ τῶν εἰδῶν, τὴν δὲ ἀπὸ τούτου τελευταίαν φύσιν τὴν τῶν αἰσθητῶν οὖσαν μηδὲ μετέχειν, ἀλλὰ κατ᾽ ἔμφασιν ἐκείνων κεκοσμῆσθαι (Simplicius, IN PHYS. I 231, 1–4 DIELS; my trans.).

[78] The specific way in which the tradition of Platonism deals with this precise constellation of participation is fascinating and might indeed be illuminating also with regard to Plato himself. However, this is not the place to pursue this question further.

[79] Though, of course, with the important difference to IP that Moderatus apparently found this constellation already in S1–4 (i.e. the first five sections in his count of nine); cf. TARRANT 1983, 84–85; TARRANT 1993, 164–165 on that issue.

[80] This also occurs in the Line and the Cave: τρόπον τινὰ πάντων αἴτιος (REP. 516c2); τοῦ παντὸς ἀρχὴ (cf. REP. 511b7); as well as REP. 517b8–c4.

|   | S1 | S2 | S2C | S3 | S4 | S5 | S6 | S7 | S8 | $p$ | DP |
|---|----|----|-----|----|----|----|----|----|----|----|----|
| + | 0 | 7 | 0 | 0 | 0 | 0 | 0 | 0 | 0 | 0.79 | 0.524 |
| – | –11 | 0 | 0 | 0 | 0 | 0 | 0 | 0 | 0 | 7.17e–06 | 0.860 |
| + | 0.000 | 0.140 | 0.000 | 0.000 | 0.000 | 0.000 | 0.000 | 0.000 | 0.000 | | |
| – | –0.679 | 0.000 | 0.000 | 0.000 | 0.000 | 0.000 | 0.000 | 0.000 | 0.000 | | |

T.20.1 μέτρον

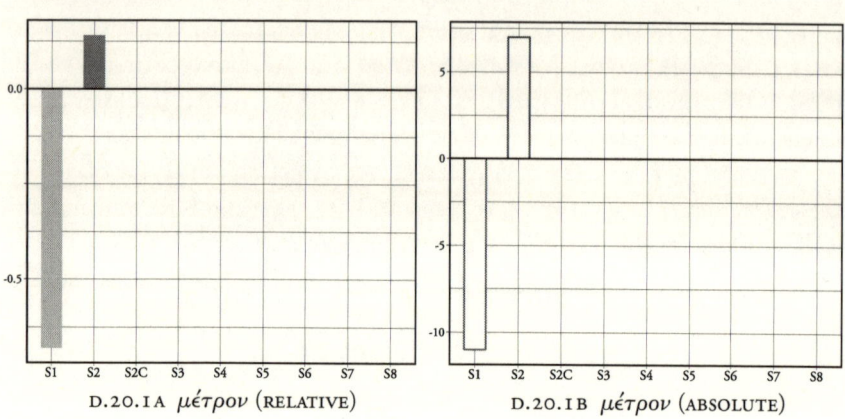

D.20.1A μέτρον (RELATIVE)      D.20.1B μέτρον (ABSOLUTE)

has to be taken in that sense, though one has to admit that S1 in itself is not the clearest of the sections with regard to this method.

Quite a strong indication, however, is to be found in the conceptual pattern of 'measure'. The role of a or the μέτρον is also closely connected to the Good in the *Republic* (504c1–d3) and we shall find another example from the *Philebus* below. The conceptual pattern of μέτρον is given in T.20.1 and D.20.1A–B. The *p*-value of the positive accounts alone is of course very high, due to its exclusive concentration in S2. The distribution of all 18 occurrences of μέτρον is perhaps still non-random, though not with the highest certainty.[81] Its moderate to high DP-value marks the pattern as quite distinct. The most remarkable thing about this pattern is obviously that it is exclusively concentrated in S1–2 and that there is not a single occurrence of this concept afterwards. This fits very well the 'ontological movement downwards' through S1–8, which has already been detected several times (§§ 9–11; 14), and confirms it *vice versa* since one naturally expects the measure to be located at the top of the hierarchy. But does the strong negative account not strongly contradict the idea of regarding S1 as describing the measure itself? In fact, it does not, but rather confirms this view. If one

[81] $p = 0.01165$ and thus p ≈ α.

takes a closer look at the instances of μέτρον in S1, it becomes evident that μέτρον occurs primarily in the plural μέτρα (8 out of 11 instances), i.e. as a multitude of units *of* this measure. μέτρα thus describes those which *are measured* in these passages. And this fits quite well the negative account in S1. Just as 1 as the principle of number is itself no number in Greek mathematics, so the μέτρον is itself not (one) of those units that are measured by it. And even for the three (negative) occurrences of the singular μέτρον it is obvious that Parmenides regards them as *instances* (containing one unit) of the measure itself (140d4–5). S2 in turn affirms the measured units, which occur in the plural throughout that section.

One more thing is remarkable with regard to this conceptual pattern. The rare term σύμμετρος is denied twice in S1 (140c1; 140c3) and this perfectly fits the present interpretation since being commensurable (σύμμετρος) presupposes the existence of at least *two* units that are measured by the same measure (cf. also δύο 138b5). The subject of S1 is hence described as something that is commensurable to nothing, and this befits an absolute first principle quite well. Of course, an additional positive occurrence of σύμμετρος in S2 would have had even further strengthened the present argument, but its negative account in S1 is definitely in the exact place where one would expect it according to IP. In fact, this constellation might receive further confirmation from the end of the *Philebus*, where within the final hierarchy the first position is labelled, among others, as μέτρον (PHLB. 66a6), while the second is said to be σύμμετρον (PHLB. 66b1).

A second, supplementary confirmation that S1 describes an incommensurable principle is to be found in the mereological pattern (§ 18), for this pattern – by the exclusively negative account in S1 – in a way excludes the subject of S1 from the ὅλον-μέρη-structure discussed in S2 and S3. This fits the exclusively negative account in S4, which, according to IP, describes the relation between the two subjects of S1 and S2 from the perspective of S1's subject. This mirrors the pattern of μέτρον to some extent since both describe an asymmetry in the sense that the principiate relates to the principle while the latter does not relate in the same way to the former. This also fits the negative accounts of μέθεξις in S1 and S4 (§ 19).

Besides these, several other patterns to some extent support IP's claim with regard to S1. Among them, the strong negative account of οὐσία especially sticks out. If one accepts the connection between the One and the Good,[82] this may be seen as mirroring the famous claim of the *Republic*

---

[82] Cf. § 12; DORTER 1994, 57–58; 66–67; VON WEIZSÄCKER ²2002, 72–73.

according to which the Good lies ἔτι ἐπέκεινα τῆς οὐσίας (REP. 509b9). On the other hand, one has to admit that there are three positive occurrences of being in S1, namely τὸ εἶναι twice (139c6; 140a1–2) and the particular usage of αὐτό (137d2)[83], as well as – if one is willing to include the pattern for other than statistical reasons (§ 18) – two positive occurrences of φύσις (139d2; 139e9). This seems to contradict IP and it is indeed not what one would expect from it at first blush. However, it is possible in my eyes to include this evidence in two ways. Firstly, if one regards the argument of S1 as a process of an ever further-reaching exclusion of the subject under consideration from being, then this subject must be graspable during this process, at least to some extent. According to Plato's own premises,[84] it must hence exhibit, at least heuristically, a certain measure of being. It is only at the very end of S1's process that this measure of being is ultimately negated.[85] This very process may indeed be mirrored in the *Republic* when Socrates explains that one has to approach the Idea of the Good by excluding it from everything else.[86] And secondly, there are some hints that αὐτὸ τὸ ἕν might have indeed been the name for Plato's first principle in the Academy.[87]

In total, there are thus several conceptual patterns that allow us to understand the subject of S1 in the sense of IP. The indications for S1 are for sure not the strongest or the most remarkable ones, but they nevertheless fit the overall picture sufficiently well.

## § 21. Some Rare Terms Revisited

*The unique and rare terms fit IP very well or at least do not contradict it.*[88] Of those unique and rare terms listed in § 8, some have already been shown

---

[83] For a more deflationary reading of ἐν αὐτὸ cf. APPENDIX B s.v. καθ' αὐτό ad 137d2.

[84] Think of REP. 477a3–4 according to which (intelligible) graspability implies being.

[85] Although I shall not discuss it further, this fits the statement of Speusippus (Proclus, IN PARM. VII 501,4–9 STEEL = frg. 48 TARÁN = TEST. PLAT. 50 GAISER) according to which the first principle was ultimately exempted from being principle.

[86] Cf. τῷ λόγῳ ἀπὸ τῶν ἄλλων πάντων ἀφελὼν τὴν τοῦ ἀγαθοῦ ἰδέαν, καὶ ὥσπερ ἐν μάχῃ διὰ πάντων ἐλέγχων διεξιών (REP. 534b9–c2). It is at least remarkable that also the second part of this phrase corresponds verbatim with Zeno's anticipation of Parmenides' exercise (ταύτης τῆς διὰ πάντων διεξόδου 136e1–2). Cf. also § 10.

[87] Cf. HALFWASSEN 1993, 340 N. 4 on this issue. About the variety of Plato's usage of αὐτό cf. also BRUNSCHWIG ²2018, 16 N. 4. Note furthermore how αὐτὸ τὸ ἕν and the ἀληθῶς ἕν are virtually identified in the *Sophist* (245a5–9). Next to the term ἀληθῶς ἕν in S4 (159c5), the usage of παντελῶς ἐν in S3 (157c4) is remarkable.

[88] For the restrictions to nouns, cf. p. 50 n. 35.

to fit IP very well, namely ἰδέα (§ 5), ὄναρ/ὕπνος and φάντασμα (§ 15), as well as ἀπουσία (§ 14). Among the others, ὅρος in its occurrence in S2 (149a8) fits the interpretation quite well in possibly marking the definition and determinacy of the forms against each other.[89] In a similar sense, συζυγία might fit S2, if one thinks of the Analogy of the Sun in the *Republic*, where Socrates insinuates a ζυγόν in the intelligible realm that is analogous to the ζυγόν of light within the visible realm (cf. REP. 508a1–5 with 508b12–c2). In both cases – in S2 of the *Parmenides* and the intelligible ζυγόν in the *Republic* – συζυγία then might characterise the most fundamental relation and connection between two elements in the intelligible realm. In that sense also δυάς fits S2 quite well. The positive presence of κοινωνία in S2 and S3 (and one very negative in S8) is quite plausible too if one thinks of the κοινωνία of the forms in the *Republic* (476a6–7; cf. 500c2–5)[90] and later on in the *Sophist* (250b6; 254c4–5; 257a8–9).

The single occurrence of δεσμός in S5 is probably the one that fits the present interpretation best. Not only does it match the systematic function of interconnection very well which S5 fulfils according to IP, but it also permits comparison to dialogues before and after the *Parmenides*. If one thinks of analogy as the κάλλιστος δεσμός in the *Timaeus* (31c2)[91] and the fact that the Line in the *Republic* establishes a vertical analogy between the realm of forms and the realm of physical particulars, δεσμός in S5 occupies exactly the same position. In fact, it appears like the keyword for the chiasm of being and non-being that it introduces (162a4–b8).

Besides these, I can neither attach significance nor see any contradiction to IP for the following rare terms: μηχανή (S1, S2), πάθημα (S1, S2C), τρόπος (S1, S4), ἕδρα (S2), τὸ ἄτοπον (S2C), and ἕξις (S5).[92] One might ask whether the rare occurrences of σχῆμα in S1 and S2 suggest a bodily scheme and thus contradict the present interpretation. In S1 it is only negated twice (137d8; 137e5) and thus does not obstruct the present interpretation. In S2 it is affirmed once (145b3) to explain that the ἓν ὄν, by having ἀρχή, μέσον, and τελευτή, participates in σχῆμα, which prima facie suggests a bodily gestalt of the ἓν ὄν. Two remarks, however, have to be made.

---

[89] Cf. also before 135a2; 135b7–8; 135c7–8. It is furthermore quite noteworthy that the formulation πανταχῶς ὄντα (144b6) – that to some extent resembles the well-known formula ὄντως ὄν – again appears only in S2.

[90] Cf. GUTIÉRREZ 2017, 302–303 (with n. 11) for the very valuable observation that the *Republic*'s notion of justice among the forms reappears in S2 of the *Parmenides* (150a7–b1).

[91] Cf. also the intervals as δεσμοί inside the World Soul's substance (TIM. 36a7).

[92] With regard to §§ 16; 19, one could ask whether the occurrence of ἕξις in LEG. 893e7; 894a7 is somehow related to this term's occurrence in S5, but this is rather faint evidence.

Firstly, the use of σχῆμα is obviously qualified (σχήματος ... τινος 145b3). And secondly, this whole passage is probably an allusion to Parmenides' poem (DK 28 B 8, 42–44); and there again, εὐκύκλου σφαίρης ... ὄγκωι is clearly marked as a figurative comparison (ἐναλίγκιον B 8, 43).[93] There are thus – in both cases – definitely two *possible* ways of understanding the use of σχῆμα and a tendency to do so metaphorically. Therefore, the single positive occurrence of σχῆμα in S2 does not obstruct the present interpretation.

The other rare terms actually occur in a context of further related terms (such as verbs) and are hence not really rare in a strict sense. These terms include: ἀλλοίωσις (S1), διαφορότης (S1), ἀνισότης (S1, S5), δύναμις (S2), γένεσις (S2), προαίρεσις (S2), τέλος (S2), στάσις (S2C), ἀπειρία (S3), ἡσυχία (S5), ἑτεροίοτης (S5, S6).

To consider the unique and rare terms in total: while these terms are of course not adequately addressable by statistical means, it is nevertheless very remarkable that the overwhelming majority of them either fit the systematic scheme proposed both by IP and the conceptual patterns quite well, or at least do not contradict that bigger picture. In a sense, they all fall into the right places, so to speak. The occurrences of the rare terms may thus count as a further argument in support of the present interpretation.


## § 22. Concluding Remarks

Let us take a look back on the second main step, which at the same time completed the statistical evaluation of Parmenides' exercise. Of course, there are much more concepts that may be considered statistically. And of course a conclusive proof of IP can only be provided by a full line-by-line analysis of the dialogue's second part. But given the scope of the present study, let me add three more general remarks and observations.

First of all, I think it has become obvious that there *are* in any case remarkable conceptual patterns to be discovered in great number in the *Parmenides*, once we take a bird's-eye view of the text. These have so far not received scholarly attention. But they cannot be dismissed as merely accidental due to the proof of their non-randomness on a statistical basis. We thus possess strong new and quite objective evidence that Plato has his Par-

---

[93] For the historical Parmenides, I shall not decide in the present context whether this is ultimately a literal or a metaphorical use and whether one should hence advocate a physical or an immaterial interpretation of Parmenides' ἐόν. Cf. the helpful remarks by GABRIEL 2009, 70–84.

menides shift thematically and hence has him very likely deal with different subjects throughout the second part of the dialogue (§ 10). This new evidence also suggests some crucial reconsiderations and specifications of Plato's systematic ontology (§ 19).

Secondly, I consider it as evident that these findings are quite coherently interpretable in a systematic sense by IP. In general, the patterns provide strong evidence of a movement 'downwards' on an ontological scale, though it is no simple linear movement through S1–8 or S1–4. Instead, the distribution of subject and relation sections that is proposed by IP fits the conceptual patterns much better and thus suggests that the second part should be considered as dealing with four main elements, each in itself and in relation to its direct principle or principiate respectively. However, I do not claim that IP is the only way to make further systematic sense of the patterns. What I do claim is that these patterns strongly call for a *systematic* interpretation in the given sense and for an interpretation that includes *multiple* subjects. In my eyes, these patterns are furthermore a very strong, and – on account of their objective character – even lethal argument against any interpretation that considers the second part as completely senseless, some awkward joke, a caricature, or a simple parody.[94]

And thirdly, it is very remarkable in my eyes that in a kind of 'second order observation' the discussed conceptual patterns *in total* provide a quite coherent and unanimous picture. Different patterns support each other, as, for instance, in the case of the resemblance between S2C and S5. Or with regard to the general tendency of a tripartite ontological hierarchy, which is furthermore emphasised by other conceptual fields, such as the one of μέθεξις. There is little to nothing in the patterns that disturbs or even

---

[94] This line of interpretation was upheld especially in the early 20th century by e.g. BURNET 1914, 263–264; 272 (the second part primarily as a kind of caricature of the Megarian position, "highly entertaining" for Plato's followers; IBID., 263) and TAYLOR 1934, 10–11; 29 (cf. also PALMER 1999, 149 N. 2 for further discussions). It seems to be out of fashion nowadays. To my knowledge, among the latest works only TABAK 2015, who sees the second part as "a satirical criticism of Plato's philosophical opponents" (IBID., 2) in which Plato wants "to parody the doctrines of his [Eleatic and Sophistic] opponents" (IBID., 3), follows this path in some sense. Above all, I consider it impossible that of all figures in the dialogues Plato should put such a simple parody in Parmenides' mouth, whom he held in the highest esteem (THT. 183e5–184a1; SOPH. 217c4–7), peer to Socrates and close to the Pythagoreans. However, I consider it possible (and even quite likely to some extent; cf. § 13) that Plato may have creatively adopted an Eleatic method that is not fully evident to us anymore. I do therefore not generally dismiss the possibility that the second part actually had a slightly humorous aspect to it for those who were familiar with this specific Eleatic method. But even if there were such humorous overtones, this does not prevent Plato from offering serious systematic thoughts in the second part of the dialogue.

contradicts the bigger picture and the overall impression. This concluding second order observation may thus count as a further argument in favour of the present approach.

We have thus finished the second main step of this study, which has offered a more detailed interpretation of the evidence. In the concluding third main step, this evidence will now be considered with a view to addressing the question how the dialogue's second part may help to solve the aporias, if it is understood according to IP.

# 6. A WAY OF SOLVING THE APORIAS?

In the previous chapters, I provided a new method and new evidence concerning the notoriously difficult second part of Plato's *Parmenides*. This was an attempt to answer in general the first of the two most pressing questions regarding this dialogue, namely what the second part is in fact all about. In the present chapter, I shall now try to tentatively approach the second major question: how does the second part help to solve the problems of the first and how are the two parts actually connected? Therefore I shall first approach this question as such (§ 23), and then turn to two exemplary aporias, which are analysed in greater detail. This includes what Parmenides calls the 'Greatest Aporia' (§ 24) and the first regress argument in 132a1–b2, famously known as the first 'Third Man Argument' (§ 26). Subsequent to each analysis, there will be an evaluation and characterisation of the proposed solution in order to highlight the specifics of the present approach and to deal with possible objections to it (§§ 25; 27). Ultimately, I shall discuss in general this attempt to solve the aporias, thereby also providing a brief sketch of how the other aporias might be specifically addressed within the present approach (§ 28).

## § 23. The Second Major Question

As is known, the first part of the *Parmenides* shows young Socrates defending a Theory of Forms that seems to resemble the position which Plato – via the same, but older Socrates[1] – holds in the so-called 'middle dialogues', first

---

[1] This internal consequence of a Socrates sticking to the Theory of Forms throughout all his life may, in my eyes, be interpreted in the sense that Plato never saw the objections in the *Parmenides* as lethal ones (cf. the very good remarks by GRAESER 1996, 160–161 on this point). It is no objection to this argument that the *Parmenides* is written after the *Phaedo*

and foremost the *Symposium*, the *Phaedo*, and the *Republic*. And famously this young Socrates is thrown into difficulty after difficulty through objections raised by the old Parmenides. In the following I shall not engage in the discussion whether or not the position of young Socrates actually fits the position of the middle dialogues and whether the criticism is thus directed against Plato himself as a form of self-criticism. (I think that it does not fit, for the reason that our reconstructions of this 'Middle Theory' remain incomplete in a decisive respect – but this is to a large extent subject to a future study.[2]) Instead, I shall mostly concentrate on the *Parmenides*. For Parmenides, albeit launching attack after attack on Socrates' Theory, still emphasises that one has to maintain the forms, for otherwise dialectics will vanish (135b5–c3). With regard to this remark he ultimately agrees to demonstrate an exercise which promises to provide the means to solve the aporias and counter the objections (135c8–136e4). But since it is far from obvious how this solution is intended to work, the question of how the dialogue's second part relates to the first forms the second major question with regard to Plato's *Parmenides*.[3] In fact, every interpretation that approaches the dialogue as a whole is obliged to answer this question and J. WAHL was hence right in stating that "toute interprétation du dialogue qui laissera séparées les deux parties de l'œuvre ne pourrait nous satisfaire."[4]

In the following, I shall face this second major question with regard to the results of the previous chapters and the interpretation I offered based on the conceptual patterns. With a detailed analysis of two exemplary aporias, I mainly argue for the following claim in this chapter: if the second part is to be understood in the way I have so far proposed, then this second part is able to answer the aporias of the first part. Note that this claim remains conditional since it is of course subject to acceptance of the interpretation

---

for Plato could have easily taken another person to advocate the Theory of Forms in the first part of the *Parmenides*. Hence, if one supposes that Plato consciously chose Socrates in the *Parmenides* and that he was by then still aware of what he had written in the *Phaedo*, we have quite a strong argument as to how we should evaluate the criticism in the *Parmenides*.

[2] To give one brief example: the entanglement of the forms that Socrates denies (129e2–3; 130a1) is clearly present already in the *Republic* (476a6–7; also 485b6; 500c4–5 both imply at least some closer relation among them). In total, the common reconstructions of the 'Middle Theory of Forms' largely lack, in my eyes, an adequate inclusion of the soul's ontological position. In § 25, I shall provide some evidence that this inclusion is crucial for the discussion of how the *Parmenides* relates to the dialogues prior to it. A full reconstruction of the 'Middle Theory' is, however, way beyond the scope of the present study.

[3] Cf. e.g. the statements by NIEWÖHNER 1971, 81; MILLER 1986, 71; MEINWALD 1992, 366–367; FRANCES 1996, 47; PALMER 1999, 148; RICKLESS 2007, 4.

[4] WAHL [2]1951, 8–9. SCOLNICOV 2003, 1 chooses this statement of J. WAHL as the motto of his very instructive study.

offered before. But if the analysis in the present chapter succeeds in support-ing this conditional claim, it may likewise strengthen the suggested approach in total since the approach then also allows us to explain the relation of the dialogue's two parts.

In the present context, I shall concentrate on two aporias of the first part, the 'Greatest Aporia' and the first 'Third Man Argument'. I concentrate on these for two reasons. Firstly, because they are quite prominent among the aporias, and secondly, because they may be considered – each in a specific respect – quite characteristic of the problems that the Theory of Forms faces in the first part. In general, the relation between forms and particulars may count as the leitmotif of Parmenides' criticism. However, each aporia obvi-ously provides specific difficulties and the question is hence in which way the second part helps to address each of them. The main claim stated above therefore implies that the present approach is able to solve the problems, on the one hand, in a *differentiated* manner with regard to the different aporias and, on the other hand, in a *specific way* to be characterised in detail later on (§§ 25; 27). I hence advocate the view that there is not a single feature in the second part which provides a solution to all aporias. Rather, there are different aspects in what is unfolded in the second part that all provide help in countering the objections. With regard to the Greatest Aporia this will especially be the intermediate position of the soul; for the first Third Man Argument it will be the decisive difference between being and appearance.

## § 24. The Greatest Aporia

The 'Greatest Aporia' (cf. μέγιστον 133b4), which Parmenides unfolds as the climax of his objections against Socrates' Theory of Forms, consists of ba-sically three aspects. One could heuristically label them the 'ontological', the 'epistemological', and the 'theological' aspect. All three are based on a very rigid understanding of the χωρισμός between forms and particulars.[5] With regard to the *ontological* aspect, this strong separation implies that forms and particulars are both only related among themselves, without any rela-tion to the other realm. Forms are what they are in relation to other forms (133c8–9), and likewise particulars are what they are solely with regard to other particulars (133d2–5), independent of the forms. The *epistemological*

---

[5] In fact, this mirrors the ways in which Parmenides had already characterised Socrates' Theory at the very beginning when entering the discussion (cf. 130a7–b6, where esp. χωρίς occurs very often).

aspect emphasises the implication that this absolute separation also separates us as human beings from knowledge and truth itself and limits us to knowledge and truth 'in our realm' (134a3–b1; 134b9–c2). The reason for this limitation is that knowledge itself is said to be among the forms and is solely directed towards them (134b6–7).[6] The consequences become even "worse" (δεινότερον 134c4) with regard to the *theological* aspect, for this absolute separation implies a strict separation between human beings on the one side and God on the other – hence there is no reign of God (or the gods) over us (134e1–6). These three aspects are in fact closely linked together since God is said to have the most accurate knowledge (134c10–11; 134d10) and this knowledge is obviously directed towards the forms as the 'most knowable' objects of knowledge (134b6–7).[7]

---

[6] Admittedly, within the Greatest Aporia, Plato has Parmenides not simply say that there is knowledge among the forms, but, more precisely, that the form 'Knowledge' actually possesses knowledge of the forms (γιγνώσκεται δέ γέ που ὑπ᾽ αὐτοῦ τοῦ εἴδους τοῦ τῆς ἐπιστήμης αὐτὰ τὰ γένη ἃ ἔστιν ἕκαστα; 134b6–7). This statement is quite obscure and definitely difficult to interpret. Does it really mean that there is exactly one single form that possesses knowledge of all forms? What can it mean that one form 'knows' the others? Does this include that knowing the form 'Knowledge' automatically implies knowing all forms? Is Plato serious about the statement in the way it is phrased? Is it rather a deliberate distortion of a position that Plato would otherwise take? Or is the form 'Knowledge' to be understood *pars pro toto* for the *whole* cosmos of forms? I tend to cling to the latter for three reasons. Firstly, there are other instances where Plato seemingly uses a single form to name the cosmos of forms as a whole, namely the form 'Being' (SOPH. 254a8–9; without denying that there is also a specific form 'Being' among the μέγιστα γένη) and the form 'Life' (TIM. 39e8). Both forms in their generality side quite well with 'Knowledge' as a third *pars pro toto*, especially in the light of SOPH. 248e6–249a2. Secondly, Parmenides says only a little later that God possesses the most accurate knowledge (134c10–11; 134d10: ἡ ἀκριβεστάτη ἐπιστήμη). But a form may not be surpassed in what itself is (there is, for instance, nothing that is more a horse than the form 'Horse', since the latter actually encodes what it is to be a horse and hence, in that specific sense, forms the very standard for all horses). Therefore, it seems that one either has to identify God with the form 'Knowledge' (since there is little other chance to reconcile the two superlatives, the one implicit in the form 'Knowledge', the other stated explicitly in 134d10) or understand 'Knowledge' as another description, a *pars pro toto* for what God is. The former alternative seems quite odd to me (though this would include a further discussion of what being παρὰ τῷ θεῷ, 134d9, exactly means), while the latter works probably best if one understands both 'Knowledge' and 'God' as referring to the realm of forms as a whole (one might, in this respect, even consider the difference between God and the gods, which is present in the aporia; cf. MÄNNLEIN-ROBERT 2022, 270–272). This would again lead to understanding 134b6–7 as referring to the forms in total. Thirdly, all this obviously comes close to some extent to what Plato writes in the much-discussed passages SOPH. 248e6–249a2 and PHDR. 247c6–d1; 247d7; 247e1–2 and hence receives further support from them; cf. SCHWABE 2001 on the latter (cf. IBID., 204 N. 47 for a short note on the *Parmenides*).

[7] This mirrors quite closely the connection between ontology and epistemology, as famously expressed in REP. 477a3–4.

For sure, this is a more general characterisation of the Greatest Aporia as a whole, which, in itself, contains further detail. Besides the difficult question of how knowledge is said to be among the forms (134b6–7),[8] Parmenides discusses for instance in remarkable length the specific single forms 'Master' and 'Slave' (133d7–134a1; 134d9–e6). Of course, a great deal could be said about this specific example in itself. In my eyes it seems to be first of all a vivid hint to the asymmetrical hierarchy as such that Plato posits between forms and particulars, but also among the forms themselves.[9] Hence also the discussion of the specific forms 'Master' and 'Slave' have at least one aspect that points to the general relation between the two main ontological realms, whose connection is at stakes in the Greatest Aporia.

With regard to these realms, there can be little to no doubt that the separation in this aporia is meant to express a *complete* separation between them.[10] However, Parmenides formulates this separation in terms of a (disrupted) relation between human beings and God. What is supposedly the realm of forms is described as the realm of (the) God(s) (134d4–e6), while the particulars are τὰ παρ' ἡμῖν and τὰ ἐν ἡμῖν.[11] This terminological decision is remarkable for three reasons: firstly, because it mirrors those passages in the Platonic corpus which at least suggest that Plato thought of the forms as gods and of the realm of forms in its totality as God.[12] Secondly, because this theme of the relation between human beings and gods is to be found in several other passages of Plato's dialogues which might be of help to further enlighten our understanding of the Greatest Aporia in the *Parmenides* – we shall come back to these passages in § 25. And thirdly, because the mentioning of 'us' as human beings should remind us of the fact that to Plato a human being is primarily characterised not by his or her physical body, but by the *soul* (as, for instance, the *Phaedo* emphasises time and again). 'Our' realm, which is separated from the forms in the aporia, thus not only includes the physical but also – and to some extent primarily – the ontological level of the immaterial soul(s).[13] This is also remarkable because the above

---

[8] Cf. p. 104 n. 6.

[9] Cf. REP. 485b6 for a hierarchy among the forms. Also the last steps in the Cave (REP. 516a8–b2) obviously imply some hierarchy among the forms.

[10] E.g. MEINWALD 1992, 376–377.

[11] Cf. for these expressions 133c5; 133c9–d1; 133d2; 133e5; 134a1; 134a9; 134a10; 134b4; 134c7; 134d1; 134d5; 134d6; 134e1; 134e2.

[12] Cf. TIM. 37c6 (with the very instructive arguments by KARFÍK 2004, esp. 123–126); to some extent also REP. 521c3 (though with regard to the position of others). TIM. 92c5–7 implies in my eyes that the realm of forms in its totality is God.

[13] Cf. again TIM. 37a1–2, quoted in § 12.

quoted expressions τὰ παρ' ἡμῖν and alike resemble some other expressions Plato uses to describe this presence of the soul in relation to the body.[14] If we closely analyse the terminology of the aporia, we thus already find, at second glance, some potential hints that 'our' realm is not only a physical realm, but includes the psychic level of reality.

But how to deal with the Greatest Aporia against the backdrop of the conceptual patterns in the second part of the *Parmenides*? The easy way is – obviously – blocked since F. M. CORNFORD rightly emphasised that there is, for instance, not even a single mention of explicit theological vocabulary in the second part.[15] However, the conceptual pattern's overall approach may provide a possible solution. In general, if the exercise promises to provide a solution, this must first and foremost include a possibility to bridge the gap which is unfolded in the Greatest Aporia. And, as becomes clear from the results in the previous chapters, the solution proposed by the conceptual patterns is to locate the realm of the soul between the noetical and the physical realm and to take S2C and S5 as descriptions of this intermediate level.

One of the most unambiguous and striking results so far is S2C's and S5's resemblance in a remarkable number of conceptual patterns (§§ 5–6; 16). Furthermore, these patterns were characteristically those that fit the soul quite well, such as those of motion and rest. Hence it has been argued that S2C and S5 can reasonably be supposed to describe the ontological level of the soul (§ 16). S2C/S5 can thus help to solve the Greatest Aporia. In order for that we have to trace, on the one hand, how these sections relate and connect to the realm of forms and, on the other, in what way they are related to the physical realm of appearance.

To begin with the relation to the realm of forms. As has been argued, the realm of being is concentrated in S2/3 and it is quite prominently characterised by the concept of οὐσία.[16] If we now look at S2C and S5 we find remarkably similar descriptions in both sections. In S2C, in the very beginning, Parmenides is obviously anxious to circumscribe how the One in question does temporarily participate in οὐσία and how, for some time, it does not (155e10). This is primarily expressed by participation in οὐσία, but it is also described as participating "in the same" (τοῦ αὐτοῦ μετέχοι 155e11).

---

[14] Cf. the similar expression περί + acc. which is found as describing very likely the presence of the soul on the level of the body in REP. 510a5 (cf. in detail POETSCH 2019, 67–74); TIM. 35a2–3 (cf. the very useful remarks by OPSOMER 2020, 171 N. 4); PHDR. 246d8 (deleting ψυχή is misleading in my eyes).

[15] Cf. CORNFORD 1939, IX.

[16] Cf. §§ 5; 17; as well as APPENDIX A.

We might interpret the latter as likewise pointing to the forms, especially since αὐτός is elsewhere, in S2, apparently employed in the well-known sense to describe forms.[17] This partial and temporal participation in being is furthermore characterised as "taking hold of being in some time" and "letting it go in another"[18], and the rest of S2C obviously analyses this alternating process as a process of becoming and passing away (esp. 156a4–b4; § 18). It is furthermore very remarkable that, at the end of S2C (156e7–157b3), Parmenides seems to also circumscribe a kind of 'substratum' which is not affected by this process of change, becoming, and passing away, and we may suspect that this describes the substance of the soul in itself, within which this process takes place, while the soul itself does not alter.

In S5, there is very similar evidence with regard to the connection to being. For Parmenides makes it clear that the One discussed in S5, τὸ μὴ ὂν ἕν, "needs to participate in being in some respect" (οὐσίας γε δεῖ αὐτὸ μετέχειν πῃ 161e3). This is then elaborated by a complex chiasm of being and non-being (162a4–b3), which remarkably employs the unique term δεσμός (162a4; § 21), and which concludes with the statement that οὐσία may indeed appear to the One in question (162b6). It is true that the concept of time is not explicitly employed in S5 (as it is in S2C), but these considerations in S5 nevertheless lead to a characteristic alternation of being and non-being which is very similar to that in S2C. οὐσία is not only present, but also absent (162b7), and change and alteration (but no change of place) is essential for the One in question (162b9–163a7). All this ultimately leads to the same pair of becoming and passing away (163b2–3) that has likewise been very characteristic of S2C (§§ 6; 16). As in S2C, we find an allusion to the Same (162d2–3), which is linked to Being and thus different from the non-being One, but which remains in connection to it somehow (162b6). Besides that, we also find a description of both some unchangeable aspects of the One in question (162d5–e3; 163b1–5) and of change and alteration (162b6–c6; 163b1–5). This again is very similar to what we found in S2C. Given the presence of alternation between κίνησις and στάσις – and hence of spontaneous motion – all this sounds very much like Plato's concept of the soul.[19] Moreover, the characteristic constellation of change and some unchanging substratum, which is to be found in both sections, could very well be understood as a description of the soul if one thinks, for instance, of a hint given in the *Symposium* (207d4–e1).

---

[17] Esp. 150b7; 150c1; 150c4; 150c5; 150c5–6.

[18] Cf. ὅτε μεταλαμβάνει τοῦ εἶναι καὶ ὅτε ἀπαλλάττεται αὐτοῦ (156a1–2).

[19] Cf. e.g. PHDR. 245c5–246a2; 246c3–4 as well as § 16 for more details.

It is true, however, that none of these passages, neither S2C nor S5, explains *how* a soul can participate in the realm of being or how it works *in detail* that οὐσία may be (temporally) present in it.[20] Yet, two things have to be noted. Firstly, there is no text at all in Plato's written works that explains in greater technical detail how these relations of participation do actually work.[21] Hence we cannot blame the *Parmenides* in particular for not being more detailed on that point. The lack of technical detail in S2C/S5 is hence no objection to the present interpretation. And secondly, it remains nevertheless quite obvious in my eyes that both S2C and S5 intend to *circumscribe* such a constellation of partial participation in οὐσία.

So far, two sections of the exercise can be understood as dealing with the relation between the soul and the realm of forms. According to the interpretation based on the conceptual patterns, the connection between the physical realm and the soul can also be detected in the second part of the *Parmenides*, in particular in S6–7 and their relation to S5. The key thought lies in the idea explained in §§ 12–14 with regard to IP. S6 describes a subject solely *in itself* and S7 describes the same subject, but now *in relation* to its direct principle in S5. Considered solely in itself, the physical realm remains nothing and is characterised by the total absence of οὐσία (οὐσίας ἀπουσίαν 163c3). In itself, it lacks the participation in οὐσία (οὐδέ πῃ μετέχει οὐσίας 163c6–7; cf. 163c8–d1). This is more or less exactly the crucial point of the Greatest Aporia's ontological aspect. In consequence, becoming and passing away are absent (163d1–8), as is change (163d8–e3). On the contrary, in S7 – when the physical realm is considered in relation to its direct principle –, appearance is present and the great majority of statements in S7 is made in the mode of φαίνεσθαι. This time, unlike in S6, becoming and passing away are present, they appear to be (165d7).[22] In general, there are thus again positive statements in S7 and no complete absence of being, though this time in a mode of dream-like appearance. As has been argued in § 15, this constellation between the complete absence of οὐσία on the one hand (S6), and the appearance of some φαντάσματα of being on the other (S7), ties in very well with TIM. 52c2–5, which likewise describes the relation of the physical to the noetical in terms of dream, appearance, and image.

As with the relation between being and soul, it is again true that there is no exact *technical* description of how the physical realm may be regarded as

---

[20] To be fair, it has to be said that even today this question of how something psychic can interact with other, non-psychic parts of reality remains a hitherto unsolved problem.

[21] Cf. the explicit gap in TIM. 50c4–6.

[22] These participles in 165d5–7 remain depending on φαίνεσθαι (165d4).

being connected to soul. But again it is likewise true that this description is nowhere to be found in Plato's writings.[23] It is thus no objection to the present interpretation that it lacks an exact description of the connection between the psychic and the physical.

The gap that forms the Greatest Aporia's core issue is thus bridged by the intermediate level of the soul. οὐσία may be temporally present within the soul and is in turn displayed in the physical world of appearance. The general solution to the Greatest Aporia which the second part offers is thus to unfold an ontological constellation within which the soul forms the decisive intermediate step. The soul provides the ontological link between the physical and the noetic realm. Furthermore, this is obviously crucial for understanding the epistemological issues of the Greatest Aporia, although this aspect is less prominent in the exercise.[24] And – even though there is no theological terminology in the second part – the constellation described can even be seen as indirectly relevant for the theological aspect. With regard to this, it might be helpful to recall, for instance, that the rational soul is τὸ θειότατον within a human being (REP. 589e4; cf. also 590c9–d1; 590e4) and that this rational soul is a δαίμων given to us by God (TIM. 90a2–5). In both cases, the soul obviously plays a crucial part in our relation to the gods and God. Hence, locating the soul between both realms has theological implications. In that sense, the constellation of the second part offers an answer to all three aspects of the Greatest Aporia.

## § 25. Evaluation of the Solution to the Greatest Aporia

If the present approach is correct, the second part's solution to the Greatest Aporia would mainly consist in deducing a complex ontological stratification within which this difficulty does not arise anymore. In a very general sense, the Greatest Aporia is thus based on two main misconceptions, which are linked to one another. On the one hand, it supposes too strict a separation

---

[23] There are some hints in the *Timaeus*, but these remain hints: TIM. 34b3–4; 36d8–e3 (cf. also PHDO. 81c6).

[24] In that respect, S1 and S2 both resemble the Divided Line in discussing ontological questions in a very lengthy way and then adding, rather briefly, epistemological remarks to it. There are only very brief epistemological remarks at the end of S6 (164a7–b2), but not in S7. However, there is nothing in S7 that would actively obstruct epistemological accounts – on the contrary, the terminology of δοκέω and δοξάζειν even to some extent demands them, though the argument in S6–7 is obviously very much abridged.

between the realm of the forms ('the realm of the gods') and the realm of the physical particulars ('our realm'), while, on the other hand, it completely misses the soul's decisive role in this constellation. The second part then deduces an ontological constellation, within which the soul plays a crucial intermediate role to connect these two realms.

One might object that it is hardly possible for young Socrates to arrive at this solution by simply listening to the arguments and deductions of the exercise, for it is e.g. quite difficult to identify the soul in S2C/S5. I agree to some extent and I do, of course, not claim that Socrates should have used something like the statistical analysis provided here to approach the second part – this is only our scientific way of reconstructing things. However, I do not think that this objection causes insurmountable problems to the present interpretation. Firstly, because there is in any case no simple solution to be found on the surface of the exercise's text (for otherwise the lengthy scholarly discussions of how the second part provides help would have been rather pointless). Therefore, *every* interpretation needs to 'delve deeper' in one sense or another and thus implies the problem of how Socrates should have arrived at exactly the solution he arrives at. And secondly, it seems highly likely to me that the exercise has to some extent a *hypomnematic function*.[25] If we take into account the clear and repeated allusions to the intimate situation in Pythodoros' house,[26] it seems quite likely that Plato is alluding to the situation of his students in the Academy. This becomes even more likely since the prologue of the *Parmenides* provides a clear hint to the Academy, which must have been quite obvious to the contemporary reader who was familiar with the city map of Athens.[27] If the *Parmenides* is hence directed – at least *inter alia* – at Plato's students, we may indeed suppose that he provides at times only hints and reminders in the dialogue's second part, while these readers were still able to grasp the intended solution. Since hints and clues may very well work via key terms and concepts, this fits the present approach quite well.

One may furthermore object that the soul may not really count as a solution to the aporia, for soul is present in us as human beings and hence is clearly located not *between* the two realms, but *in one* of the two realms whose separation is at stakes, especially since we found allusions to the soul

---

[25] Cf. ERLER 2007, 228 for this aspect of the *Parmenides*.

[26] Esp. 136d6–e3, 137a6–7; cf. also 127c1–6, 129d1.

[27] Cf. POETSCH 2019, 161–167. In a sense, this is the same walk that is visualised in the drawing in LONG/SEDLEY 1987, I 4 (though of course in a different context and years later than the dramatic date of the *Parmenides*).

in expressions like τὰ παρ' ἡμῖν and τὰ ἐν ἡμῖν (§ 24).[28] I agree to some extent, as long as the souls of individual human beings are concerned. However, there are, at least, two rejoinders to this objection. Firstly, the proposed solution refers to the World Soul, but not to individual human souls. Although they are in principle (and literally) cast in the same mould,[29] it is doubtlessly the World Soul that fulfils the systematic task of connecting both realms, but not the souls of individual human beings. Hence, the allusions τὰ παρ' ἡμῖν and τὰ ἐν ἡμῖν ultimately do not obstruct the present solution. And secondly, it has to be remarked that these allusions are in fact no more than allusions. It is not stated explicitly that this refers to or includes the soul. It is thus anything but clear that Socrates (or any other person being struck by the Greatest Aporia) does in fact recognise that τὰ ἐν ἡμῖν in a Platonic context inevitably implies an immaterial soul. After all, it is perfectly possible that a human being considers him- or herself as being completely corporeal.[30] The implication of expressions like τὰ ἐν ἡμῖν may thus be understood as hints where to look for the solution, but do not obstruct the present interpretation.

Besides all that, we may furthermore ask: is it *plausible* that the solution in § 24 meets Plato's intention to solve the Greatest Aporia? I think there is one argument that strongly encourages this view: the proposed solution is the very same answer that Plato provides after and, very likely, also before the *Parmenides*. For the period after this dialogue, the clearest evidence comes from the *Timaeus*, where the World Soul clearly forms a crucial intermediate step between the forms and the physical cosmos.[31] The same – or at least something quite similar – is stated very briefly in the *Philebus* (30c9–10). In the case of the dialogues before (or roughly contemporary to) the *Parmenides*, things are a bit more difficult. However, there are clues that Plato held this view in those dialogues as well. The most important hint is to be found in the *Symposium*, a dialogue that is in some sense a 'twin' of the *Parmenides*.[32] The crucial passage is located at the beginning of Socrates' speech,

---

[28] I would like to thank B. STROBEL for making this point.

[29] Cf. TIM. 41d5–7; and also PHLB. 30a3–7.

[30] This is the state of the chained prisoners in the Cave (cf. POETSCH 2019, 328–334).

[31] Cf. esp. TIM. 30b3–5 (~ PHLB. 30c9–10); 31b8–c4 (with regard to the employment of the arithmetic and harmonic mean in the mixture of the soul in TIM. 36a2–7).

[32] There are at least three decisive parallels on a macroscopic level: 1) both dialogues stick out in the Platonic corpus and resemble each other by their very complex framings, which can be coordinated in greater detail (cf. POETSCH 2019, 172–176); 2) both dialogues are the only instances in the Platonic corpus where Socrates is clearly depicted as an inexperienced and inferior junior partner; 3) the concept of love, which is omnipresent in the *Symposium*, is also employed as a kind of title for the second part of the *Parmenides* (137a4).

where he reports Diotima's statement that τὸ δαιμόνιον is "in between both [sc. human beings and gods], filling (both)[33] up, so that the All is bound together with itself."[34] If we understand τὸ πᾶν in a broad sense as embracing both the physical realm and the realm of forms (as Plato does, for instance, in the *Cratylus*[35]), this σύνδεσμος reminds us quite literally of the systematic function the World Soul later fulfils in the *Timaeus*.[36] This especially holds true if we recall that Plato can sometimes identify δαίμων and soul,[37] for Diotima literally calls Eros a δαίμων μέγας (SYMP. 202d13). According to the Mantinean priestess, it is hence a 'great daemon' – and thus possibly: a 'great soul' – that binds the All together. This comes remarkably close to the idea of the World Soul's intermediate function. There are even more hints in this direction, especially since there is a close parallel to the Greatest Aporia. As the *Parmenides*, also the *Symposium* extensively uses the relation between human beings and gods as a motif and describes Eros as mediating between them (SYMP. 202d13–203a4). If the systematic relation between forms and particulars, which clearly is behind this motif in the *Parmenides* (§ 24), also applies to this motif in the *Symposium*, it becomes even more likely that Eros in its intermediate position[38] in fact mediates between the physical realm and the realm of forms.

Besides these parallels, there are more passages to support this argument. In the *Gorgias*, Socrates famously states that "the geometric equality has great power amongst both gods and human beings"[39]. If one recalls that geometric equality is mathematically based on the concept of a continuous geometric analogy,[40] the Divided Line forms a clear parallel in this respect since it employs exactly the same theorem to relate the physical realm and the realm

---

[33] The verb συμπληροῖ is not easy to understand here. It might either be understood as filling up the space in between both or as (additionally) pervading both realms and thereby connecting them. With regard to the present interpretation, I prefer the second option.

[34] ἐν μέσῳ δὲ ὂν ἀμφοτέρων συμπληροῖ [sc. τὸ δαιμόνιον], ὥστε τὸ πᾶν αὐτὸ αὑτῷ συνδεδέσθαι (SYMP. 202e6–7).

[35] Cf. the etymology of the twofold god 'Pan' (CRAT. 408b8–d5), which again takes up the motif of human beings and gods in a sense that fits the present argument remarkably well (CRAT. 408c5–7). PHLB. 30d8 and TIM. 30b5 probably allude to the same understanding of τὸ πᾶν. With Eros' function as translator (SYMP. 202e3) and the role of λόγος in the *analogia entis* (cf. FRIEDLÄNDER ³1964, 45–46), also the etymology of 'Hermes' – directly preceding the one of 'Pan' – might possibly be of further interest (CRAT. 407e5–6; 408a6).

[36] This is, of course, not to claim that Eros and the World Soul are simply identical.

[37] Esp. TIM. 90a2–4; 90c5; cf. also PLTC. 309c7–8 and to some extant REP. 614c1. Cf. the very good remarks by KARFÍK 2004, 101–102 on this issue.

[38] The crucial term μεταξύ occurs several times (SYMP. 202d11; 202e1; 204b1; 204b5).

[39] ἡ ἰσότης ἡ γεωμετρικὴ καὶ ἐν θεοῖς καὶ ἐν ἀνθρώποις μέγα δύναται (GORG. 508a6–7).

[40] I.e. a | b = b | c (as opposed to a discrete geometric analogy a | b = c | d).

of forms.[41] This becomes even clearer if one recalls the relation between the World Soul and mathematical analogy as a δεσμός later in the *Timaeus*.[42] From this perspective, the motif of human beings and gods,[43] which is employed again in the *Gorgias* fits the usage of that motif in the *Parmenides* and the *Symposium* quite well. Moreover, the very same motif reoccurs in the *Theaetetus* (which remains a bit difficult to date in relation to the *Parmenides*). In interpreting the famous golden chain from the *Iliad* (8.17–27), Socrates there quite clearly alludes – via Zeus[44] – to the World Soul and, again, employs the motif of human beings and gods in a very similar sense (THT. 153c8–d5).[45] Other passages from the middle period, such as the so-called 'Tyrant Number' (REP. 587b12–588a10), also point to an intermediate psychic realm.[46]

There are thus numerous passages before (and roughly contemporary to) the *Parmenides* that all employ the same motif as the Greatest Aporia. And they all hint to the psychic realm as a possible bridge between the physical and the forms. How likely is it thus that Plato intended the solution to the Greatest Aporia proposed here? At least, this solution has some plausibility to it since Plato clearly advocates it after the *Parmenides* and – at least – hints at it several times in the dialogues before.

## § 26. The First Regress Argument

The first regress argument (132a1–b2) that Parmenides raises against the Theory of Forms is commonly known as the first 'Third Man Argument'.[47]

---

[41] The λόγοι of the Line do, in fact, implement the transition from a discrete to a continuous geometric analogy. The Line is hence to be interpreted as emphasising the *connection* between the noetical and the physical, as has rightly been emphasised by AUBENQUE 1992. In consequence, the equality of the Line's middle segments is no unintended flaw, but ultimately the punchline of the whole Analogy; cf. more in detail POETSCH 2019, 92–98.

[42] On the horizontal and vertical employment of analogy in that respect, cf. the important remarks by DÖRRIE/BALTES 1996, 324.

[43] Cf. also before GORG. 507e6–508a4, where the relation and harmony between gods and human beings is once more stressed.

[44] Some connection between Zeus and the all-embracing vital function of the World Soul is alluded to in the *Cratylus* (397a6–b2) as well as in the *Philebus* (30d1–2).

[45] For a more detailed analysis of this passage, cf. POETSCH 2021A, 244.

[46] A detailed reconstruction of this obscure passage and a proof of the importance of the intermediate psychic realm for its understanding is given in POETSCH 2022.

[47] As early as 1941, P. WILPERT pointed to the fact that the title 'Third Man' may have applied to a variety of arguments and objections and that this title is thus at least in danger of being historically vague (WILPERT 1941, 61; cf. also MIGNUCCI 1990, 144; FINE 1993,

The well-known objection runs, in a very first sketch, as follows: suppose that there is a form for every plurality of things (in a wide sense) that are[48] in some respect the same (132a2–4).[49] For example, if there is a plurality of large things, then there is a form 'Largeness'. This form causes the common respect in all given things (132a7–8). But if someone now looks at all those things that are the same in some respect *and* at the form just mentioned (132a6–7), there is, according to the initial premise (and if the form itself exhibits the shared feature), yet another form through which those things and the first form share the common respect in question; there is hence another form next and above all of them (132a7–11). Obviously, it is possible to iterate this process indefinitely: if one now looks at those two forms and all those things that are the same in some respect, there is yet another form above them all, and so forth (132a11–b1). We thus end up with an indefinite multitude of forms. And this obviously contradicts a crucial claim of the Theory of Forms according to which every form exists only once. The initial premise – which sounds like the very principle of Plato's Theory of Forms – thus seems to lead to an aporia of this Theory.

With regard to the present study, I shall provide a solution to this aporia that rests, on the one hand and first of all, on the part that appearance plays in this argument. This allows to answer the second major question for this aporia (§ 23). On the other hand, I will put some emphasis on the position of the soul within this argument. The latter aspect will be treated subsequently, when evaluating the present solution (§ 27). Before that, in the present paragraph, I shall first provide a more formal reconstruction of the argument to then explain how the second part, read according to IP and the conceptual patterns, could help to avoid the aporia. After that, I shall relate this approach to previous solutions. One possible way to reconstruct the argument in a more formal and general way is the following:[50]

203–224; LIENEMANN 2010, 24 N. 20 on this issue). Besides that, one cannot exclude that 'Largeness' is a non-arbitrary pick with further hints and implications and hence switching to the form 'Man' or something alike at least risks blurring things. Some – as for instance SCOLNICOV 2003, 1 – have argued that especially the first regress argument "received more than [a] fair share of effort and ingenuity". A helpful overview of the most important steps of the discussion is provided with the analysis by LIENEMANN 2010.

[48] For the moment I stick to the common terminology of being, though we shall see that there is almost certainly significance in Parmenides' use of terms of appearance.

[49] Cf. MARTENS ²2001, 163 N. 10.

[50] This reconstruction obviously benefits from the many attempts that have preceded it. Since my main aim is to emphasise the importance of appearance in this argument (and hence to provide a possible link to Parmenides' exercise), I shall limit myself mainly to this aspect. It

(1) Whenever there are several F(-things), then there is one separate form F through which all these F(-things) are F.

(2) There are several F(-things).

($c_1$) There is one separate form $F_1$. [follows from (1), (2)]

<3> (A and each) Form F is itself (an) F(-thing).

(4) There are several F(-things); these consist of several F(-things) and one form $F_1$. [follows from (2), ($c_1$), <3>]

(5) There is one separate form $F_{1+1}$ (= $F_2$). [follows from (1), (4)]

($c_2$) There is an indefinite multitude of forms $F_{1...\infty}$.

[results from infinitely iterating (4), (5) with (1), <3>]

A few remarks on this reconstruction, before I propose a solution based on the conceptual patterns. Premise (1) is a general form of 132a2–3[51] and could be regarded as something like the general principle of the Theory of Forms, as known, in its general impetus, also from other dialogues.[52] It is a version of the so-called 'One-over-Many'-premise. By including 'separate', it implies what has been called early on in the discussion the 'Non-Identity-Assumption'.[53] The addition 'things' is obviously to be taken in a very wide sense[54] since it remains implicit in the Greek text and since the argument ultimately presupposes that it includes both particulars and forms.[55] The causal aspect of F in (1) is not stated in 132a2–3, but it is, firstly, implied in 132a7 (ᾧ) and, secondly, it will play a rather minor role in the present reconstruction. (2) follows the obvious implication of 132a2.[56] Within (2), 'several' indicates that there is more than one and hence a certain multitude of F-things.[57]

is hence not possible in the present context to follow all the detailed and manifold discussions that arose around this argument. Implicit premises are indicated by <...>.

[51] ὅταν πόλλ' ἄττα μεγάλα σοι δόξῃ εἶναι, μία τις ἴσως δοκεῖ ἰδέα ἡ αὐτὴ εἶναι ἐπὶ πάντα ἰδόντι (132a2–3).

[52] Cf. e.g. REP. 596a6–7; admittedly, in this case emphasis is put on the same ὄνομα for a multitude of things, but the general impetus obviously remains the same.

[53] Cf. VLASTOS 1954, 325. I do not put this assumption separately since it will play no major role in the present reconstruction.

[54] For a similar usage of 'things', cf. PENNER 1987, 280.

[55] Cf. on this issue instructively FERRARI 2022, 72–75.

[56] πόλλ' ἄττα μεγάλα σοι δόξῃ εἶναι (132a2). To some extent one could regard (2) as implicit since 132a2–3 only states the conditional expressed in (1). However, it is obvious that both Parmenides and Socrates accept (2).

[57] Note that this is obviously not intended to mean that the form F only causes *exactly* *these* several things to be F, but ultimately all F-things. What is needed, as some kind of trigger, is that there is more than only one F-thing. In that sense 'these' in the consequence of (1) might be omitted.

Since Parmenides introduces it in that way in 132a1 and 132a3–4,[58] $(c_1)$ is considered to be a first conclusion drawn from (1) and (2).[59] I take both formulations of $(c_1)$ to mean that *exactly one* form F exists and that both interlocutors understand it in this way.[60] Hence, $(c_1)$ expresses the famous feature of the Theory of Forms according to which every form exists only once, and (1)–(2) provide the reason for this. Also <3> is a version of another well-known and much discussed feature of the Theory of Forms: self-predication, according to which each form F is itself F. This premise remains implicit in Parmenides' argument. However, a version of it obviously has to be taken into account in order to count the form F among the F-things in the argument's next step and to set the regress in motion. This next step is formulated in (4), which is a general form of 132a6–7.[61] As <3> allows to regard the form F from $(c_1)$ as an F-thing, step (4) clusters this form F from $(c_1)$ and the several F-things from (2) to again apply principle (1) to this new group. This results in (5), which Parmenides formulates in 132a7–8 and 132a10–11.[62] Subsequently, the iteration of (4) and (5) is indicated in 132a11–b1[63], which then results in $(c_2)$ and the infinite multitude of F. In total, Parmenides thus derives – or better: has the immature Socrates derive – two contradictory conclusions from the initial premise (1): there is exactly *one* form F (= $c_1$), while ultimately there is not one single form F, but an *infinite multitude* of it (= $c_2$), καὶ οὐκέτι δὴ ἓν ἕκαστόν σοι

---

[58] οἶμαί σε ἐκ τοῦ τοιοῦδε ἓν ἕκαστον εἶδος οἴεσθαι εἶναι (132a1); ὅθεν ἓν τὸ μέγα ἡγῇ εἶναι (132a3–4). Both ἐκ τοῦ τοιοῦδε and ὅθεν indicate that the existence of that one form F is considered as a *consequence* of (1) and (2).

[59] For the sake of brevity and since it does not affect the further reconstruction, I leave out the causal role of the form, which is included in the consequence of (1) and may hence also be transferred to $(c_1)$. Note that within both of Socrates' ways to meet the aporia (which will be given below, pp. 118–120) there is no obligation to provide a causal explanation for <3>, i.e. why a certain form F is F, in order to avoid the aporia. Obviously, there must be a different explanation than the one in (1), which, in both ways, will only apply to those F which appear.

[60] On this issue, cf. COHEN 1971, 451; 455; LIENEMANN 2010, 102–105; STROBEL 2018, 202–203. $(c_1)$ is obviously echoed at the end by ἓν ἕκαστόν σοι τῶν εἰδῶν ἔσται (132b1–2). This (negated) statement according to which "each form is one" only makes sense if it means that each form exists only *once*, for it is intended as an opposition to ἄπειρα τὸ πλῆθος (132b2).

[61] τί δ' αὐτὸ τὸ μέγα καὶ τἆλλα τὰ μεγάλα, ἐὰν ὡσαύτως τῇ ψυχῇ ἐπὶ πάντα ἴδῃς (132a6–7).

[62] οὐχὶ ἕν τι αὖ μέγα φανεῖται, ᾧ ταῦτα πάντα μεγάλα φαίνεσθαι (132a7–8); ἄλλο ἄρα εἶδος μεγέθους ἀναφανήσεται, παρ' αὐτό τε τὸ μέγεθος γεγονὸς καὶ τὰ μετέχοντα αὐτοῦ (132a10–11).

[63] καὶ ἐπὶ τούτοις αὖ πᾶσιν ἕτερον, ᾧ ταῦτα πάντα μεγάλα ἔσται (132a11–b1). Note that it seems fruitful to compare this to the principle of complete induction; a principle whose employment has been convincingly detected behind 149a7–c3 by ACERBI 2000.

τῶν εἰδῶν ἔσται, ἀλλὰ ἄπειρα τὸ πλῆθος (132b1–2). The aporia thus basically consists in the fact that the initial premise, intended to provide a reason for the existence of a unique form F, turns out to produce an infinite multitude of it.

How to avoid this aporia within the present approach and the conceptual patterns? If one takes a closer look at the text of the argument, one thing is very remarkable: the dominant *terminology of appearance*. In (1), it is to some extent a matter of appearance when there "seem" (cf. δόξῃ 132a2) to be several particulars that have something in common (in this case: they all seem to be large) and, in consequence, the first form $F_1$ (Largeness) "seems" (δοκεῖ 132a2) to exist as well. In the following, in (4)–(5), the second form $F_2$ "appears" (φανεῖται 132a7) and it is through this form that $F_1$ and the particulars "appear" (φαίνεσθαι 132a8) to possess the common feature. The emergence of $F_2$ is described a second time as "appearing above" (ἀναφανήσεται 132a10) the first form $F_1$ and the particulars. Hence, until the final conclusion $(c_2)$ is drawn in 132b1–2, virtually every existence and emergence within the argument is expressed or accompanied by a term of appearance.[64] This indisputable terminological dominance is doubtlessly remarkable; especially since it would have been easily possible for Plato to put things differently. On the other hand, there seems to have been mutual agreement among scholars that, throughout the whole argument, this terminology of appearance can be substituted by a terminology of being ever since G. VLASTOS very briefly mentioned this change in terms.[65] Many approaches since then applied this change without further remark.[66] However,

---

[64] The only exception is $(c_1)$ which seems to be no coincidence, cf. the remarks below on Socrates' first way to avoid the aporia.

[65] "I say 'are,' where Plato's text above says only 'seem.' But the difference is immaterial to the argument. A few lines later Plato speaks of the large things as 'participating' in Largeness (132a11), which is his way of saying that they are large (so far as particulars *are* anything at all) and do not merely appear such." (VLASTOS 1954, 320 N. 3; emph. orig.).

[66] If I see it correctly, this tacit switch in terminology is to be found e.g. in GEACH 1956 (note esp. the silent substitution IBID., 77–78); MORAVCSIK 1963; PETERSEN 1973 (cf. esp. IBID., 452–452 with N. 3–4); MIGNUCCI 1990 ("But 'appear' may very well simply mean 'be' here." IBID., 147 N. 8; cf. also IBID., 149); MEINWALD 1992; FRANCES 1996; HUNT 1997 (note esp. how being and appearance are used without any differentiation IBID., 4). Given the vast amount of studies on this argument, this list of course only indicates a certain tendency; it does not claim exhaustiveness. Besides those mentioned, COHEN 1971, 468 made a very brief remark on δοκέω/φαίνω, interpreting this vocabulary as pointing to the momentary and transitory situation where *just one* new form F appears over the given set of many F-things, while it later turns out that there are actually many more forms. For S. M. COHEN, these terms thus emphasise the *illusionary* character of the situation where one is inclined to believe that one has reached the one and unique form above all. However, if I see it correctly, he does not implement these terms more explicitly in his reconstruction.

this change – which is, heuristically, applied in the reconstruction above[67] – decisively levels the ways in which particulars and forms exist.[68] After all, in Plato, this is no trivial change or just a matter of quibbling, for the very way in which all particulars exist consists just in appearing. This appearance is distinguished from being, which is the forms' proper and peculiar mode of existence.[69]

If we now take a look at the conceptual patterns, there is obviously potential to deal with these issues. One of the clearest patterns (recall the very high DP-value) and one that is certainly no result of mere accident was the conceptual pattern of appearance (§§ 5; 7; 15). This pattern concentrates its positive accounts in S7 and it is to a very large extent made up of the terms φαίνω and δοκέω, i.e. the very same terms that we find in the present aporia. The pattern of appearance was clearly distinguished from the field of being and the forms (§§ 5; 14; 18). A Socrates instructed by the exercise as it is understood by IP was hence taught a clear distinction between being and appearance from the exercise. Accordingly, there are at least two ways for Socrates in which he could counter Parmenides' argument and avoid the aporia. The first way criticises how Parmenides phrases the aporia and is hence, in a sense, at odds with the reconstruction given above. The second way accepts this reconstruction, but uses the differentiation established by the exercise to modify the premises and to avoid aporia. These two ways are not mutually exclusive, but the former puts greater emphasis on Parmenides' *presentation*, while the latter focuses more on how Socrates should *modify* his position with regard to the driving principles of the argument.

Socrates' *first way* would entail the insistence that, in a more specific sense, only forms *are*, while particulars *appear*. They both exist in a certain way, but their modes of existence differ from one another. It is therefore incorrect to indiscriminately treat forms and particulars in the very same mode of appearance. If forms do not appear in the sense that particulars do, a view ἐπὶ πάντα becomes much more difficult or in fact even impossible. Hence, Socrates would avoid especially his consent to step (4), which lumps particulars and forms together indiscriminately, without properly clarifying their mode of existence. Accordingly, he would insist that the appearance of a form – esp. ἔν τι αὖ μέγα φανεῖται (132a7) and ἄλλο … εἶδος μεγέθους

---

[67] Cf. p. 114 n. 48.

[68] There can be no doubt that both forms and particulars *exist*, in some sense, for Plato. It is, however, crucial to understand in *which* sense and hence in which *mode* they exist. Besides that, it is important not to understand existence as something purely binary.

[69] Cf. the very helpful remarks by FERRARI 2000, 371–372 on these issues.

ἀναφανήσεται (132a10) – may not be conflated with its proper mode of existence, i.e. being. Either a form *appears*, then we are to do with an instantiation of it, which does not disturb the being and the uniqueness of the one single form, i.e. $(c_1)$.[70] Or a form *is*, then it cannot be counted among the things that appear, and $(c_2)$ in consequence does not apply. In that sense, Socrates could also point to the remarkable fact that Parmenides seems to – deliberately? – switch between being and appearance throughout his argument. A closer look at the text reveals that especially in the conclusions $(c_1, c_2)$ the terminology of being is present, while in the premises it is virtually exclusively the terminology of appearance. Therefore, Parmenides commits a fallacy by deducing facts about being from premises about appearance.

Socrates' *second way* could consist in a solution that puts a bit less emphasis on Parmenides' wording and on how the argument is presented strategically. In that sense, Socrates would understand the premises of the reconstruction above as his own (immature) position and would take these as a starting point for considering where to modify his own position in order to avoid aporia.[71] Being educated by the exercise as interpreted by IP, he could again make use of the difference between being and appearance. In particular, this differentiation would help him to modify his initial premise (1) – and the second premise as well, since it was more or less implicit in the former.[72] These modified versions would read as follows:

(1')  Whenever there *appear* several F(-things), there *is* one
       separate form F through which all these F(-things) *appear* as F.
(2')  There *appear* several F(-things).

With these modifications, Socrates could still deduce a crucial feature of his Theory of Forms, namely the existence of a unique form F in $(c_1)$.[73] However, his modified principle (1') would no longer be applicable to the cluster given in (4) since either the 'are' would obstruct the application, or – if it is changed to 'appear' – he would insist that $F_1$ from $(c_1)$ cannot be counted among the entities that appear. Therefore, neither (5) nor $(c_2)$ could be deduced anymore and Socrates would avoid the aporia. Of course, he

---

[70] Cf. also the discussion of REP. 476a4–7 below.

[71] This may relate to the 'epistemological' version of the argument, given pp. 121–122.

[72] Cf. p. 115 n. 56.

[73] Hence, Socrates could probably even advocate a stronger version of his first premise, namely (1″): Whenever there appear several F(-things), then there is *exactly* one separate Form F through which all these F(-things) appear as F. As discussed above, p. 115 n. 57, he could furthermore also leave out 'these' in the consequence.

would thereby insist that the relation 'Form F is itself F', expressed in <3>, happens in the mode of being, but not in the mode of appearance in order not to again allow a clustering of forms and particulars as in (4) under the mode of appearance. For this would again allow to apply (1') to (4). But sticking to <3> as a mode of being is hardly problematic since – however self-predication is to be understood in detail – it doubtlessly belongs to the form's 'inner core' so to speak, and hence is related to being, but not to appearance.[74] All in all, it is thus the general difference between being and appearance which permits to control the aporia. On the other hand, to a person who *does* conflate being and appearance, the aporia remains in this respect much more oppressive.

Especially with regard to Socrates' second way, but also with regard to the first, there is a dense and remarkable passage in the *Republic*, and hence in a dialogue prior to the *Parmenides*, which emphasises a similar constellation of being and appearance, as well as unity and multitude. Socrates there says the following: "And with regard to the Just and the Unjust, the Good and the Bad, and all forms the same *logos* applies – each is in itself one, but because of their communion with actions, with bodies, and with each other they appear everywhere, and hence each one appears as many."[75] A form *is,* and in that sense it is one. And it *appears*, in that sense it is many. This is quite a similar constellation as in the *Parmenides* and one may note that it also applies to

---

[74] Of course, 'is' in <3> is employed as a copula and relating this usage in greater detail to the mode of being (as opposed to the mode of appearance) is not an easy task. However, I think it is in principle feasible, though this would demand a much more detailed discussion of self-predication, which is beyond the scope of the present study. To provide at least a rough sketch: I tend to think that what is expressed in self-predicative statements (such as 'Form F is F') is best understood in the sense that each Form F *encodes primordially* what it is to be F – just as Plato can indicate forms by the formula (αὐτὸ) ὃ ἔστιν F (e.g. ὃ ἔστιν ἴσον PHDO. 75b1–2; αὐτὸ ἕκαστον ὃ ἔστιν 78d3–4). This encoding, and its information, is implemented and realised in noetical being (οὐσία). Hence, there is a certain link to the copula in self-pre-dicative statements (understood in the mode of being), for the copula might in these cases be taken to express exactly the implementation of this encoding. And Plato can consider these self-predicative statements as true since, among other reasons, he can regard 'Form F is F' as a short cut of, for instance, 'Form F is what it is to be F' or 'Form F encodes primordially what it essentially is to be F'.

[75] καὶ περὶ δὴ δικαίου καὶ ἀδίκου καὶ ἀγαθοῦ καὶ κακοῦ καὶ πάντων τῶν εἰδῶν πέρι ὁ αὐτὸς λόγος, αὐτὸ μὲν ἓν ἕκαστον εἶναι, τῇ δὲ τῶν πράξεων καὶ σωμάτων καὶ ἀλλήλων κοινωνίᾳ πανταχοῦ φανταζόμενα πολλὰ φαίνεσθαι ἕκαστον. (REP. 476a4–7; my trans.). I left λόγος untranslated since it may hint at the same time to the 'argument' which applies to all forms and to the 'relation' which exists between the one form and its many appearances. Note that τῶν πράξεων καὶ σωμάτων καὶ ἀλλήλων may indeed refer to the three levels discussed in § 19, if one accepts that πράξεων refers to the soul as source of every motion and action.

the forms among themselves, but crucially still does not deny the claim that a form as such *is* only one in itself and *remains one* in its proper mode of existence. On the other hand, a form's appearance among the forms is therefore most plausibly understood in the sense that one form F is implied by other forms in order for them to encode what it is to be G or H. For instance, the form 'Living Being' is implied and hence present in the forms 'Goose' and 'Horse'. Therefore, the form 'Living Being' may *appear* as many, even among the forms themselves, although the form 'Living Being' as such remains a unique form in itself.[76] Thus, the difference that is decisively blurred in the first regress argument is already present quite pointedly in the *Republic*. In fact, it might even be possible to understand the very rare and remarkable occurrences of φαίνω in S2 and S5 (§§ 5; 7; 15), i.e. among the forms and in the World Soul according to IP, in the sense of the appearance described by Socrates in this passage.

Before turning to the evaluation of the proposed solution (§ 27), let me at least briefly and tentatively try to locate this solution within the copious discussion on this argument. A distinction that shaped this discussion early on is the difference between an 'ontological' and an 'epistemological' reading of the argument. Broadly speaking, the latter consists in putting emphasis on the relevance of the *epistemic subject* within the argument, while the former denies, or at least downplays this importance. In this sense, a prominent proponent of the ontological version, W. SELLARS, emphasised that his reconstruction omits "all reference to apprehension"[77] and hence to the subject. Furthermore, the epistemological version puts greater emphasis on the *explanatory role* of the forms under discussion. In this respect, a prominent spokesman of the epistemological interpretation, G. VLASTOS, used exactly the terminology of appearance as core evidence of Plato's intention that the property in question *appears to a subject* and that this appearance refers to an *explanatory role* of the form.[78] Or, as T. PENNER, another prominent proponent of the epistemological version, puts it: "what the text makes clear by its epistemological locutions is that Parmenides is describing in Socrates

---

[76] Cf. the instructive remarks by ADAM ²1963, II 336 and SZLEZÁK 2021, 465–466; 477 on this passage.

[77] SELLARS 1955, 408.

[78] "Don't they [sc. the words ᾧ ταῦτα πάντα μεγάλα φαίνεσθαι in 132a7–8] make it clear that Plato *is* thinking of the epistemological function of the form in the course of his argument? For if not, why should he say that it is in virtue of this (second) Largeness that large things *appear* large, instead of just saying that in virtue of it they *are* large?" (VLASTOS 1955, 442; emph. orig.). G. VLASTOS, however, seems to have oscillated between the ontological and the epistemological version (cf. also PENNER 1987, 280–281).

a process of thought taking him from all the things he first sees as large to a new object 'through which' they [sc. the original large things] all 'appear' large."[79] In this view, what is described in the steps of the argument is something that appears, due to wrong premises and principles, to an immature subject.[80] If one puts it a bit more loosely, then to the ontological version the regress is happening 'out there' in reality, while, for the epistemological version, it happens within the subject and through its intention to explain a given multitude's common appearance as F.

Obviously, the present approach sympathises more with the epistemological version since it takes into account the terminology of appearance much more than the ontological version does. I agree with T. PENNER that quite a lot of the appearances throughout the argument are phrased in relation to a subject,[81] and hence there is quite some textual support for the epistemological approach. However, there are two further remarks to be made – which to some extent might even reconcile the epistemological and the ontological version.

Firstly, I do not see in Plato such a strict dichotomic division between ontology and epistemology as T. PENNER seems to presuppose.[82] To Plato, as I understand him, epistemology and ontology are intrinsically linked in the sense that a certain epistemic status depends on the ontological status of its object.[83] Likewise, an explanation can only be a (correct) explanation if it points to or tracks a given structure in reality. (This presupposes, of course, that reality is *in itself* logical and reasonable in a certain sense – but that is, in my eyes, one of the core thoughts of Plato's philosophy.) Therefore, one cannot draw such a clear line between ontology and epistemology, or answer epistemological questions without implying ontology. In the same vein, the epistemic subject and its content are themselves entities of some sort – in fact, to Plato, this subject is more persistent than physical particulars.

---

[79] PENNER 1987, 280 (addition in squared brackets in orig.); cf. also IBID., 281 for "the notion of the explanatory and the notion of the epistemological functioning". Especially with regard to this second quote, I can see no reason why T. PENNER (IBID., 279) considers the ᾧ in 132b1 as explanatory (by capitalizing it), but not the ᾧ in 132a7.

[80] I would like to thank B. STROBEL for emphasising this aspect of the epistemological version as well as for directing my attention to the approach of PENNER 1987 and his treatment of the terminology of appearance.

[81] σοι δόξῃ εἶναι (132a2); μία τις ἴσως δοκεῖ ἰδέα ἡ αὐτὴ εἶναι ἐπὶ πάντα ἰδόντι (132a2–3); τῇ ψυχῇ ἐπὶ πάντα ἴδῃς (132a7); οὐκέτι δὴ ἓν ἕκαστόν σοι τῶν εἰδῶν ἔσται (132b1–2). Cf. PENNER 1987, 279 (who furthermore emphasises the expressions of subjective belief, such as ἡγῇ in 132a3).

[82] Cf. esp. PENNER 1987, 279.

[83] REP. 477a3–4 and the Analogy of the Line may be two *loci classici* for this.

Secondly, it seems very remarkable that – at least as far as I can see – there has not even been the *proposal* or the *attempt* to consider the dominant terminology of appearance other than in relation to a subject. For, as stated above already, appearance is also a mode of existence as such in Plato, without any subject being involved.[84] In Plato, a single physical tree remains an appearance (of the form 'Tree'), no matter whether there is actually an epistemic subject to which this tree appears (or appears in a specific or distorted way, or in a certain angle or perspective).[85] In that sense – and given that the conceptual pattern of appearance is indeed very distinct – it is in my eyes telling that this option has not even been considered.[86] That being said, I do not deny, of course, that φαίνω or δοκέω *can* signify the appearance to an epistemic subject in Plato.[87] And neither do I deny that he can describe a discrepancy between an entity's physical being and its (distorted) appearance to or its wrong apprehension by a subject in these terms.[88]

[84] Admittedly, δοκέω seems to be more subject-directed than φαίνω. However, the former may still signify an appearance to any potential subject not specified any further.

[85] In that sense the present proposal also sides to some extent with the ontological version. To put things in yet another manner: the ontological version reads the terms of appearance without any relation to a subject – but thereby substitutes them instantly by terms of being. The epistemological version acknowledges these terms of appearance and reads them as expressing a relation to a subject – but reduces appearance exclusively to this relation. None of them thus uses the full systematic potential of appearance in Plato.

[86] Cf. esp. G. VLASTOS in his paper from 1969: "I must emphasize here that the words I have translated 'will show up' (ἀναφανεῖται) and 'come into view' (ἀναφανήσεται) [...] are not used to denote psychological events: Parmenides' point is not that it would *look* to Socrates, or *seem* to him, that there was another Largeness, but in point of logic there *has* to be one for him. There are many contexts in Greek argumentative prose in which this verb (with or without the prefix) is used without the slightest subjective hue, so that what it means is not that something *appears to be* the case, but *evidently is* the case." (VLASTOS 1969, 299–300 n. 32; emph. orig.). At first glance, G. VLASTOS seems to switch to an objective mode of appearance (i.e. where appearance denotes a mode of existence as such, without any subject involved). However, since he writes that there "has to be one *for him*" (emph. mine), he obviously still conceives appearance in relation to a subject. The differentiation he points to in this note is thus a differentiation *within* the subjective mode of appearance (i.e. appearance with a subject involved in some sense), namely between, on the one hand, the very *personal* (and perhaps misled) impression of a subject and, on the other hand, the appearance of what is *actually and in fact* the case to a subject. From here it is only a small step to the objective mode, but it is obviously not taken. Besides that, there is no doubt that the employment of φαίνω that G. VLASTOS points to is possible in Greek. In fact, this is one of the two meanings I distinguished in the second half of the dialogue since Parmenides employs it time and again (cf. APPENDIX B s.v. φαίνω; δοκέω).

[87] Both as a very personal or distorted impression and as one that reveals the facts (cf. G. VLASTOS' remark in n. 86). This is how δοκέω is used in S1 (cf. APPENDIX B s.v. δοκέω).

[88] SOPH. 236a4–b7 is a *locus classicus* for this. But here again there are several arguments that this situation analogically hints to the more fundamental relation between physical and non-physical entities (cf. POETSCH 2019, 199–210).

These two remarks aside, I think that ultimately the epistemological version and the solution provided above are not mutually exclusive. For even if the terminology of appearance is primarily used in the argument to indicate something that happens to an immature subject (as the epistemological version suggests), one may still *furthermore* understand this doubtlessly dominant terminology as a hint to the direction where and how this immature subject needs to modify his or her premises in order to avoid the apparent regress. This especially fits Socrates' second way described above. In order to be consistent with the epistemological approach, this presupposes, on a hermeneutical level, nothing more than the idea that Plato may have used the terminology of appearance to actually indicate *two* aspects at the same time, a relation to a subject *and* a (hint to a) distinction which allows to avoid the regress. If this hermeneutical premise is accepted, one can do justice to the way in which the argument is obviously phrased *and* find a decisive link to the second part with the aid of conceptual patterns in the exercise.

## § 27. Evaluation of the Solution
to the First Regress Argument

If the proposed approach is feasible, then the second part's solution would bank on several factors: the difference between being and appearance, the terminological connections between the first and the second part of the dialogue, and again, to some extent, the deduction of an ontological stratification. In the following, I shall first deal with this stratification and especially the soul's position both within this stratification and within the argument. After that, I shall deal with an objection regarding the emphasis on Parmenides' wording of the argument to then ultimately add two final remarks on the expression $\check{\alpha}\pi\epsilon\iota\rho\rho\nu$ $\pi\lambda\hat{\eta}\theta\sigma$ and on self-predication.

The difference between being and appearance obviously resides within an ontological stratification.[89] In a similar way as in the Greatest Aporia, the soul's position is also noteworthy in the stratification of the regress argument. Evidently, the soul plays a crucial role in this argument since, in the exact formulation of (4), the infinite iteration arises when "you look with

---

[89] Cf. also how this quasi-spatial arrangement of the elements within the argument is furthermore alluded to through the prepositions and prefixes: the new form(s) which emerge(s) oscillate between, on the one hand, being coordinated and "next" to the other entities ($\pi\alpha\rho$' 132a10) and, on the other hand, being "above" them ($\dot{\alpha}\nu\alpha\phi\alpha\nu\dot{\eta}\sigma\epsilon\tau\alpha\iota$ 132a10; $\dot{\epsilon}\pi\grave{\iota}$ 132a11), which again indicates a stratification.

your soul at all those (things)" (cf. τῇ ψυχῇ ἐπὶ πάντα ἴδῃς 132a7), i.e. at the first form F₁ and all things that were considered before, in (1)–(2). Hence, the soul and its epistemic intention(s) towards the form(s) and the things is one decisive motor of the process.[90] If it is accepted that IP is in general correct, the second part would indeed describe a vertical ontological alignment within which the soul occupies an intermediate position between the forms above it and the physical particulars beneath it. One single epistemic intention of the soul towards form(s) *and* particulars is therefore not possible within this constellation. This has already been remarked especially by A. GRAESER, who rightly emphasised that such a perspective is "platonisch gesehen unhaltbar"[91]. As the conceptual patterns suggest, the second part thus describes an ontological constellation within which the epistemic intention of one's soul that causes the regress is in fact impossible. Besides the distinction between being and appearance (§ 26), Parmenides' exercise may hence teach Socrates to not accept premise (4), according to which – if we stick once more to the exact wording of Parmenides within the regress argument – the soul is able to look ἐπὶ πάντα and hence allows an indiscriminate clustering of forms and particulars.[92] Besides switching to (1')–(2') and a more specific understanding of <3>, as described above (pp. 119–120), Socrates can thus learn from the exercise to not accept (4) with regard to the soul's function in it.

One very remarkable thing about this aspect regarding the soul's position is that it is again quite literally anticipated in the *Republic*. Here, within the Analogy of the Sun, Socrates explicitly mentions these two epistemic intentions of the soul: one towards the forms, the other towards the sensible particulars.[93] And the turning (περιαγωγή cf. REP. 518d4) from one inten-

---

[90] By 'epistemic intention' I heuristically mean the soul's directedness towards any object that it can deal with in a cognitive way.

[91] GRAESER 2002, 133.

[92] Since in the proposed interpretation S2C/S5 are primarily concerned with the World Soul, this implies of course an implicit premise: to align the human soul(s) to the World Soul with regard to their principal ontological status. This is, however, rather easily acceptable since in the *Timaeus* it is explicitly stated that the human soul is in fact of the same 'material' as the World Soul, though of inferior quality and thus less pure (TIM. 41d5–7; cf. PHLB. 30a3–7). Recall furthermore the *Phaedrus*, where the argument about the World Soul's immortality (PHDR. 245c5–246a3) seems to be closely connected to the treatment of the individual soul afterwards (cf. esp. ψυχὴ πᾶσα PHDR. 245c5; 246b6).

[93] "Well, then, think that the soul is also characterized in this way. When it fixes itself on that which is illumined by truth and that which *is*, it intellects, knows, and appears to possess intelligence. But when it fixes itself on that which is mixed with darkness, on coming into being and passing away, it opines and is dimmed, changing opinions up and down, and seems at such times not to possess intelligence." οὕτω τοίνυν καὶ τὸ τῆς ψυχῆς ὧδε νόει· ὅταν

tion to the other forms a constant motif in *Republic* VI and VII. Hence there can be little doubt that Plato is trying to avoid here, in a dialogue prior to the *Parmenides*, a systematic position according to which an epistemic intention of the soul is possible that grasps both forms *and* physical particulars within the very same intention. If this line of reasoning is correct, it would entail – even if I am not primarily concerned with this question – that the first regress argument is neither a self-criticism of Plato nor a sign of "honest perplexity"[94], but rather someone else's objection against Plato's position.[95]

Let us dwell for another moment on the soul's position. Does it not remain possible to accept the necessarily twofold 'view of the soul' towards forms and particulars and still formulate in some sense an objection like the first regress argument? Such an objection could run as follows: conceding that the soul cannot 'look' at a form and physical particulars in a single grasp, one could still suppose that the soul is able to create some kind of inner-psychic 'copies' of both of them. Accordingly, these copies were then – as inner-psychic entities – of the *same* sort and status. The soul was therefore again perfectly able to perform a view ἐπὶ πάντα with regard to these inner-psychic copies and hence to cause the regress again.[96] The regress could thus be performed, in a sense, within the soul and the argument seems to remain a valid objection.

However, the second part of the *Parmenides* would still be able to counter this objection within IP. A rejoinder could begin by stating that a form is a being, and that there can be no doubt that this is being in the sense of οὐσία.[97] This ontological level of reality, which is identified by the conceptual

μὲν οὗ καταλάμπει ἀλήθειά τε καὶ τὸ ὄν, εἰς τοῦτο ἀπερείσηται, ἐνόησέν τε καὶ ἔγνω αὐτὸ καὶ νοῦν ἔχειν φαίνεται· ὅταν δὲ εἰς τὸ τῷ σκότῳ κεκραμένον, τὸ γιγνόμενόν τε καὶ ἀπολλύμενον, δοξάζει τε καὶ ἀμβλυώττει ἄνω καὶ κάτω τὰς δόξας μεταβάλλον, καὶ ἔοικεν αὖ νοῦν οὐκ ἔχοντι. (REP. 508d4–9; trans. A. BLOOM).

[94] Thus the famous formula of VLASTOS 1954, 343 (original in capital letters).

[95] GRAESER 2002 proposed to see Speusippus behind this objection. Furthermore, it has to be remarked that if it is true that Plato actually depicts the argument *of someone else*, this has consequences for considering possible inconsistencies in the argument (such as an inconsistent set of premises). These defects may then well be due to the fault of this person. Or they might even be a deliberate distortion by Plato in order to make the argument look worse than it actually was. Or to put it differently: we cannot presuppose for our reconstruction that Plato *did in fact* intend to provide a – perfectly or even only approximately – valid and consistent objection in 132a1–b2.

[96] It might be no coincidence that Socrates' subsequent attempt in 132b3–6 turns to a very similar position. The question remains how he thinks that this move helps to get rid of the problems of the first regress argument. Perhaps Socrates is trying to avoid some kind of coordinated account of forms and particulars which he might have perceived within this regress argument.

[97] Cf. 133c4; 133c9; 135a8. For further details, cf. § 5.

field of being, is in itself found in S2/S3 (§§ 5–6). Since the realm of the soul as an intermediate level – again fitting REP. 508d4–9 – differs specifically from this realm (but remains connected to it, especially via S2C), the second part's constellation can also handle the modified objection, for it can insist that a form's being *as such* must still mean its existence in the realm of Being. And *this* entity cannot be multiplied in the sense of the modified objection since the decisive multiplication remains restricted to the copies within the soul. In other words, a Socrates instructed by the second part could allow that regress *within* the soul, but would insist that every 'new' form that appears (within the soul) still remains a copy of that one single form in the realm of being, to which the soul has access, but which remains (as a transsubjective realm) different from it – as is described by the relation between S2/S3 and S2C/S5.

So much for the soul's position. Let us now turn to the terminological connection between the dialogue's two parts, which the present solution identifies especially with regard to being and appearance. Emphasising this connection obviously implies that the specific way in which Parmenides expresses the aporia is of greater importance. One could object that this clings to the wording too much and tends to lose sight of the systematic problems which form the core of the argument. However, firstly, we have to keep in mind that we simply cannot decide *a priori* in what respect Parmenides intends the exercise to provide solutions, i.e. whether the second part helps to counter the exact formulations of the aporias or a more general understanding of them. This implies that *any* plausible solution from the second part – no matter how close it sticks to the wording – is in fact a solution supported by the second part and hence provides an answer to the second major question of how the second part helps to solve the problems of the first. Secondly, we have at least further hints in the first regress argument that the terminology is of some importance.[98] Besides that, there is another instance in the aporias of the first part where Parmenides seemingly indicates a 'predetermined breaking point' through his terminology.[99] And thirdly, even if one does pay closer attention to Parmenides' wording, there remains still a possible access to the more systematic aspects of the argument, as has been shown in § 26.

---

[98] Cf. p. 124 n. 89.
[99] Cf. the employment of ἐν τῇ φύσει in the second regress argument (132d2). If one understands φύσις in a conventional way as referring to the physical world, the regress is much more likely to happen than if one understands φύσις as referring to the realm of forms as Plato repeatedly does (e.g. PHDR. 254b6; REP. 476b7; 597c2; 597e4). Cf. also § 28.

Let me finally add two additional remarks. The first one suggests even more connections to the conceptual patterns within the few lines of this aporia. It is concerned with the expression of ἄπειρον πλῆθος. The second is in regard to self-predication.

With regard to the way in which the conceptual patterns of the second part could possibly take up aspects of the aporias in the first part, it is remarkable that Parmenides concludes the present aporia with the expression ἄπειρα τὸ πλῆθος (132b2). This is particularly remarkable for the reason that this formula of 'infinite multitude' occurs only once in the first part, but is to be found again as a conceptual pattern in the second.[100] The absolute majority, 7 out of 9 instances, is to be found in S2 (5 times) and S3 (2 times), i.e. those sections that describe the realm of forms according to the proposed interpretation. The remaining two instances occur in S7, directly connected to issues that are concerned with bodies and that are closely related to appearance (164d1; 165c2). This evidence might be interpreted in two ways. Firstly, one could put emphasis on the fact that the great majority of these instances occur where the realm of forms is supposedly described. Hence, there would *indeed* be an ἄπειρον πλῆθος of forms, though, of course, in a different sense than in the argument – but nevertheless the single occurrence in 132b2 could be interpreted as a kind of disguised hint to that fact. This means: there *is* in fact an ἄπειρον πλῆθος of forms,[101] but in another sense than in the argument. Secondly, one could argue that this repeats the general flaw of the regress argument by treating forms and particulars as though they exist on the same level. The second part would then point out that an 'infinite multitude' is in fact to be found on *two* levels of reality (in S2/3 and S7 respectively), while the aporia merges these two levels by putting forms and particulars next to each other.

My ultimate remark with regard to this aporia is concerned with one aspect of 'self-predication'.[102] As G. VLASTOS remarked early on with credits

---

[100] For further details, cf. § 16. In the second part, the formula is found in S2: 143a2; 144a6; 144e4–5; 145a3; S3: 158b6; 158c6–7; S7: 164d1; 165c2.

[101] That Plato is committed to an infinite multitude of forms is already implied in the fact that there is a form of every natural number. Since there are infinitely many of these, there must also be an infinite multitude of forms. An important passage in the *Sophist* (256e5–257a9) provides a remarkable, probably confirming parallel to the formula of ἄπειρον πλῆθος in S2 and S3; cf. esp. ἄπειρον ... πλήθει (SOPH. 256e6) and ἀπέραντα ... τὸν ἀριθμὸν τἆλλα (SOPH. 257a6).

[102] This is of course only one aspect of a much broader issue. For another caveat with regard to 'self-predication' cf. SELLARS 1955, 414. For detailed analyses of this topic cf. LIENEMANN 2010, 117–239 (with regard to the regress arguments in the *Parmenides*) and STROBEL 2007 (in a more general account).

to A. E. Taylor,[103] one crucial premise of the argument is that the form needs to be *itself* that specific aspect which is common to all particulars. This feature is commonly addressed as 'self-predication' of the form and I do not deny that the systematic point addressed by this term is a necessary part of the argument. However, with regard to the position of the soul in that argument, one could ask whether the concept of self-*predication* is in fact suitable, for one has to suppose a certain entity or subject that performs this predication. Within the Platonic approach this seems to be most naturally the soul, but not the form itself, for it is doubtlessly rather strange to say that a form predicates something of itself. *We* can predicate something of a form (though, of course, by employing this form and others). Hence, I do not deny that forms do ultimately form the very core of our predicates and thus render predication as such possible, but the expression 'self-predication' at least tends to intermingle the levels of forms and souls by, in some sense, ascribing something to the former that is found in the latter. The term thus, at least, tends to merge two things that have to be kept apart with regard to the present aporia.

## § 28. General Characterisation of the Proposed Solution

How to characterise and evaluate the proposed solution as such? In a very general sense, the present solution posits that Parmenides deduces a complex ontological structure within which the aporias of the first part do not apply or with regard to which they can be countered. Within this solution special emphasis is placed on the concrete phrasing of the aporias and the terminology involved.

One may object and count it as a disadvantage that the present approach seems to imply the presupposition that all deductions and arguments in S1–8 need to be correct in order to secure a well-established ontological constellation, which then helps to solve the aporias. This objection is correct insofar the present approach indeed regards S1–8 as providing positive – or to put it broader: useful – information in every section. It is correct that it does not permit to dismiss entire sections. Yet, it is perfectly able to deal with negative accounts such as, say, the ones in S4 or S6. However, one important thing has to be noted with regard to the given objection. The present

---

[103] Cf. Vlastos 1954, 324.

approach does *not* imply that every single argument in the second part is Plato's last word on the issue in question and hence his master argument to ground and deduce that ontological structure in question. It is in my eyes possible that Plato did not regard all arguments as the best ones possible. Quite the contrary is likely in my eyes given the brevity and negligible quality of some arguments, given the negligible philosophical capacities of young Aristotle[104] and given that Parmenides seems to be readily willing to employ rather dubious dodges and convenient short-cuts in order to reach some seemingly intended goal[105]. Hence an incorrect or dubious argument does not *eo ipso* permit to immediately dismiss Plato's commitment to the claim which is supported by that dubious argument. A fallacious, an incomplete, or even an absurd argument in the second part of the *Parmenides* does therefore not obstruct the view that Plato regarded the ontological constellation which he has his Parmenides circumscribe through his arguments *in general* as sound. The present approach is thus not committed to necessarily regarding every single argument as correct, neither as such nor in Plato's own eyes. The second part therefore remains to some extent a sketch. And we have at least two reasons to regard this as plausible. Firstly, because there can be no doubt that especially in S3–8 things are often and explicitly abridged. And secondly, because the allusions to Plato's critique of writing in the first part render it quite likely that he had further arguments at hand with regard to what he wrote in the second part of the *Parmenides*.[106]

In an overall evaluation of the present approach, one may count it as a general advantage that according to its interpretation the second part does not provide one generic rejoinder to all aporias, but *specific* ones.

---

[104] One has to recall that young Aristotle is a tyrant *in spe* (127d2–3), and hence is definitely no philosophical mind in Plato's eyes (*pace* MILLER 1986, 10). Without any doubt, the second part would have looked rather different if one young Theaetetus would have been the interlocutor (cf. 137b6–7).

[105] Cf. e.g. the argumentative steps in 150e4–5 (the identification of the One with the Others comes quite out of blue sky); 161e4–6 (obviously a short-cut or trick relying on τὰ ὄντα λέγειν) or 163c2–d1 (quite a short-cut after everything that Parmenides had argued in S5, esp. 162a2–b7).

[106] Ultimately, if one remembers the critique of writing in the *Phaedrus* and some clear allusions to the problems of written work in the *Parmenides* (128d6–e1 – PHDR. 275d9–e3), one might even ask, whether there is *anything* in the second part that can be regarded as an exhaustive and definitive treatment. I have provided a new argument that the critique applies to Plato's writings as well by pointing to an Egyptian text that in all likelihood forms the concrete source of this passage in the *Phaedrus* (cf. POETSCH 2021B). Note that by taking into account the critique of writing the present reconstruction does not rely on any detailed reconstruction of Plato's inner-academic teachings since all elements of the present interpretation are derived from the written dialogues (§ 13).

C. C. Meinwald, for instance, has to admit that according to her interpretation there is ultimately *one* key feature to resolve *all* aporias, in her case the *pros heauto/pros ta alla*-distinction.[107] Compared to this interpretation, I think that the present approach provides a more specific reaction to the single aporias, though of course the second part in total provides one single framework to discuss these problems. The differences in the responses to the two exemplary aporias analysed in §§ 24–27 are evident from their respective analyses. Besides that, it is possible to provide at least a brief sketch of how a response to the other problems might look like:

For the very first aporia, the question regarding of what things there are actually forms (130a3–e4), once again the formula of ἄπειρον πλῆθος in the second part could be of help since it is concentrated in S2/3 and would answer this question in the sense that there are forms of everything, at least within the range of things that Parmenides refers to in his objection. This fits his very obvious hint in this direction (130e1–4) quite well. This solution, however, needed further discussion since it contradicts the testimonies of Aristotle, according to which Plato did, for instance, not posit forms of artefacts.[108]

With regard to the complex mereological issues in the second aporia (130e4–131e7), at least two things are of potential importance in the present approach. Firstly, one could particularly take into account those passages in the second part which deal with apparently similar questions.[109] Secondly and more importantly, it seems to be especially promising to take TIM. 52c2–d1 into account with regard to this aporia, for there seems to be, as has been shown in § 15, a close and even partially literal relation between this passage and the constellation of S6–8. This is of the utmost importance for the aporia in question since TIM. 52d1 takes up literally the very same question that is formulated in Parmenides' aporia.[110] This parallel is especially remarkable since yet another passage, in the *Philebus*,[111] might hint to the fact that Plato's intended solution is to actually suppose that the

---

[107] Cf. Meinwald 1991, 163.

[108] E.g. Aristotle, META. M 5, 1080a5–6.

[109] One could take into account, for instance, 149d8–150e4 where apparently the form 'Largeness' is discussed in relation to others forms (esp. Smallness) and in relation to the particulars.

[110] Cf. ἓν ἄρα ὂν καὶ ταὐτὸν ἐν πολλοῖς (131b1) and ἕκαστον τῶν εἰδῶν ἓν ἐν πᾶσιν ἅμα ταὐτὸν εἴη (131b5–6) with ἓν ἅμα ταὐτὸν καὶ δύο γενήσεσθον (TIM. 52d1).

[111] Cf. ὅλην αὐτὴν αὑτῆς χωρίς, ὃ δὴ πάντων ἀδυνατώτατον φαίνοιτ᾽ ἄν, ταὐτὸν καὶ ἓν ἅμα ἐν ἑνί τε καὶ πολλοῖς γίγνεσθαι (PHLB. 15b6–8). With regard to the *Timaeus* (cf. n. 110 above), I consider the superlative as pointing in fact to Plato's intended solution.

form remains one in itself and still is present as a whole in all particulars. If a solution lies in this direction, the exercise would of course not provide an explicit account of how this is technically possible.[112] But this is probably more than we have to expect from Parmenides' exercise, as has been remarked with regard to the technical details of participation above (§ 24).

The discussion of Socrates' response to the first regress argument, according to which forms are thoughts within the soul (132b3–c12), may again benefit from the correct vertical alignment of the different ontological realms. As analysed in detail with regard to both aporias, the position of the soul is again obviously of greater importance to Socrates' proposal. The ontological stratification that is outlined by S1–8 according to IP is thus perfectly able to deal with Parmenides' first objection that the soul's thought needs to be directed towards a form, which is hence 'outside' of the soul (132b7–c8). In this case, it has to be remarked that Socrates' proposal is obviously not in accordance with Plato's Theory of Forms in the middle dialogues, for e.g. REP. 508d4–9 proves that the forms are located somewhere beyond the soul and the soul's thoughts are thus directed towards something 'outside' of it. Parmenides' first objection is therefore not even an objection to Plato's Theory. Furthermore, the ontological stratification in S1–8 can also deal with Parmenides' second objection (132c9–11), which raises the problem that Socrates' proposal implies the absurdity that "everything thinks" (πάντα νοεῖν 132c11). In this case, the ontological stratification could point to the fact that the ontological realm circumscribed in S7 does not entail thinking. But again we have to take into account that Socrates' proposal does not fit Plato's Theory. It rather seems to be an *ad hoc* assumption which he develops with regard to the results of the first regress argument.

Dealing with the idea that forms are παραδείγματα ... ἐν τῇ φύσει (132d2) and hence the second regress argument, one may especially point to the role of the term φύσις in this argument. As the first regress argument works 'best' if one understands forms as the same (physical) entities as particulars, the second 'Third Man Argument' also seems to work best if one understands φύσις as pointing to the physical realm. If this is the case, then the second part of the dialogue would indeed correct this view since the conceptual pattern of φύσις quite remarkably restricts this term to S1–3, while there is not a single mention of it in S4–8 (§ 18). Admittedly one would then have to deal with the further problem that this conceptual field may not

---

[112] As I proposed in POETSCH 2019, 238–242, there is in fact a possible – and quite an easy – solution to this at first glance paradoxical demand if one takes into account the mathematics of dimensions that underlie Plato's ontology.

be regarded as significant for *statistical* reasons in particular. However, there are other ways at hand to handle this issue, for instance by including other passages[113] in order to support the claim that the distribution of φύσις is in fact not arbitrary.

Of course, these remarks do not settle the issue for each aporia. But this overview provides at least an idea of how the present approach, based on conceptual patterns, may actually be able to react specifically to each aporia. Hence, I hope to have shown that my main conditional claim is correct, according to which the second part of the *Parmenides* may indeed help solving the aporias of the first part if one interprets the exercise according to IP and the conceptual patterns.

---

[113] Such as PHDO. 103b5; PHDR. 254b6; REP. 476b7; 597c2; 597e4.

# 7. CONCLUSION AND OUTLOOK

The aim of this study was to introduce in general a new approach to Plato's *Parmenides* and to answer, within this scope, the two main questions regarding this most enigmatic of his dialogues: what is the second part all about? How does the second part help to solve the problems raised in the first part? Since the answer to the latter depends inevitably on the answer to the former, emphasis was put on answering the first question. Nevertheless, I hope to have shown, at least in outline, how the approach is also able to address the second question. The present conclusion will summarise the main results and provide a tentative outlook in several respects.

A main second-order aim of this study was to distinguish the objective evidence as such from a more far-reaching interpretation. This evidence, offered mainly in the third chapter (supplemented by patterns in the fifth), included, first of all, a clear ontological shift throughout the sections (§§ 5–7). This shift followed the main realms of reality that Plato proposes in his philosophy, it was obviously vertical and it was remarkably not bipartite, but tripartite. As I proposed subsequently, this may have important consequences for a detailed assessment of Plato's ontology in general as well as of the concept of participation in particular (§ 19). Notably, this shift is not a linear, but a more complex one. This in turn strongly opposes those approaches, ancient and modern, which try to establish a one-on-one correspondence between sections and subjects (§§ 10; 13). However, the present results still strongly encourage a multiple-subject approach (§ 10).

As was the case with many others, one of the firmest results was not even on my radar when I started conducting this study: the strong relation between S2C and S5 (§ 6). I offered an interpretation of this evidence which refrains from declaring S2C a full section in its own right, but which permits both to give the corollary a specific function within the array of sections and to include it in an answer to the aporias in the first part (§§ 12–13; 16; 19).

Regardless of how one considers this specific solution (§ 24), I hope that the evidence regarding S2C and S5 can be of help to other approaches as well, especially in assessing the notorious corollary.

Chapters 4 and 5 provided, in the form of IP, a more systematic interpretation of the patterns, while chapter 6 proposed exemplarily how this helps to approach the aporias. *In nuce*, IP rests on four main elements that we know from other dialogues of Plato, both prior and posterior to the *Parmenides*. These four main elements are related in a way that is again well-known in Plato, namely in that of a geometric analogy. I hope to have shown in some detail how this analogy, with its elements, provides a concise key to explaining the general constellation of the sections (§ 14) and the four different subjects (§§ 15–16; 18; 20). Again, this constellation is not simply linear, but a more complex one. It crucially distinguishes between the physical world, the realm of the soul, the forms, and a first principle of the latter. This constellation can in turn be regarded as one possible answer to the aporias in the first part of the dialogue, both with regard to the Greatest Aporia (§§ 24–25) and the first Third Man Argument (§§ 26–27).

\*

Since this study's aim was a general introduction of a new approach, there are several directions in which further analysis can go. Firstly, this includes the investigation of further conceptual patterns since the list of the ones analysed in this study is of course not exhaustive. It might be interesting, for instance, to evaluate why three very similar epistemological passages are concentrated at the end of S1, S2, and S6. Secondly, it may seem promising to also analyse the *internal* structure of S2 by help of the method provided here since this section is the most complex one and makes up roughly one half of the exercise. Besides that, there is, thirdly, the option to cross-check the present method by applying it to other dialogues about whose topics in the different passages we feel more secure than we do in the case of the *Parmenides*. This option entails difficulties in itself[1] and it remains doubtlessly very laborious, but it is in principle feasible.

An important subsequent step of the present approach – to which I already alluded several times, especially in the second and the fourth chapter – is to take the present results as a starting point of a line-by-line analysis of

---

[1] An important difficulty is to find an equivalent to the sections of the *Parmenides*. To solve this one could look for clear caesurae in the text, to take the division in books (in the case of the *Republic* and the *Nomoi*), to use the Stephanus-pages, or letter-/word-counts.

the second part. This means to take IP and the conceptual patterns as a framework for approaching in detail every section, passage, and argument in Parmenides' exercise. If such an attempt succeeds in aligning the details with IP, it would be quite a strong argument for the interpretation offered in chapters 4 and 5 (and indirectly for the approach in chapter 6). This argument would then be grounded both in an objective evaluation of the bigger picture *and* a comprehensive analysis of its details.

It is, however, quite important to correctly identify the precise burden of proof for such an approach. Such an attempt only has to argue for *one plausible* interpretation of every passage – or at least as many passages as possible – which is in alignment with IP and thus fits the bigger picture of the exercise as a whole. It does *not* need to prove that the interpretation it proposes is the *only* possible interpretation of each single passage or argument in question. The latter is neither needed to support IP as a coherent interpretation nor is it probably possible as such, for – given the generality and abstractness of the second part – there will definitely always be *several* plausible interpretations of a certain passage or argument considered solely in itself. The greater challenge is therefore to provide an interpretation that is coherent with regard to the exercise *as a whole*. This in turn presupposes of course that one does regard the second part not as a loose collection of arguments (let alone some kind of intentional non-sense), but as a more unified and carefully composed whole. Obviously, this presupposition cannot be made *a priori*. However, I think the patterns and their coherence strongly support such a more unified approach. Were the arguments only loosely connected or their sequence ultimately accidental, would Plato have given them such a remarkably coherent structure, within which a great deal, even the rare terms, is consistent with the bigger picture?

If the *Parmenides* is "a mountain that must be climbed"[2], I hope to have offered, by the present approach, some new perspectives on it. Perhaps, these can help to develop new assaults and routes to its summit. A summit – if it is one – that hitherto remains shrouded in mist.

---

[2] GERSON 1984, 377.

# APPENDICES

The following appendices contain the main data on which the argument of the present study is based. APPENDIX A provides the absolute and relative counts of the concepts that are part of a conceptual field. APPENDIX B lays open all decisions that have been made with regard to the occurrences of these concepts. As explained in § 1, this is at times accompanied by a short explanation or comment in order to clarify the decision. APPENDIX C provides a full list of all lemmata in Parmenides' exercise and the absolute counts of each.

| | S1 | S2 | S2C | S3 | S4 | S5 | S6 | S7 | S8 | $p$ | DP |
|---|---|---|---|---|---|---|---|---|---|---|---|
| οὐσία | 3 | 34 | 5 | 0 | 0 | 7 | 8 | 0 | 0 | 5.999e-05 | 0.285 |
| τὸ εἶναι | 2 | 13 | 4 | 1 | 0 | 8 | 0 | 0 | 0 | 0.044 | 0.285 |
| τὸ μὴ εἶναι | 0 | 0 | 1 | 0 | 0 | 6 | 0 | 0 | 0 | 1.580e-04 | 0.869 |
| τὸ ὄν, τὰ ὄντα | 1 | 28 | 0 | 0 | 0 | 8 | 3 | 1 | 0 | 3.686e-03 | 0.342 |
| τὸ μὴ ὄν, τὰ μὴ ὄντα | 1 | 0 | 0 | 0 | 0 | 7 | 5 | 0 | 5 | 3.428e-12 | 0.811 |
| καθ᾽ αὑτό, αὐτό | 2 | 15 | 1 | 4 | 0 | 0 | 0 | 0 | 0 | 0.287 | 0.317 |
| εἶδος | 0 | 2 | 0 | 1 | 2 | 0 | 0 | 0 | 0 | 0.097 | 0.507 |
| ἰδέα | 0 | 0 | 0 | 1 | 0 | 0 | 0 | 0 | 0 | 0.259 | 0.953 |
| φύσις | 2 | 4 | 1 | 3 | 0 | 0 | 0 | 0 | 0 | 0.297 | 0.331 |
| φύω | 0 | 4 | 0 | 0 | 0 | 0 | 0 | 0 | 0 | 0.928 | 0.524 |
| μετέχω, μέθεξις | 14 | 23 | 11 | 13 | 8 | 5 | 5 | 0 | 0 | 6.925e-07 | 0.307 |
| μεταλαμβάνω, λαμβάνω* | 0 | 2 | 4 | 3 | 0 | 0 | 2 | 0 | 0 | 2.322e-04 | 0.682 |
| γίγνομαι, προσ-, ἐγ- (total) | 43 | 99 | 9 | 3 | 1 | 6 | 3 | 1 | 0 | 8.000e-08 | 0.224 |
| γίγνομαι ** | 0 | 0 | 6 | 0 | 1 | 6 | 3 | 1 | 0 | 4.736e-09 | 0.747 |
| ἀπόλλυμι | 0 | 0 | 7 | 0 | 1 | 6 | 5 | 1 | 0 | 2.362e-11 | 0.747 |
| μεταβάλλω, μεταβολή | 0 | 0 | 17 | 0 | 0 | 4 | 0 | 0 | 0 | 4.273e-19 | 0.869 |
| ἀλλοιόω, ἀλλοίωσις, ἀλλοῖος | 4 | 5 | 0 | 0 | 0 | 16 | 2 | 0 | 0 | 9.474e-08 | 0.548 |
| μεταβαίνω | 0 | 1 | 0 | 0 | 0 | 2 | 0 | 1 | 0 | 0.164 | 0.615 |
| μεθίστημι | 0 | 0 | 0 | 0 | 0 | 1 | 0 | 0 | 0 | 0.356 | 0.921 |
| ἀπαλλάττω, ἀφίημι | 0 | 1 | 4 | 0 | 0 | 0 | 0 | 0 | 0 | 2.741e-03 | 0.764 |
| αὐξάνω | 0 | 0 | 2 | 0 | 0 | 0 | 0 | 0 | 0 | 0.018 | 0.968 |
| φθίω | 0 | 0 | 2 | 0 | 0 | 0 | 0 | 0 | 0 | 0.018 | 0.968 |

* without subjective grasping   ** only where paired with ἀπόλλυμι   T.A.I   TOTAL COUNTS (ABSOLUTE)

| | S1 | S2 | S2C | S3 | S4 | S5 | S6 | S7 | S8 | p | DP |
|---|---|---|---|---|---|---|---|---|---|---|---|
| φαίνω (total) | 3 | 15 | 0 | 1 | 2 | 4 | 1 | 12 | 3 | 7.369e-06 | 0.314 |
| φαίνω*** | 0 | 2 | 0 | 0 | 0 | 1 | 0 | 12 | 3 | 9.490e-13 | 0.779 |
| δοκέω (total) | 2 | 0 | 0 | 0 | 0 | 0 | 0 | 6 | 0 | 5.270e-06 | 0.809 |
| δοκέω*** | 0 | 0 | 0 | 0 | 0 | 0 | 0 | 6 | 0 | 2.681e-07 | 0.970 |
| ὄγκος | 0 | 0 | 0 | 0 | 0 | 0 | 0 | 7 | 0 | 1.396e-08 | 0.970 |
| ὄναρ, ὕπνος | 0 | 0 | 0 | 0 | 0 | 0 | 0 | 2 | 0 | 0.015 | 0.970 |
| φάντασμα | 0 | 0 | 0 | 0 | 0 | 0 | 0 | 2 | 1 | 1.649e-03 | 0.949 |
| σκιαγραφέω | 0 | 0 | 0 | 0 | 0 | 0 | 0 | 1 | 0 | 0.140 | 0.970 |
| κίνησις, κινέω | 8 | 3 | 14 | 1 | 1 | 12 | 2 | 2 | 0 | 4.972e-12 | 0.509 |
| φέρω, περιφέρω | 8 | 0 | 0 | 0 | 0 | 0 | 0 | 0 | 0 | 4.849e-04 | 0.860 |
| ἀλλάττω, μεταλλάττω, ἀμείβω | 3 | 0 | 0 | 0 | 0 | 0 | 0 | 0 | 0 | 0.125 | 0.860 |
| στρέφω | 0 | 0 | 0 | 0 | 0 | 3 | 0 | 0 | 0 | 0.029 | 0.921 |
| στάσις, ἡσυχία, ἵστημι | 4 | 6 | 14 | 1 | 1 | 4 | 3 | 1 | 0 | 1.338e-08 | 0.446 |
| πολυς****, πολλάκις | 13 | 35 | 9 | 8 | 3 | 2 | 0 | 9 | 8 | 3.437e-05 | 0.206 |
| ἄπειρος, ἀπέραντος, ἀπειρία | 1 | 6 | 0 | 6 | 0 | 0 | 0 | 3 | 0 | 4.207e-03 | 0.455 |
| πλῆθος, πλεονάκις, πλεονεκτέω | 0 | 13 | 0 | 4 | 0 | 0 | 0 | 3 | 0 | 0.028 | 0.405 |
| πέρας, περαίνω | 1 | 4 | 0 | 5 | 0 | 0 | 0 | 3 | 0 | 5.479e-03 | 0.509 |
| ἀρχή***** | 3 | 6 | 0 | 0 | 0 | 0 | 0 | 3 | 0 | 0.282 | 0.312 |
| μέσος | 7 | 7 | 0 | 0 | 0 | 0 | 0 | 4 | 0 | 0.031 | 0.412 |
| τελευτή, τέλος, τέλειος | 3 | 7 | 0 | 2 | 0 | 3 | 0 | 2 | 0 | 0.650 | 0.221 |
| ἔσχατος | 2 | 4 | 0 | 0 | 0 | 0 | 0 | 0 | 0 | 0.949 | 0.363 |

T.A.I (CONTINUED) TOTAL COUNTS (ABSOLUTE)

*** only where appearance of subject is indicated          **** without πολλὴ ἀνάγκη   ***** without ἐξ ἀρχῆς

| | S1 | S2 | S2C | S3 | S4 | S5 | S6 | S7 | S8 | $p$ | DP |
|---|---|---|---|---|---|---|---|---|---|---|---|
| ὄνῳ | 10 | 41 | 0 | 14 | 4 | 0 | 0 | 0 | 0 | 4.403e–06 | 0.270 |
| σοφμή | 19 | 39 | 0 | 0 | 0 | 0 | 0 | 0 | 1 | 1.215e–05 | 0.346 |
| μόριον | 0 | 28 | 0 | 31 | 6 | 0 | 0 | 0 | 0 | 1.798e–21 | 0.475 |
| μερίζω, μεριστός | 0 | 4 | 0 | 0 | 0 | 0 | 0 | 0 | 0 | 0.928 | 0.524 |
| μέτρον | 11 | 7 | 0 | 0 | 0 | 0 | 0 | 0 | 0 | 0.012 | 0.463 |
| μέν | 15 | 44 | 4 | 6 | 4 | 7 | 1 | 5 | 1 | 0.985 | 0.054 |
| δέ | 30 | 117 | 9 | 15 | 7 | 24 | 8 | 11 | 2 | 0.888 | 0.053 |
| ἄν | 47 | 115 | 9 | 17 | 7 | 25 | 7 | 9 | 3 | 0.793 | 0.051 |
| οὖν | 6 | 27 | 4 | 1 | 1 | 3 | 1 | 1 | 0 | 0.778 | 0.170 |
| γε | 29 | 49 | 5 | 13 | 3 | 14 | 4 | 7 | 3 | 0.227 | 0.129 |
| γάρ | 10 | 32 | 5 | 9 | 5 | 11 | 3 | 6 | 4 | 0.136 | 0.153 |
| μήν | 22 | 26 | 2 | 5 | 1 | 10 | 3 | 2 | 2 | 0.049 | 0.205 |
| δή | 5 | 26 | 7 | 7 | 1 | 7 | 3 | 8 | 1 | 0.024 | 0.198 |
| οὔτε | 73 | 63 | 21 | 1 | 13 | 6 | 18 | 3 | 6 | < 1.000e–08 | 0.351 |
| μή | 11 | 45 | 6 | 4 | 1 | 54 | 13 | 10 | 11 | < 1.000e–08 | 0.375 |
| καί | 54 | 285 | 43 | 38 | 14 | 53 | 3 | 38 | 2 | 2.000e–08 | 0.112 |
| τε | 9 | 76 | 17 | 14 | 3 | 13 | 1 | 8 | 0 | 1.813e–04 | 0.164 |

T.A.I (CONTINUED) TOTAL COUNTS (ABSOLUTE)

| | S1 | S2 | S2C | S3 | S4 | S5 | S6 | S7 | S8 |
|---|---|---|---|---|---|---|---|---|---|
| οὐσία | 0.185 | 0.680 | 0.942 | 0.000 | 0.000 | 0.698 | 2.439 | 0.000 | 0.000 |
| τὸ εἶναι | 0.124 | 0.260 | 0.753 | 0.145 | 0.000 | 0.798 | 0.000 | 0.000 | 0.000 |
| τὸ μὴ εἶναι | 0.000 | 0.000 | 0.188 | 0.000 | 0.000 | 0.598 | 0.000 | 0.000 | 0.000 |
| τὸ ὄν, τὰ ὄντα | 0.062 | 0.560 | 0.000 | 0.000 | 0.000 | 0.798 | 0.915 | 0.195 | 0.000 |
| τὸ μὴ ὄν, τὰ μὴ ὄντα | 0.062 | 0.000 | 0.000 | 0.000 | 0.000 | 0.698 | 1.524 | 0.000 | 2.358 |
| καθ' αὑτό, αὐτό | 0.124 | 0.300 | 0.188 | 0.581 | 0.000 | 0.000 | 0.000 | 0.000 | 0.000 |
| εἶδος | 0.000 | 0.040 | 0.000 | 0.145 | 0.528 | 0.000 | 0.000 | 0.000 | 0.000 |
| ἰδέα | 0.000 | 0.000 | 0.000 | 0.145 | 0.000 | 0.000 | 0.000 | 0.000 | 0.000 |
| φύσις | 0.124 | 0.080 | 0.188 | 0.436 | 0.000 | 0.000 | 0.000 | 0.000 | 0.000 |
| φύω | 0.000 | 0.080 | 0.000 | 0.000 | 0.000 | 0.000 | 0.000 | 0.000 | 0.000 |
| μετέχω, μέθεξις | 0.865 | 0.460 | 2.072 | 1.890 | 2.111 | 0.499 | 1.524 | 0.000 | 0.000 |
| μεταλαμβάνω, λαμβάνω* | 0.000 | 0.040 | 0.753 | 0.436 | 0.000 | 0.000 | 0.610 | 0.000 | 0.000 |
| γίγνομαι, προσ-, ἐγ- (total) | 2.656 | 1.981 | 1.695 | 0.436 | 0.264 | 0.598 | 0.915 | 0.195 | 0.000 |
| γίγνομαι** | 0.000 | 0.000 | 1.130 | 0.000 | 0.264 | 0.598 | 0.915 | 0.195 | 0.000 |
| ἀπόλλυμι | 0.000 | 0.000 | 1.318 | 0.000 | 0.264 | 0.598 | 1.524 | 0.195 | 0.000 |
| μεταβάλλω, μεταβολή | 0.000 | 0.000 | 3.202 | 0.000 | 0.000 | 0.399 | 0.000 | 0.000 | 0.000 |
| ἀλλοιόω, ἀλλοίωσις, ἀλλοῖος | 0.247 | 0.100 | 0.000 | 0.000 | 0.000 | 1.595 | 0.610 | 0.000 | 0.000 |
| μεταβαίνω | 0.000 | 0.020 | 0.000 | 0.000 | 0.000 | 0.199 | 0.000 | 0.195 | 0.000 |
| μεθίστημι | 0.000 | 0.000 | 0.000 | 0.000 | 0.000 | 0.100 | 0.000 | 0.000 | 0.000 |
| ἀπαλλάττω, ἀφίημι | 0.000 | 0.020 | 0.753 | 0.000 | 0.000 | 0.000 | 0.000 | 0.000 | 0.000 |
| αὐξάνω | 0.000 | 0.000 | 0.377 | 0.000 | 0.000 | 0.000 | 0.000 | 0.000 | 0.000 |
| φθίω | 0.000 | 0.000 | 0.377 | 0.000 | 0.000 | 0.000 | 0.000 | 0.000 | 0.000 |

* without subjective grasping  ** only where paired with ἀπόλλυμι   T.A.2  TOTAL COUNTS (RELATIVE)

| | S1 | S2 | S2C | S3 | S4 | S5 | S6 | S7 | S8 |
|---|---|---|---|---|---|---|---|---|---|
| φαίνω (total) | 0.185 | 0.300 | 0.000 | 0.145 | 0.528 | 0.399 | 0.305 | 2.335 | 1.415 |
| φαίνω *** | 0.000 | 0.040 | 0.000 | 0.000 | 0.000 | 0.100 | 0.000 | 2.335 | 1.415 |
| δοκέω (total) | 0.124 | 0.000 | 0.000 | 0.000 | 0.000 | 0.000 | 0.000 | 1.167 | 0.000 |
| δοκέω *** | 0.000 | 0.000 | 0.000 | 0.000 | 0.000 | 0.000 | 0.000 | 1.167 | 0.000 |
| ὄγκος | 0.000 | 0.000 | 0.000 | 0.000 | 0.000 | 0.000 | 0.000 | 1.362 | 0.000 |
| ὄναρ, ὕπνος | 0.000 | 0.000 | 0.000 | 0.000 | 0.000 | 0.000 | 0.000 | 0.389 | 0.000 |
| φάντασμα | 0.000 | 0.000 | 0.000 | 0.000 | 0.000 | 0.000 | 0.000 | 0.389 | 0.472 |
| σκιαγραφέω | 0.000 | 0.000 | 0.000 | 0.000 | 0.000 | 0.000 | 0.000 | 0.195 | 0.000 |
| κίνησις, κινέω | 0.494 | 0.060 | 2.637 | 0.145 | 0.264 | 1.196 | 0.610 | 0.389 | 0.000 |
| φέρω, περιφέρω | 0.494 | 0.000 | 0.000 | 0.000 | 0.000 | 0.000 | 0.000 | 0.000 | 0.000 |
| ἀλλάττω, μεταλλάττω, ἀμείβω | 0.185 | 0.000 | 0.000 | 0.000 | 0.000 | 0.000 | 0.000 | 0.000 | 0.000 |
| στρέφω | 0.000 | 0.000 | 0.000 | 0.000 | 0.000 | 0.299 | 0.000 | 0.000 | 0.000 |
| στάσις, ἡσυχία, ἴστημι | 0.247 | 0.120 | 2.637 | 0.145 | 0.264 | 0.399 | 0.915 | 0.195 | 0.000 |
| πολυς****, πολλάκις | 0.803 | 0.700 | 1.695 | 1.163 | 0.792 | 0.199 | 0.000 | 1.751 | 3.774 |
| ἄπειρος, ἀπέραντος, ἀπειρία | 0.062 | 0.120 | 0.000 | 0.872 | 0.000 | 0.000 | 0.000 | 0.584 | 0.000 |
| πλῆθος, πλεονάκις, πλεονεκτέω | 0.000 | 0.260 | 0.000 | 0.581 | 0.000 | 0.000 | 0.000 | 0.584 | 0.000 |
| πέρας, περαίνω | 0.062 | 0.080 | 0.000 | 0.727 | 0.000 | 0.000 | 0.000 | 0.584 | 0.000 |
| ἀρχή***** | 0.185 | 0.120 | 0.000 | 0.000 | 0.000 | 0.000 | 0.000 | 0.584 | 0.000 |
| μέσος | 0.432 | 0.140 | 0.000 | 0.000 | 0.000 | 0.000 | 0.000 | 0.778 | 0.000 |
| τελευτή, τέλος, τέλεως | 0.185 | 0.140 | 0.000 | 0.291 | 0.000 | 0.299 | 0.000 | 0.389 | 0.000 |
| ἔσχατος | 0.124 | 0.080 | 0.000 | 0.000 | 0.000 | 0.000 | 0.000 | 0.000 | 0.000 |

T.A.2 (CONTINUED) TOTAL COUNTS (RELATIVE)

*** only where appearance of subject is indicated     **** without πολλὴ ἀνάγκη     ***** without ἐξ ἀρχῆς

| | S1 | S2 | S2C | S3 | S4 | S5 | S6 | S7 | S8 |
|---|---|---|---|---|---|---|---|---|---|
| ὅλος | 0.618 | 0.820 | 0.000 | 2.035 | 1.055 | 0.000 | 0.000 | 0.000 | 0.000 |
| μέρος | 1.174 | 0.780 | 0.000 | 0.000 | 0.000 | 0.000 | 0.000 | 0.000 | 0.472 |
| μόριον | 0.000 | 0.560 | 0.000 | 4.506 | 1.583 | 0.000 | 0.000 | 0.000 | 0.000 |
| μερίζω, μεριστός | 0.000 | 0.080 | 0.000 | 0.000 | 0.000 | 0.000 | 0.000 | 0.000 | 0.000 |
| μέτρον | 0.679 | 0.140 | 0.000 | 0.000 | 0.000 | 0.000 | 0.000 | 0.000 | 0.000 |
| μέν | 0.926 | 0.880 | 0.753 | 0.872 | 1.055 | 0.698 | 0.305 | 0.973 | 0.472 |
| δέ | 1.853 | 2.341 | 1.695 | 2.180 | 1.847 | 2.393 | 2.439 | 2.140 | 0.943 |
| ἄν | 2.903 | 2.301 | 1.695 | 2.471 | 1.847 | 2.493 | 2.134 | 1.751 | 1.415 |
| οὖν | 0.371 | 0.540 | 0.753 | 0.145 | 0.264 | 0.299 | 0.305 | 0.195 | 0.000 |
| γε | 1.791 | 0.980 | 0.942 | 1.890 | 0.792 | 1.396 | 1.220 | 1.362 | 1.415 |
| γάρ | 0.618 | 0.640 | 0.942 | 1.308 | 1.319 | 1.097 | 0.915 | 1.167 | 1.887 |
| μήν | 1.359 | 0.520 | 0.377 | 0.727 | 0.264 | 0.997 | 0.915 | 0.389 | 0.943 |
| δή | 0.309 | 0.520 | 1.318 | 1.017 | 0.264 | 0.698 | 0.915 | 1.556 | 0.472 |
| οὔτε | 4.509 | 1.261 | 3.955 | 0.145 | 3.430 | 0.598 | 5.488 | 0.584 | 2.830 |
| μή | 0.679 | 0.900 | 1.130 | 0.581 | 0.264 | 5.384 | 3.963 | 1.946 | 5.189 |
| καί | 3.335 | 5.702 | 8.098 | 5.523 | 3.694 | 5.284 | 0.915 | 7.393 | 0.943 |
| τε | 0.556 | 1.521 | 3.202 | 2.035 | 0.792 | 1.296 | 0.305 | 1.556 | 0.000 |

T.A.2 (CONTINUED) TOTAL COUNTS (RELATIVE)

| | + | | | | | | | | | − | | | | | | | | | $p_+$ | $p_-$ | $DP_+$ | DP |
|---|---|---|---|---|---|---|---|---|---|---|---|---|---|---|---|---|---|---|---|---|---|---|
| | S1 | S2 | S2C | S3 | S4 | S5 | S6 | S7 | S8 | S1 | S2 | S2C | S3 | S4 | S5 | S6 | S7 | S8 | | | | |
| οὐσία | 0 | 33 | 3 | 0 | 0 | 4 | 0 | 0 | 0 | −3 | −1 | −2 | 0 | 0 | −3 | −8 | 0 | 0 | 9.65e-04 | 3.19e-08 | 0.37 | 0.62 |
| τὸ εἶναι | 2 | 12 | 2 | 1 | 0 | 6 | 0 | 0 | 0 | 0 | −1 | −2 | 0 | 0 | −2 | 0 | 0 | 0 | 0.392 | 0.065 | 0.24 | 0.66 |
| τὸ μὴ εἶναι | 0 | 0 | 1 | 0 | 0 | 5 | 0 | 0 | 0 | 0 | 0 | 0 | 0 | 0 | −1 | 0 | 0 | 0 | 8.21e-04 | 0.356 | 0.87 | 0.92 |
| τὸ ὄν, τὰ ὄντα | 0 | 26 | 0 | 0 | 0 | 5 | 0 | 1 | 0 | −1 | −2 | 0 | 0 | 0 | −3 | −3 | 0 | 0 | 9.78e-03 | 0.011 | 0.39 | 0.55 |
| τὸ μὴ ὄν, τὰ μὴ ὄντα | 1 | 0 | 0 | 0 | 0 | 5 | 5 | 0 | 0 | 0 | 0 | 0 | 0 | 0 | −2 | 0 | 0 | −5 | 3.59e-07 | 1.48e-08 | 0.80 | 0.90 |
| καθ' αὑτό, αὐτό | 1 | 15 | 1 | 4 | 0 | 0 | 0 | 0 | 0 | −1 | 0 | 0 | 0 | 0 | 0 | 0 | 0 | 0 | 0.176 | 0.514 | 0.36 | 0.86 |
| εἶδος | 0 | 2 | 0 | 1 | 0 | 0 | 0 | 0 | 0 | 0 | 0 | 0 | 0 | −2 | 0 | 0 | 0 | 0 | 0.704 | 4.16e-03 | 0.46 | 0.98 |
| ἰδέα | 0 | 0 | 0 | 1 | 0 | 0 | 0 | 0 | 0 | 0 | 0 | 0 | 0 | 0 | 0 | 0 | 0 | 0 | 0.259 | — | 0.95 | — |
| φύσις | 2 | 4 | 1 | 3 | 0 | 0 | 0 | 0 | 0 | 0 | 0 | 0 | 0 | 0 | 0 | 0 | 0 | 0 | 0.297 | — | 0.33 | — |
| φύω | 0 | 4 | 0 | 0 | 0 | 0 | 0 | 0 | 0 | 0 | 0 | 0 | 0 | 0 | 0 | 0 | 0 | 0 | 0.928 | — | 0.52 | — |
| μετέχω, μέθεξις | 0 | 20 | 6 | 11 | 0 | 5 | 0 | 0 | 0 | −14 | −3 | −5 | −2 | −8 | 0 | −5 | 0 | 0 | 1.07e-05 | 1.89e-11 | 0.31 | 0.60 |
| μεταλαμβάνω etc.* | 0 | 2 | 4 | 2 | 0 | 0 | 0 | 0 | 0 | 0 | 0 | 0 | −1 | 0 | 0 | −2 | 0 | 0 | 4.46e-03 | 2.59e-03 | 0.65 | 0.92 |
| γίγνομαι** | 0 | 0 | 6 | 0 | 0 | 3 | 0 | 1 | 0 | 0 | 0 | 0 | 0 | −1 | −3 | −3 | 0 | 0 | 1.38e-06 | 6.04e-05 | 0.82 | 0.85 |
| ἀπόλλυμι | 0 | 0 | 6 | 0 | 0 | 3 | 0 | 1 | 0 | 0 | 0 | −1 | 0 | −1 | −3 | −5 | 0 | 0 | 1.38e-06 | 4.05e-07 | 0.82 | 0.80 |
| μεταβάλλω, μεταβολή | 0 | 0 | 15 | 0 | 0 | 4 | 0 | 0 | 0 | 0 | 0 | −2 | 0 | 0 | 0 | 0 | 0 | 0 | 8.60e-17 | 0.018 | 0.87 | 0.97 |
| ἀλλοιόω etc. | 0 | 3 | 0 | 0 | 0 | 8 | 0 | 0 | 0 | −4 | −2 | 0 | 0 | 0 | −8 | −2 | 0 | 0 | 9.90e-04 | 2.61e-04 | 0.64 | 0.60 |
| μεταβαίνω | 0 | 0 | 0 | 0 | 0 | 0 | 0 | 1 | 0 | 0 | −1 | 0 | 0 | 0 | −2 | 0 | 0 | 0 | 0.140 | 0.282 | 0.97 | 0.58 |
| μεθίστημι | 0 | 0 | 0 | 0 | 0 | 0 | 0 | 0 | 0 | 0 | 0 | 0 | 0 | 0 | −1 | 0 | 0 | 0 | — | 0.356 | — | 0.92 |
| ἀπαλλάττω, ἀφίημι | 0 | 1 | 4 | 0 | 0 | 0 | 0 | 0 | 0 | 0 | 0 | 0 | 0 | 0 | 0 | 0 | 0 | 0 | 2.74e-03 | — | 0.76 | — |
| αὐξάνω | 0 | 0 | 1 | 0 | 0 | 0 | 0 | 0 | 0 | 0 | 0 | −1 | 0 | 0 | 0 | 0 | 0 | 0 | 0.192 | 0.192 | 0.97 | 0.97 |
| φθίω | 0 | 0 | 1 | 0 | 0 | 0 | 0 | 0 | 0 | 0 | 0 | −1 | 0 | 0 | 0 | 0 | 0 | 0 | 0.192 | 0.192 | 0.97 | 0.97 |

* without subjective grasping    ** only paired with ἀπόλλυμι

T.A.3  POSITIVE AND NEGATIVE COUNTS (ABSOLUTE)

| | + | | | | | | | | | − | | | | | | | | | $p_+$ | $p_-$ | $DP_+$ | $DP_-$ |
|---|---|---|---|---|---|---|---|---|---|---|---|---|---|---|---|---|---|---|---|---|---|---|
| | S1 | S2 | S2C | S3 | S4 | S5 | S6 | S7 | S8 | S1 | S2 | S2C | S3 | S4 | S5 | S6 | S7 | S8 | | | | |
| φαίνω *** | 0 | 2 | 0 | 0 | 0 | 1 | 0 | 12 | 0 | 0 | 0 | 0 | 0 | 0 | 0 | 0 | 0 | -3 | 4.36e-11 | 9.21e-06 | 0.77 | 1.00 |
| δοκέω *** | 0 | 0 | 0 | 0 | 0 | 0 | 0 | 6 | 0 | 0 | 0 | 0 | 0 | 0 | 0 | 0 | 0 | 0 | 2.68e-07 | — | 0.97 | — |
| ὄγκος | 0 | 0 | 0 | 0 | 0 | 0 | 0 | 7 | 0 | 0 | 0 | 0 | 0 | 0 | 0 | 0 | 0 | 0 | 1.40e-08 | — | 0.97 | — |
| ὄναρ, ὕπνος | 0 | 0 | 0 | 0 | 0 | 0 | 0 | 2 | 0 | 0 | 0 | 0 | 0 | 0 | 0 | 0 | 0 | 0 | 0.015 | — | 0.97 | — |
| φάντασμα | 0 | 0 | 0 | 0 | 0 | 0 | 0 | 2 | 0 | 0 | 0 | 0 | 0 | 0 | 0 | 0 | 0 | -1 | 0.015 | 0.021 | 0.97 | 1.00 |
| σκιαγραφέω | 0 | 0 | 0 | 0 | 0 | 0 | 0 | 1 | 0 | 0 | 0 | 0 | 0 | 0 | 0 | 0 | 0 | 0 | 0.140 | — | 0.97 | — |
| κίνησις, κινέω | 0 | 3 | 9 | 1 | 0 | 6 | 0 | 2 | 0 | -8 | 0 | -5 | 0 | -1 | -6 | -2 | 0 | 0 | 1.60e-07 | 2.15e-07 | 0.62 | 0.64 |
| φέρω, περιφέρω | 0 | 0 | 0 | 0 | 0 | 0 | 0 | 0 | 0 | -8 | 0 | 0 | 0 | 0 | 0 | 0 | 0 | 0 | — | 4.85e-04 | — | 0.86 |
| ἀλλάττω etc. | 0 | 0 | 0 | 0 | 0 | 0 | 0 | 0 | 0 | -3 | 0 | 0 | 0 | 0 | 0 | 0 | 0 | 0 | — | 0.125 | — | 0.86 |
| στρέφω | 0 | 0 | 0 | 0 | 0 | 0 | 0 | 0 | 0 | 0 | 0 | 0 | 0 | 0 | -3 | 0 | 0 | 0 | — | 0.029 | — | 0.92 |
| στάσις, ἡσυχία, ἵστημι | 0 | 4 | 9 | 1 | 0 | 4 | 0 | 1 | 0 | -4 | -2 | -5 | 0 | -1 | 0 | -3 | 0 | 0 | 3.23e-06 | 7.88e-05 | 0.55 | 0.60 |
| πολυς ****, πολλάκις | 0 | 27 | 6 | 4 | 0 | 2 | 0 | 9 | 0 | -13 | -8 | -3 | -4 | -3 | 0 | 0 | 0 | -8 | 2.28e-05 | 9.40e-09 | 0.31 | 0.47 |
| ἄπειρος etc. | 1 | 6 | 0 | 6 | 0 | 0 | 0 | 3 | 0 | 0 | 0 | 0 | 0 | 0 | 0 | 0 | 0 | 0 | 4.21e-03 | — | 0.46 | — |
| πλῆθος etc. | 0 | 13 | 0 | 4 | 0 | 0 | 0 | 3 | 0 | 0 | 0 | 0 | 0 | 0 | 0 | 0 | 0 | 0 | 0.028 | — | 0.40 | — |
| πέρας, περαίνω | 0 | 4 | 0 | 5 | 0 | 0 | 0 | 2 | 0 | -1 | 0 | 0 | 0 | 0 | 0 | 0 | -1 | 0 | 6.32e-03 | 0.171 | 0.53 | 0.81 |
| ἀρχή ***** | 0 | 6 | 0 | 0 | 0 | 0 | 0 | 2 | 0 | -3 | 0 | 0 | 0 | 0 | 0 | 0 | -1 | 0 | 0.371 | 0.065 | 0.47 | 0.81 |
| μέσος | 0 | 6 | 0 | 0 | 0 | 0 | 0 | 3 | 0 | -7 | -1 | 0 | 0 | 0 | 0 | 0 | -1 | 0 | 0.143 | 8.81e-03 | 0.47 | 0.70 |
| τελευτή, τέλος, τέλεος | 0 | 7 | 0 | 2 | 0 | 3 | 0 | 2 | 0 | -3 | 0 | 0 | 0 | 0 | 0 | 0 | 0 | 0 | 0.238 | 0.125 | 0.31 | 0.86 |
| ἔσχατος | 0 | 4 | 0 | 0 | 0 | 0 | 0 | 0 | 0 | -2 | 0 | 0 | 0 | 0 | 0 | 0 | 0 | 0 | 0.928 | 0.254 | 0.52 | 0.86 |

T.A.3 (CON.) POSITIVE AND NEGATIVE COUNTS (ABS.)

*** only where appearance of subject is indicated    **** without πολλὴ ἀνάγκη    ***** without ἐξ ἀρχῆς

| | + | | | | | | | | | − | | | | | | | | | $p_+$ | $p_-$ | $DP_+$ | $DP_-$ |
|---|---|---|---|---|---|---|---|---|---|---|---|---|---|---|---|---|---|---|---|---|---|---|
| | S1 | S2 | S2C | S3 | S4 | S5 | S6 | S7 | S8 | S1 | S2 | S2C | S3 | S4 | S5 | S6 | S7 | S8 | | | | |
| ὅλος | 0 | 28 | 0 | 14 | 0 | 0 | 0 | 0 | 0 | -10 | -13 | 0 | 0 | -4 | 0 | 0 | 0 | 0 | 2.89e-08 | 7.95e-03 | 0.46 | 0.33 |
| μέρος | 0 | 24 | 0 | 0 | 0 | 0 | 0 | 0 | 0 | -19 | -15 | 0 | 0 | 0 | 0 | 0 | 0 | -1 | 5.05e-03 | 3.20e-05 | 0.52 | 0.40 |
| μόριον | 0 | 22 | 0 | 31 | 0 | 0 | 0 | 0 | 0 | 0 | -6 | 0 | 0 | -6 | 0 | 0 | 0 | 0 | 1.30e-21 | 3.09e-04 | 0.53 | 0.49 |
| μερίζω, μεριστός | 0 | 4 | 0 | 0 | 0 | 0 | 0 | 0 | 0 | 0 | 0 | 0 | 0 | 0 | 0 | 0 | 0 | 0 | 0.928 | — | 0.52 | — |
| μέτρον | 0 | 7 | 0 | 0 | 0 | 0 | 0 | 0 | 0 | -11 | 0 | 0 | 0 | 0 | 0 | 0 | 0 | 0 | 0.794 | 7.17e-06 | 0.52 | 0.86 |

T.A.3 (CONTINUED)  POSITIVE AND NEGATIVE COUNTS (ABSOLUTE)

| | + | | | | | | | | | − | | | | | | | | |
|---|---|---|---|---|---|---|---|---|---|---|---|---|---|---|---|---|---|---|
| | S1 | S2 | S2C | S3 | S4 | S5 | S6 | S7 | S8 | S1 | S2 | S2C | S3 | S4 | S5 | S6 | S7 | S8 |
| οὐσία | 0.000 | 0.660 | 0.565 | 0.000 | 0.000 | 0.399 | 0.000 | 0.200 | 0.000 | -0.185 | -0.020 | -0.377 | 0.000 | 0.000 | -0.299 | -2.439 | 0.000 | 0.000 |
| τὸ εἶναι | 0.124 | 0.240 | 0.377 | 0.145 | 0.000 | 0.598 | 0.000 | 0.300 | 0.000 | 0.000 | -0.020 | -0.377 | 0.000 | 0.000 | -0.199 | 0.000 | 0.000 | 0.000 |
| τὸ μὴ εἶναι | 0.000 | 0.000 | 0.188 | 0.000 | 0.000 | 0.499 | 0.000 | 0.300 | 0.000 | 0.000 | 0.000 | 0.000 | 0.000 | 0.000 | -0.100 | 0.000 | 0.000 | 0.000 |
| τὸ ὄν, τὰ ὄντα | 0.000 | 0.520 | 0.000 | 0.000 | 0.000 | 0.499 | 0.000 | 0.195 | 0.000 | -0.062 | -0.040 | 0.000 | 0.000 | 0.000 | -0.299 | -0.915 | 0.000 | 0.000 |
| τὸ μὴ ὄν, τὰ μὴ ὄντα | 0.062 | 0.000 | 0.000 | 0.000 | 0.000 | 0.499 | 1.524 | 0.300 | 0.000 | 0.000 | 0.000 | 0.000 | 0.000 | 0.000 | -0.199 | 0.000 | 0.000 | -2.358 |
| καθ' αὐτό, αὐτό | 0.062 | 0.300 | 0.188 | 0.581 | 0.000 | 0.000 | 0.000 | 0.300 | 0.000 | -0.062 | 0.000 | 0.000 | 0.000 | 0.000 | 0.000 | 0.000 | 0.000 | 0.000 |
| εἶδος | 0.000 | 0.040 | 0.000 | 0.145 | 0.000 | 0.000 | 0.000 | 0.000 | 0.000 | 0.000 | 0.000 | 0.000 | 0.000 | -0.528 | 0.000 | 0.000 | 0.000 | 0.000 |
| ἰδέα | 0.000 | 0.000 | 0.000 | 0.145 | 0.000 | 0.000 | 0.000 | 0.000 | 0.000 | 0.000 | 0.000 | 0.000 | 0.000 | 0.000 | 0.000 | 0.000 | 0.000 | 0.000 |
| φύσις | 0.124 | 0.080 | 0.188 | 0.436 | 0.000 | 0.000 | 0.000 | 0.000 | 0.000 | 0.000 | 0.000 | 0.000 | 0.000 | 0.000 | 0.000 | 0.000 | 0.000 | 0.000 |
| φύω | 0.000 | 0.080 | 0.000 | 0.000 | 0.000 | 0.000 | 0.000 | 0.000 | 0.000 | 0.000 | 0.000 | 0.000 | 0.000 | 0.000 | 0.000 | 0.000 | 0.000 | 0.000 |
| μετέχω, μέθεξις | 0.000 | 0.400 | 1.130 | 1.599 | 0.000 | 0.499 | 0.000 | 0.000 | 0.000 | -0.865 | -0.060 | -0.942 | -0.291 | -2.111 | 0.000 | -1.524 | 0.000 | 0.000 |
| μεταλαμβάνω, etc.* | 0.000 | 0.040 | 0.753 | 0.291 | 0.000 | 0.000 | 0.000 | 0.000 | 0.000 | 0.000 | 0.000 | 0.000 | -0.145 | 0.000 | 0.000 | -0.610 | 0.000 | 0.000 |
| γίγνομαι** | 0.000 | 0.000 | 1.130 | 0.000 | 0.000 | 0.299 | 0.000 | 0.195 | 0.000 | 0.000 | 0.000 | 0.000 | 0.000 | -0.264 | -0.299 | -0.915 | 0.000 | 0.000 |
| ἀπόλλυμι | 0.000 | 0.000 | 1.130 | 0.000 | 0.000 | 0.299 | 0.000 | 0.195 | 0.000 | 0.000 | 0.000 | -0.188 | 0.000 | -0.264 | -0.299 | -1.524 | 0.000 | 0.000 |
| μεταβάλλω, μεταβολή | 0.000 | 0.000 | 2.825 | 0.000 | 0.000 | 0.399 | 0.000 | 0.000 | 0.000 | 0.000 | 0.000 | -0.377 | 0.000 | 0.000 | 0.000 | 0.000 | 0.000 | 0.000 |
| ἀλλοιόω etc. | 0.000 | 0.060 | 0.000 | 0.000 | 0.000 | 0.798 | 0.000 | 0.000 | 0.000 | -0.247 | -0.040 | 0.000 | 0.000 | 0.000 | -0.798 | -0.610 | 0.000 | 0.000 |
| μεταβαίνω | 0.000 | 0.000 | 0.000 | 0.000 | 0.000 | 0.000 | 0.000 | 0.195 | 0.000 | 0.000 | -0.020 | 0.000 | 0.000 | 0.000 | -0.199 | 0.000 | 0.000 | 0.000 |
| μεθίστημι | 0.000 | 0.000 | 0.000 | 0.000 | 0.000 | 0.000 | 0.000 | 0.000 | 0.000 | 0.000 | 0.000 | 0.000 | 0.000 | 0.000 | -0.100 | 0.000 | 0.000 | 0.000 |
| ἀπαλλάττω, ἀφίημι | 0.000 | 0.020 | 0.753 | 0.000 | 0.000 | 0.000 | 0.000 | 0.000 | 0.000 | 0.000 | 0.000 | 0.000 | 0.000 | 0.000 | 0.000 | 0.000 | 0.000 | 0.000 |
| αὐξάνω | 0.000 | 0.000 | 0.188 | 0.000 | 0.000 | 0.000 | 0.000 | 0.000 | 0.000 | 0.000 | 0.000 | -0.188 | 0.000 | 0.000 | 0.000 | 0.000 | 0.000 | 0.000 |
| φθίω | 0.000 | 0.000 | 0.188 | 0.000 | 0.000 | 0.000 | 0.000 | 0.000 | 0.000 | 0.000 | 0.000 | -0.188 | 0.000 | 0.000 | 0.000 | 0.000 | 0.000 | 0.000 |

* without subjective grasping   ** only paired with ἀπόλλυμι

T.A.4  POSITIVE AND NEGATIVE COUNTS (RELATIVE)

| | − | | | | | | | | | + | | | | | | | | |
|---|---|---|---|---|---|---|---|---|---|---|---|---|---|---|---|---|---|---|
| | S1 | S2 | S2C | S3 | S4 | S5 | S6 | S7 | S8 | S1 | S2 | S2C | S3 | S4 | S5 | S6 | S7 | S8 |
| φαίνω *** | 0.000 | 0.000 | 0.000 | 0.000 | 0.000 | 0.000 | 0.000 | 0.000 | −1.415 | 0.000 | 0.040 | 0.000 | 0.000 | 0.000 | 0.100 | 0.000 | 2.335 | 0.000 |
| δοκέω *** | 0.000 | 0.000 | 0.000 | 0.000 | 0.000 | 0.000 | 0.000 | 0.000 | 0.000 | 0.000 | 0.000 | 0.000 | 0.000 | 0.000 | 0.000 | 0.000 | 1.167 | 0.000 |
| ὄγκος | 0.000 | 0.000 | 0.000 | 0.000 | 0.000 | 0.000 | 0.000 | 0.000 | 0.000 | 0.000 | 0.000 | 0.000 | 0.000 | 0.000 | 0.000 | 0.000 | 1.362 | 0.000 |
| ὄναρ, ὕπνος | 0.000 | 0.000 | 0.000 | 0.000 | 0.000 | 0.000 | 0.000 | 0.000 | 0.000 | 0.000 | 0.000 | 0.000 | 0.000 | 0.000 | 0.000 | 0.000 | 0.389 | 0.000 |
| φάντασμα | 0.000 | 0.000 | 0.000 | 0.000 | 0.000 | 0.000 | 0.000 | 0.000 | −0.472 | 0.000 | 0.000 | 0.000 | 0.000 | 0.000 | 0.000 | 0.000 | 0.389 | 0.000 |
| σκιαγραφέω | 0.000 | 0.000 | 0.000 | 0.000 | 0.000 | 0.000 | 0.000 | 0.000 | 0.000 | 0.000 | 0.000 | 0.000 | 0.000 | 0.000 | 0.000 | 0.000 | 0.195 | 0.000 |
| κίρνης, κιέω | −0.494 | 0.000 | −0.942 | 0.000 | −0.264 | −0.598 | −0.610 | 0.000 | 0.000 | 0.000 | 0.060 | 1.695 | 0.145 | 0.000 | 0.598 | 0.000 | 0.389 | 0.000 |
| φέρω, περιφέρω | −0.494 | 0.000 | 0.000 | 0.000 | 0.000 | 0.000 | 0.000 | 0.000 | 0.000 | 0.000 | 0.000 | 0.000 | 0.000 | 0.000 | 0.000 | 0.000 | 0.000 | 0.000 |
| ἀλλάττω etc. | −0.185 | 0.000 | 0.000 | 0.000 | 0.000 | 0.000 | 0.000 | 0.000 | 0.000 | 0.000 | 0.000 | 0.000 | 0.000 | 0.000 | 0.000 | 0.000 | 0.000 | 0.000 |
| στρέφω | 0.000 | 0.000 | 0.000 | 0.000 | 0.000 | 0.000 | 0.000 | 0.000 | 0.000 | 0.000 | 0.000 | 0.000 | 0.000 | 0.000 | 0.000 | 0.000 | 0.000 | 0.000 |
| στάσις, ἡσυχία, ἵστημι | −0.247 | −0.040 | −0.942 | 0.000 | −0.264 | 0.000 | −0.915 | 0.000 | 0.000 | 0.000 | 0.080 | 1.695 | 0.145 | 0.000 | 0.399 | 0.000 | 0.195 | 0.000 |
| πολύς ****, πολλάκις | −0.803 | −0.160 | −0.565 | −0.581 | −0.792 | 0.000 | 0.000 | 0.000 | −3.774 | 0.000 | 0.540 | 1.130 | 0.581 | 0.000 | 0.199 | 0.000 | 1.751 | 0.000 |
| ἄπειρος etc. | 0.000 | 0.000 | 0.000 | 0.000 | 0.000 | 0.000 | 0.000 | 0.000 | 0.000 | 0.062 | 0.120 | 0.000 | 0.872 | 0.000 | 0.000 | 0.000 | 0.584 | 0.000 |
| πλῆθος etc. | 0.000 | 0.000 | 0.000 | 0.000 | 0.000 | 0.000 | 0.000 | 0.000 | 0.000 | 0.000 | 0.260 | 0.000 | 0.581 | 0.000 | 0.000 | 0.000 | 0.584 | 0.000 |
| πέρας, περαίνω | −0.062 | 0.000 | 0.000 | 0.000 | 0.000 | 0.000 | 0.000 | 0.000 | 0.000 | 0.000 | 0.080 | 0.000 | 0.727 | 0.000 | 0.000 | 0.000 | 0.389 | 0.000 |
| ἀρχή ***** | −0.185 | 0.000 | 0.000 | 0.000 | 0.000 | 0.000 | 0.000 | −0.195 | 0.000 | 0.000 | 0.120 | 0.000 | 0.000 | 0.000 | 0.000 | 0.000 | 0.389 | 0.000 |
| μέσος | −0.432 | −0.020 | 0.000 | 0.000 | 0.000 | 0.000 | 0.000 | −0.195 | 0.000 | 0.000 | 0.120 | 0.000 | 0.000 | 0.000 | 0.000 | 0.000 | 0.584 | 0.000 |
| τελευτή, τέλος, τέλεως | −0.185 | 0.000 | 0.000 | 0.000 | 0.000 | 0.000 | 0.000 | −0.195 | 0.000 | 0.000 | 0.140 | 0.000 | 0.291 | 0.000 | 0.299 | 0.000 | 0.389 | 0.000 |
| ἔσχατος | −0.124 | 0.000 | 0.000 | 0.000 | 0.000 | 0.000 | 0.000 | 0.000 | 0.000 | 0.000 | 0.080 | 0.000 | 0.000 | 0.000 | 0.000 | 0.000 | 0.000 | 0.000 |

T.A.4 (CON.) POSITIVE AND NEGATIVE COUNTS (REL.)

*** only where appearance of subject is indicated     **** without πολλὴ ἀνάγκη     ***** without ἐξ ἀρχῆς

| | + | | | | | | | | | − | | | | | | | | |
|---|---|---|---|---|---|---|---|---|---|---|---|---|---|---|---|---|---|---|
| | S1 | S2 | S2C | S3 | S4 | S5 | S6 | S7 | S8 | S1 | S2 | S2C | S3 | S4 | S5 | S6 | S7 | S8 |
| ὅλος | 0.000 | 0.560 | 0.000 | 2.035 | 0.000 | 0.000 | 0.000 | 0.000 | 0.000 | -0.618 | -0.260 | 0.000 | 0.000 | -1.055 | 0.000 | 0.000 | 0.000 | 0.000 |
| μέρος | 0.000 | 0.480 | 0.000 | 0.000 | 0.000 | 0.000 | 0.000 | 0.000 | 0.000 | -1.174 | -0.300 | 0.000 | 0.000 | 0.000 | 0.000 | 0.000 | 0.000 | -0.472 |
| μόριον | 0.000 | 0.440 | 0.000 | 4.506 | 0.000 | 0.000 | 0.000 | 0.000 | 0.000 | 0.000 | -0.120 | 0.000 | 0.000 | -1.583 | 0.000 | 0.000 | 0.000 | 0.000 |
| μερίζω, μεριστός | 0.000 | 0.080 | 0.000 | 0.000 | 0.000 | 0.000 | 0.000 | 0.000 | 0.000 | 0.000 | 0.000 | 0.000 | 0.000 | 0.000 | 0.000 | 0.000 | 0.000 | 0.000 |
| μέτρον | 0.000 | 0.140 | 0.000 | 0.000 | 0.000 | 0.000 | 0.000 | 0.000 | 0.000 | -0.679 | 0.000 | 0.000 | 0.000 | 0.000 | 0.000 | 0.000 | 0.000 | 0.000 |

T.A.4 (CONTINUED) POSITIVE AND NEGATIVE COUNTS (RELATIVE)

|      | Total  | %      | Parmenides | %     | Aristotle | %    |
|------|--------|--------|------------|-------|-----------|------|
| S1   | 1,823  | 15.90  | 1,619      | 14.12 | 204       | 1.78 |
| S2   | 5,432  | 47.39  | 4,998      | 43.60 | 434       | 3.79 |
| S2C  | 573    | 5.00   | 531        | 4.63  | 42        | 0.37 |
| S3   | 745    | 6.50   | 688        | 6.00  | 57        | 0.50 |
| S4   | 408    | 3.56   | 379        | 3.31  | 29        | 0.25 |
| S5   | 1,094  | 9.54   | 1,003      | 8.75  | 91        | 0.79 |
| S6   | 372    | 3.25   | 328        | 2.86  | 44        | 0.38 |
| S7   | 559    | 4.88   | 514        | 4.48  | 45        | 0.39 |
| S8   | 236    | 2.06   | 212        | 1.85  | 24        | 0.21 |
| Sum  | 11,242 | 98.08  | 10,272     | 89.62 | 970       | 8.46 |
| IS   | 25     | 0.22   | 22         | 0.19  | 3         | 0.10 |
| TP   | 156    | 1.36   | 145        | 1.27  | 11        | 0.03 |
| FS   | 39     | 0.34   | 38         | 0.33  | 1         | 0.01 |
| Sum  | 11,462 | 100.00 | 10,477     | 91.41 | 985       | 8.59 |

T.A.5  WORD COUNTS

# APPENDIX B

*οὐσία*

## S1

1  141e7 *οὐσίας* 0–  general question, negated 141e9
2  141e9 *οὐσίας* –
3  141e11 *οὐσίας* 0–  hypothetical consideration, negated 141e9

## S2

1  142b6 *οὐσίας* 0+  rhetorical question, affirmed 142c5–6 and 143a4–5
2  142b7 *ἡ οὐσία* +
3  142b8 *οὐσία* 0+  hypothetical consideration, affirmed 142c5–6; 143a4–5
4  142c5 *οὐσίας* +
5  142d3 *οὐσία* +
6  143a4 *οὐσίας* +
7  143a6 *οὐσίας* +
8  143b1 *οὐσίαν* +  from here to 143c2: counted as positive if *ἕν* and *οὐσία* are described positively as two different aspects of *τὸ ἓν ὄν*; cf. 142d9–e3
9  143b2 *οὐσία* –  negative since it is emphasised that *τὸ ἕν* is not *οὐσία* (but in fact participates in it; cf. also 143b3)
10  143b3 *οὐσίας* +
11  143b3 *ἡ οὐσία* +
12  143b4 *τῆς οὐσίας* +
13  143b5 *τῷ οὐσία εἶναι* +
14  143b5 *ἡ οὐσία (τοῦ ἑνὸς)* +
15  143b7 *τῇ οὐσίᾳ* +
16  143c1 *τὴν οὐσίαν* +
17  143c2 *τὴν οὐσίαν* +
18  143c5 *οὐσίαν* 0+  from here to 143c8: general consideration, affirmed 142c5–6; 142d9–e3
19  143c7 *οὐσία* 0+
20  143c8 *οὐσία* 0+
21  144a7 *οὐσίας* +  from here to

144e7: counted as positive since *ἕν* and *οὐσία* again appear as two aspects of *τὸ ἓν ὄν* with regard to number/parts; cf. 144c6–8, 144d5–e3
22  144a8 *οὐσίας* +
23  144b1 *ἡ οὐσία* +
24  144b4 *οὐσία* 0+  rhetorical question, affirmed 144b1–2
25  144c1 *τῆς οὐσίας* +
26  144c3 *οὐσίας* 0+  general consideration, affirmed 144c1; 144c6–8
27  144c6 *τῆς οὐσίας* +
28  144d3 *τῆς οὐσίας* 0+  hypothetical consideration, affirmed 144e1–3
29  144d6 *ἡ οὐσία* +  the negation refers to *πλεῖστα* (144d6) and *πλείω* (144d7)
30  144e4 *τῆς οὐσίας* +  cf. 144e1–3
31  149e3–4 *ταῖς οὐσίαις* 0+  hypothetical consideration, affirmed 149e8–9
32  149e10–150a1 *τοῖς οὖσιν* 0+  hypothetical consideration, affirmed 149e8–9
33  151e8 *οὐσίας* 0+  general definition, affirmed 152a2–3
34  152a2 *οὐσίας* 0+  general definition, affirmed 152a2–3

## S2C

1  155e7 *οὐσίας* +
2  155e8 *οὐσίας* –
3  156a4 *οὐσίας* 0+  general definition, affirmed 156a7–b1
4  156a6 *οὐσίας* 0–  general definition, counted as negative due to *ἀπαλλάττεσθαι* (156a6); used in 156a7–b1
5  156a7 *οὐσίαν* +  could also be counted twice (+/–) due to *λαμβάνον τε καὶ ἀφιὲν* (156a7)

**S5**

1    161e3 οὐσίας +
2    162a8 οὐσίας (τοῦ εἶναι ὄν) 0+
    from here to 162b2: general con-
    sideration; according to the chiasm
    in 162b6–7 counted twice as 0+
    and twice as 0– for the complex
    consideration in 162a8–b2 to map
    the chiasm statistically
3    162a8 οὐσίας ... (τοῦ εἶναι
    μὴ ὄν) 0–
4    162b1 οὐσίας ... (τοῦ μὴ εἶναι
    μὴ ὄν) 0–
5    162b2 οὐσίας ... (τοῦ εἶναι
    μὴ ὄν) 0+
6    162b6 οὐσία +
7    162b7 οὐσία –

**S6**

1    163c3 οὐσίας 0–  from here to
    163d1: general consideration,
    negated 163d5–8; ἀπουσίαν could
    be counted as another negative
    occurrence
2    163c7 οὐσίας 0–
3    163d1 οὐσίας 0–
4    163d2 οὐσίας 0–  here, and 163d3:
    general definition, negated subse-
    quently in 163d5–8
5    163d3 οὐσίαν 0–
6    163d6 οὐσίας –
7    163d8 οὐσίας –
8    164a1 οὐσίας 0–  hypothetical
    consideration, negated 163d5–8

### τὸ εἶναι

Only those occurrences are counted where εἶναι is nominalised.

**S1**

1    139c6 τῷ ... (ἐν) εἶναι 0+  positive
    tendency here and mostly through-
    out S1 (cf. 137d1–2), yet ultimately
    negated (cf. 141e10–12)
2    140a1–2 τοῦ (ἐν) εἶναι 0+  very
    similar to 139c6 before

**S2**

1    142d1 τὸ ἔστι +  obviously nomi-
    nalising ὄντος in τοῦ ἑνὸς ὄντος as
    does τὸ ἓν with regard to τοῦ ὄντος
    ἑνός (142d2), cf. also 142d5
2    142d5 τὸ εἶναι +
3    142e2 τοῦ εἶναι (μορίου) 0+  gen-
    eral question, affirmed 142e3–143a1
4    147a2 τὸ (μὴ ἕτερα) εἶναι 0–
    difficult; said about τὰ μὴ ἓν
    (146e6); ultimately, ἐκφεύγοι
    suggests negative tendency; how
    ever, the whole passage 147a1–6
    remains quite hypothetical
5    148b2 τὸ εἶναι (ταὐτὸν) 0+  gener-
    al consideration, affirmed 148b4–5
6    148b2 τῷ (ἕτερον) εἶναι 0+  gener-
    al consideration, affirmed 148b4–5
7    149b5 τὸ (πλείω) εἶναι 0+  general
    consideration, affirmed 149c2–3

8    149e1–2 τῷ ... (ἐν) εἶναι +
9    149e4 τῷ (τοιαῦτα) εἶναι 0+
    slightly hypothetical, affirmed
    149e5–9
10    151e7 τὸ ... εἶναι 0+  general defi-
    nition, affirmed 152a2–3
11    152a3 τοῦ εἶναι +
12    152e1 τοῦ εἶναι +
13    154a8 τοῦ εἶναι +

**S2C**

1    156a2 τοῦ εἶναι +  implicitly also
    negated by ὅτε ἀπαλλάττεται
    (156a2), could be counted +/–
2    156b3 τὸ (πολλὰ) εἶναι 0–  count-
    ed as 0– since 'being many' is ac-
    companied by ἀπόλλυται (156b3)
3    156b3 τὸ (ἓν) εἶναι 0–  counted as
    0– since 'being one' is accompanied
    by ἀπόλλυται (156b4)
4    156e8 τοῦ εἶναι +  parallel to τοῦ
    μὴ εἶναι (157a1)

**S3**

1    158a1–2 τό ... (ἕκαστον) εἶναι +

**S5**

1    162a2–3 τοῦ εἶναι 0–  general con-

sideration, negated to some degree by ἀνήσει and hence counted as 0- instead of - (yet also affirmed with regard to εὐθὺς ἔσται ὄν, 162a3, and 162a4–5; cf. also 156a2; 156e8–157a1)

2  162a4 τὸ εἶναι (μὴ ὄν) +

3  162a8 τοῦ εἶναι (ὄν) 0+ from here to 162b2: complex general consideration, counted as 0+ with regard

to the chiasm in 162a4–5 and esp. 162b3–6; 162a8 and 162b2 are counted as 0-/0+ accordingly to map the chiasm statistically

4  162a8 τοῦ εἶναι (μὴ ὄν) 0-

5  162b2 τοῦ εἶναι (μὴ ὄν) 0+

6  162b4 τοῦ εἶναι 0+ general consideration, affirmed in 162b5–6

7  162b5 τοῦ εἶναι +

8  162c6 τοῦ εἶναι +

### τὸ μὴ εἶναι

Only those occurrences are counted where μὴ εἶναι is nominalised.

#### S2C

1  157a1 τοῦ μὴ εἶναι + parallel to τοῦ εἶναι (156e8)

#### S5

1  162a3 τὸ μὴ εἶναι + cf. also s.v. τὸ εἶναι S2C 156a2; 156e8–157a1

2  162a4 τοῦ μὴ εἶναι +

3  162b1–2 τοῦ μὴ εἶναι (μὴ ὄν) 0- complex general consideration, cf. also s.v. τὸ εἶναι S5 162a8

4  162b4 τοῦ μὴ εἶναι 0+ general consideration, affirmed in 162b5–6

5  162b5–6 τὸ μὴ εἶναι +

6  162c6 τὸ μὴ εἶναι +

### τὸ ὄν, τὰ ὄντα

Only those occurrences are counted where ὄν is nominalised. τὸ ... ὄν in τὸ ἐν ὄν is not taken into account where τὸ ἐν ὄν is explicitly stated.

#### S1

1  142a6 τῶν ὄντων –

#### S2

1  142e1 τὸ ὄν 0+ here, and 142e2: general question, affirmed 142e3–143a1

2  142e2 τὸ ὄν 0+

3  142e4 τὸ ὄν +

4  142e7 τὸ ὄν +

5  142e7 τὸ ὄν +

6  144a6 τῶν ὄντων +

7  144b1 (πάντα ... πολλὰ) ὄντα + counted as positive since parallel to τῶν ὄντων (144b2; b4)

8  144b2 τῶν ὄντων 0+ ultimately positive since none is missing (οὐδενὸς ἀποστατεῖ 144b2)

9  144b4 τῶν ὄντων 0+ rhetorical question, affirmed 144b1–2

10  144b6 (σμικρότατα καὶ μέγιστα καὶ πανταχῶς) ὄντα + counted as

positive since parallel to τῶν ὄντων (144b2; 144b4)

11  144e1 τὸ ὄν +

12  144e2 τοῦ ὄντος +

13  144e5 τὸ ὄν (ἐν πολλά) 0+ difficult instance since one can understand {τὸ ὄν} {ἐν πολλά} ἐστιν or {τὸ ὄν ἐν} {πολλά} ἐστιν; counted as positive since a) the former would mirror τὸ ἐν ὑπὸ τοῦ ὄντος in 144e6 and b) both readings are ultimately positive in their tendency (though the latter is a compositum)

14  144e6 τοῦ ὄντος +

15  146a2–3 τὸ ... (ἐν τῷ αὐτῷ) ... ὄν 0+ general consideration, affirmed 146a1–2

16  146a3–4 τὸ (ἐν ἑτέρῳ) ... ὄν 0+ general consideration, affirmed 146a6–8

17  146c4–5 τὸ (ἑτέρωθι) ὂν 0+ general consideration, affirmed 146c7–8

18  146d9 τῶν ὄντων 0– hypothetical
consideration about τὸ ἕτερον
(146d8), ultimately negated
146e2–4

19  146e3 τῶν ὄντων – again about
τὸ ἕτερον; cf. 146d8–e2

20  149c2 τὰ ὄντα +

21  150b5 τῶν ὄντων 0+ difficult
passage; τι … σμικρὸν is negated
but αὐτή ἡ σμικρότης is ultimately
affirmed as existing there
(cf. 150b6–7), hence a slightly
positive tendency

22  151a4–5 τό … ὂν +

23  151a5 τό … (ἔν τω) ὂν +

24  154b4 τὸ (νεώτερον) ὂν +

25  154b7 τὸ ὂν +

26  154b7 τοῦ ὄντος + following the
text of BURNET and MORESCHINI

27  154c3–4 τῶν (ἄλλων) ὄντων +
named as comparative object to τὸ
ἓν … ὂν (150c3), which becomes
neither older nor younger than
them

28  154e5–6 τὸ (πρότερον γεγονός τε
καὶ πρεσβύτερον) ὂν 0+ general
consideration, affirmed 155c4–6

S5

1  162a1 ὄντα 0+ ultimately in the
sense of τὰ ὄντα λέγειν

2  162a5 τὸ ὂν 0+ from here to
162a8: complex general consideration, counted as 0+ with regard
to the chiasm in 162a4–5; esp.
162b3–6

3  162a6–7 τό … ὂν 0+

4  162a7–8 τὸ … ὂν 0+

5  162b3–4 τῷ … ὄντι +

6  162c7 τῶν ὄντων –

7  162d3 τῶν ὄντων 0– general
consideration, counted as 0– with
regard to 162c7

8  162d6 τὸ ὂν – ultimately, τὸ ὂν
means τὸ ἓν ὂν

S6

1  163e7 τῶν ὄντων –

2  164a1 <τοῦ> ὄντος 0– following
the text of MORESCHINI; hypothetical consideration, negated 163d8

3  164b2 τῶν ὄντων –

S7

1  165b5 (πᾶν) τὸ ὂν +

τὸ μὴ ὂν, τὰ μὴ ὄντα

Only those occurrences are counted where μὴ ὂν is nominalised. τὸ μὴ ὂν in τὸ μὴ ὂν ἕν is not
taken into account where τὸ μὴ ὂν ἕν is explicitly stated.

S1

1  142a2 τῷ μὴ ὄντι +

S5

1  162a5 τὸ μὴ ὂν 0+ complex
general consideration, counted as
0+ with regard to the chiasm in
162a4–5; esp. 162b3–6 (perhaps
even to be understood as τὸ ὂν τὸ
μὴ ὂν, i.e. 'the non-being being'?)

2  162a7 τὸ μὴ ὂν 0– complex general consideration, counted as 0– to
map the chiasm statistically

3  162b1 τὸ … μὴ ὂν 0+ here and
162b2: complex general consider-

ation, counted as 0+ since τὸ μὴ
ὂν is subject and with regard to the
chiasm in 162a4–5; esp. 162b3–6

4  162b2 τὸ μὴ ὂν 0+

5  162b4 τῷ μὴ ὄντι +

6  162d3 τὸ … μὴ ὂν 0+ general
consideration, counted as 0+ due
to affirmation before, cf. 162b3–6;
162c3

7  162d6 τὸ μὴ ὂν – ultimately, τὸ
μὴ ὂν means τὸ μὴ ὂν ἓν

S6

1  163c7 τό … μὴ ὂν 0+ here and
163c8: general definition, affirma-

tion of this (negative) subject; ultimately, τὸ μὴ ὄν probably means τὸ μὴ ὄν ἕν, cf. 163d7–8

2  163c8 τὸ μὴ ὄν 0+
3  163e3–4 τὸ μηδαμοῦ ὄν 0+ general definition, same as 163c7; 163c8
4  163e5 τὸ μὴ ὄν 0+ general definition, cf. 163c7; 163c8
5  164b2 τὸ μὴ ὄν 0+ cf. 163c7; 163c8

**S8**

1  166a1–2 τῶν μὴ ὄντων –
2  166a3 τῶν μὴ ὄντων –
3  166a4 τοῖς μὴ οὖσιν – could also be counted as negative in οὐσία
4  166a4–5 τοῦ μὴ ὄντος –
5  166a6 τὸ μὴ ὄν 0– counted as 0– since δοξάζεται is negated (cf. 166a4–5)

## καθ' αὑτό, αὐτό

Only those occurrences are counted that form the well-known expression to denote a form. Reflexive, emphatic formulations such as αὐτο ἑαυτῷ (cf. e.g. 145c7 145e4; 145e5 145e8; 146a6–7; 146b5–6; 148e1; 150e1; 165d3) are not included; both κατ' αὐτὸ 148a1; 148a4 are difficult and most likely do not fit the terminology of forms; they are thus not included; the same applies to the even more difficult expressions in 150a4; 158a5.

**S1**

1  137d2 (ἐν) αὐτὸ +
2  138b2–3 αὐτὸ (τὸ περιέχον) 0– hypothetical consideration, negated 138b5–6

**S2**

1  142d4 (ἐν ὄν) ... αὐτό +
2  143a6 αὐτὸ (τὸ ἕν) + probably points to the One of S1; cf. also 144e3; 144e6; 153c3–4; 153d1–2
3  143a7 αὐτὸ ... καθ' αὐτὸ +
4  144e3 (τὸ ἕν) ... αὐτὸ +
5  144e6 αὐτὸ (τὸ ἕν) +
6  145c5 αὐτὸ (τὸ ὅλον) +
7  146d5 αὐτό ... (ταὐτὸν) +
8  150b7 αὐτῆς (σμικρότητος) +
9  150c1 αὐτοῦ (μεγέθους) +

10  150c4 αὐτὸ (μέγεθος) +
11  150c5 αὐτῆς (σμικρότητος) +
12  150c5–6 αὐτοῦ (μεγέθους) +
13  153c3–4 αὐτοῦ (τοῦ ἑνὸς) +
14  153d1–2 αὐτὸ (τὸ ἕν) +
15  153e6 αὐτὸ (τὸ ἕν) +

**S2C**

1  156d5 (ἡ ἐξαίφνης) αὕτη (φύσις) +

**S3**

1  158a2–3 καθ' αὐτὸ +
2  158a5 αὐτῷ (τῷ ἑνὶ) +
3  158c5 αὐτὴν καθ' αὑτὴν (τὴν ἑτέραν φύσιν τοῦ εἴδους) +
4  158d6 (ἡ ... ἑαυτῶν φύσις) καθ' ἑαυτὰ +

## εἶδος

**S2**

1  149e7 τῷ εἴδει 0+ general consideration, affirmed 149e8–9
2  149e9 εἴδη +

**S3**

1  158c6 τοῦ εἴδους 0+ counted as positive since εἶδος refers to the positive determination of all μόρια afterwards (158c7–d8) as opposed

to the ἕτερα φύσις without any determination (158c1–4)

**S4**

1  159e5 εἴδη 0– hypothetical consideration, negated 159e6–8
2  160a1 εἴδη 0– hypothetical consideration, negated 159e6–8

ἰδέα

S3
1    157d8 ἰδέας +


φύσις

S1
1    139d2 φύσις +
2    139e9 τὴν φύσιν +

S2
1    147e5 τῇ φύσει +
2    153b8 φύσιν 0+  παρὰ remains
     hypothetical, affirmed 153d1–4
3    153d2 φύσιν +
4    153e6 φύσιν +

S2C
1    156d5 ἡ (ἐξαίφνης αὕτη) φύσις 0+
     general consideration, affirmed
     156e5

S3
1    158c6 τὴν ... φύσιν +
2    158d6 φύσις +
3    158e2 τὴν ... φύσιν +


φύω

S2
1    145e7 πεφυκὸς 0+  general consid-
     eration, affirmed 146a6–7
2    153d1 πέφυκε +

3    153d3 πεφυκὸς +
4    153e6 πέφυκεν +


μετέχω, μέθεξις

S1
1    137e1 μετέχει –
2    137e6 μετέχοι 0–  hypothetical
     consideration, negated 137d8–e1
     (cf. also 137c4–6)
3    138a6 μετέχοντος –
4    140c5 μετέχον 0–  general con-
     sideration, negated 140c6–d7
5    140d4 μετέχον –
6    140d5 μετέχον –
7    140e4 μεθέξει 0–  hypothetical
     consideration, negated 140b4–5;
     140d6; 141a5–6
8    140c7 μετέχει
9    141d1 μετέχει 0–  general defini-
     tion, negated 141d3–5
10   141d8 μέθεξιν 0–  general defini-
     tion, negated 141d3–5; 141e3–7
11   141e4 μετέχει –
12   141e8 μετάσχοι 0–  general con-
     sideration, negated 141e9
13   141e9 μετέχει –

14   141e11 μετέχον 0–  hypothetical
     consideration, negated 141e9

S2
1    142b6 μετέχειν 0+  rhetorical ques-
     tion, affirmed 142c5–7; 143a4–5
2    142c1 μετεῖχεν 0+  hypothetical
     consideration, affirmed 142c5–7;
     143a4–5
3    142c6 μετέχει +
4    143a4 μετέχειν +
5    143a7 μετέχειν +
6    143a8 μετέχειν 0+  hypothetical
     and negative to some degree, but
     affirmed 143a4–7; 143b2–3
7    143b3 μετέσχεν +
8    144a7 μετέχων +
9    144a8 μετέχει +
10   144a9 μετέχοι +
11   145b4 μετέχοι +
12   146e7 μετέχοντα –

13  147a3 μετέχει –
14  147a7 μετεῖχε 0+  one of two
    possibilities, affirmed 147a8
15  149c6 μετέχει –
16  151e3 μετέχει 0+  question,
    affirmed 152a2–3
17  151e6 μετέχον 0+  question,
    affirmed 152e8–10; 155c6–7
18  151e8 μέθεξις 0+  general defini-
    tion, affirmed 152a2–3
19  152a2 μετέχει +
20  153a5 μετέχοι +
21  155c8 μετέχει +
22  155d2 μετέχειν +
23  155d3 μετέχει +

S2C

1   155e6 μετέχον +
2   155e7 μετέχειν +
3   155e7 μετέχειν –
4   155e8 μετέχει +
5   155e9 μετέχειν 0–  hypothetical
    consideration, counted as negative
    in the sense of the chiasm 155e8–9
6   155e9 μετέχει –
7   155e9 μετέχειν 0+  hypothetical
    consideration, counted as positive
    in the sense of the chiasm 155e8–9
8   155e10 μετέχει +
9   155e10 μετέχει –
10  155e11 μετέχοι +
11  155e11 μετέχοι –

S3

1   157c2 μετέχει +
2   157e3 μετέχοι +
3   157e6 μετέχειν +
4   158a3 μετέχοι +
5   158a4 μετεῖχεν 0+  hypothetical
    consideration, affirmed 157e5–6
6   158a6 μετέχειν +
7   158b1 μεθέξει +
8   158b2 τὰ μετέχοντα +
9   158b6 μετέχοντα +

10  158b8 μετέχοντα –  describes the
    moment before participation
11  158c4 μετέχοι 0–  hypothetical
    consideration with negative
    implication, yet also affirmed
    158a6–7; 158d6–8
12  158d8 μετέχει +
13  158e4 μετέχει +

S4

1   159d1 μετέχοι –
2   159d2 μετέχοντα –
3   159d7 μετέχει –
4   159e7 μετέχειν 0–  here, and
    second occurrence in 159e7:
    hypothetical consideration,
    negated 159d1–4
5   159e7 μετέχοι 0–
6   160a2 μετέχοι 0–  hypothetical
    consideration, negated 159e8
7   160a8 μεθέξει 0–  hypothetical
    consideration, negated 160a8–b1
8   160b1 μετέχειν –

S5

1   160e4 μετέχει +
2   160e8 μετέχειν +
3   161c9 μετέχει +
4   161e3 μετέχειν +
5   162a7 μετέχοντα 0+  general con-
    sideration, affirmed 162b3–7

S6

1   163c7 μετέχει 0–  here, and 163d1:
    general consideration, negated
    163c8–d1; 163d8
2   163d1 μετέχειν 0–
3   163d8 μετέχει –
4   164a1 μετέχον 0–  here, and
    second occurrence in 164a1:
    hypothetical consideration,
    negated 163c8–d1; 163d8
5   164a1 μετέχοι 0–

λαμβάνω, μεταλαμβάνω

Without counting those occurrences where the subjective act of grasping something is denoted (143a7; 164d2; 165a8; 165b3–4; 165b5; 165b6).

S2

1   152c2 ληφθείη 0+ hypothetical
    negation, affirmed 152c3–6
2   154d5 λαμβάνον +

S2C

1   156a1 μεταλαμβάνει +
2   156a4 λαμβάνη +
3   156a4–5 μεταλαμβάνειν 0+ gen-
    eral definition, affirmed 156a7–b1
4   156a7 λαμβάνον +

S3

1   158b7 τὰ μεταλαμβάνοντα +
2   158b9 μεταλαμβάνει – describes
    the moment before participation
3   158b9 μεταλαμβάνει +

S6

1   163d2 τὸ ... μεταλαμβάνειν 0–
    here, and 163d4: general definition,
    negated 163d5–8
2   163d4 λαμβάνοι 0–


γίγνομαι, προσγίγνομαι, ἐγγίγνομαι

Occurrences marked with * are paired with ἀπόλλυμι.

S1

1   138d3 γίγνεται 0– general
    hypothetical consideration,
    negated 139a2–3; 139b3
2   138d5 γίγνεσθαι 0– general
    and slightly rhetorical question,
    negated 138e7–139a3
3   138d6 γίγνεται 0– from here to
    138e7: general hypothetical consid-
    eration, negated 138e7–139a3; 139b3
4   138d7 ἐγγιγνόμενον 0–
5   138d8 ἐγγίγνεται 0–
6   138e6 ἐγγίγνεσθαί 0–
7   138e7 ἐγγιγνόμενον 0–
8   139a1 γιγνόμενον –
9   139d3 γένηταί 0– from here to
    139d7: general hypothetical con-
    sideration, negated 139e1–4
10  139d4 γίγνεται 0–
11  139d4–5 γενόμενον 0–
12  139d5 γίγνεσθαι 0–
13  139d7 ἐγίγνετο 0–
14  139d7 ἐγίγνετο 0–
15  140d2–3 γίγνοιτο 0– hypothetical
    consideration, negated 140d3–4
16  141a7 γίγνεσθαι 0– hypothetical
    consideration, negated 141a5–6
17  141b1 γιγνόμενον 0– from here
    to 141d3: general consideration,
    negated 141d3–5

18  141b2 γίγνεται 0–
19  141b3 γίγνηται 0–
20  141b4 γίγνεσθαι 0–
21  141b5 γεγονότος 0–
22  141b5 γεγονέναι 0–
23  141b6 γιγνομένου 0–
24  141b6 γεγονέναι 0–
25  141b7 γίγνεσθαι 0–
26  141c3 γιγνόμενον 0–
27  141c4 γίγνεσθαι 0–
28  141c5 γίγνεσθαι 0–
29  141c6 γίγνεσθαι 0–
30  141c6–7 γεγονέναι 0–
31  141d3 γίγνεσθαι 0–
32  141d7 γέγονε 0– from here to
    141e1: general consideration,
    negated 141e3–7
33  141d7 ἐγίγνετο 0–
34  141d8 γεγονότος 0–
35  141e1 γενήσεται 0–
36  141e1 γενηθήσεται 0–
37  141e3 γίγνεται 0– general
    definition, negated 141e3–7
38  141e5 γέγονεν –
39  141e5 ἐγίγνετο –
40  141e5 γέγονεν –
41  141e6 γίγνεται –
42  141e6 γενήσεται –
43  141e6–7 γενηθήσεται –

S2

1   142d5 γίγνεσθαι +
2   142e4 γίγνεται +
3   142e6 γένηται +
4   143a1 γιγνόμενον +
5   143d7 γίγνεται +
6   144a7 γίγνεται +
7   149a1 γένοιτο +
8   149a8 προσγένηται 0+ from here
    to 149c1: general consideration,
    affirmed 148e10–149a1; 149c2–3
9   149b2 προσγιγνομένου 0+
10  149b2 προσγίγνεται 0+
11  149c1 προσγίγνεται 0+
12  150a1 ἐγγιγνοίσθην 0+ hypotheti-
    cal consideration, affirmed 149e8–9
13  150a2 ἐγγίγνεται +
14  150a3 ἐγγίγνοιτο 0– general con-
    sideration, negated for σμικρότης
    150b1–2
15  150b6 ἐγγιγνομένη –
16  151e3–4 γίγνεται 0+ question, af-
    firmed 152b1–2; 152e2–3; 155c4–6
    (but also negated 155c6–7)
17  152a4 γίγνεται +
18  152a6 γιγνομένου 0+ here, and
    152a7: general consideration,
    affirmed 152b1–2; 152e2–3
19  152a7 γίγνεται 0+
20  152a8 γίγνεται +
21  152a8 γιγνομένου +
22  152b1 γίγνοιτο +
23  152b1 γίγνεται +
24  152b3 γιγνόμενον +
25  152b6 γίγνεσθαι +
26  152c1 γίγνεται –
27  152c5 γιγνόμενον 0+ general
    consideration, affirmed 152c1 with
    152c6–d2
28  152c7 τὸ γιγνόμενον 0+ general
    consideration, affirmed 152c1
29  152d1 τοῦ γίγνεσθαι 0– general
    consideration, negated 152d3
30  152d2 γιγνόμενον 0+ general
    consideration, affirmed 152c1
31  152d3 γιγνόμενον +
32  152d3 τοῦ γίγνεσθαι –
33  152d4 ἐγίγνετο +
34  152d5 ἐγίγνετο +
35  152d8 γιγνόμενον +

36  152e2 γίγνεται +
37  152e4 γίγνεται 0+ here, and
    152e5: general consideration,
    affirmed 152e2–3; 152e8
38  152e5 γιγνόμενον 0+
39  152e8 γιγνόμενον +
40  152e9–10 γίγνεται –
41  153a6 γίγνεσθαί 0+ here, and
    second occurrence in 153d6: gener-
    al consideration, affirmed 153b1–3
42  153a6 γεγονέναι 0+
43  153b2 γέγονε +
44  153b4 γεγονὸς 0+ from here to
    153b6: general consideration,
    affirmed 153b6–7
45  153b4 γέγονε 0+
46  153b5 γεγονότα 0+
47  153b6 γεγονότος 0+
48  153c1 γεγονός +
49  153c3 γίγνεται +
50  153c7 γεγονέναι +
51  153c8 γίγνεται +
52  153d1 γίγνεσθαι +
53  153d2 γίγνεσθαι 0+ hypothetical
    consideration, affirmed 153c8 d1;
    153d2–3; 153e6
54  153d2 γεγονὸς +
55  153d3 γίγνεσθαι +
56  153d8 τῷ ... γιγνομένῳ +
57  153d8 γίγνοιτ᾽ +
58  153e1–2 τῶν ... γιγνομένων +
59  153e2 προσγίγνηται +
60  153e3 γένηται +
61  153e7 γεγονὸς + counted as
    positive since ἅμα is affirmed
62  154a5 γεγονός +
63  154a5 τοῦ γίγνεσθαι 0+ general
    question, affirmed 155c4–6
64  154a7 γίγνεσθαι 0– general
    question, negated 154c3–4
    (but also affirmed 155c4–6)
65  154a8 τοῦ γίγνεσθαι 0+ general
    question, affirmed 155c4–6
66  154b2 γίγνεσθαί 0– general
    consideration, negated 154c3–4
67  154b2–3 τὸ ... γενόμενον 0+
    general consideration, concept
    used as such
68  154b4 γίγνεσθαι 0– general
    consideration, negated 154c3–4

69  154b7 γίγνοιτ᾽ –
70  154c2 γέγονε +
71  154c3 γίγνεται –
72  154c4 γίγνεται –
73  154c6 γίγνεται 0+ general ques-
     tion, affirmed 154e3–4
74  154c8 γέγονεν +
75  154e1 γίγνοιτ᾽ 0+ from here to
     155a3: general consideration,
     affirmed 155c4–6
76  154e5 γεγονὸς 0+
77  154e5 γίγνεται 0+
78  154e6 γεγονός 0+
79  154e7 γίγνεται 0+
80  155a1 γίγνεται 0+
81  155a3 γίγνεσθον 0+
82  155a5 γενέσθαι 0– from here to
     155d6: hypothetical consideration,
     obviously counterfactual
83  155a5 γένοιντο 0–
84  155a6 γίγνοιντο 0–
85  155a6 γίγνονται +
86  155a8 γίγνεται +
87  155b1 γεγονός +
88  155b2 γέγονε +
89  155b4 γεγονότα +
90  155b5 γίγνεται 0– general con-
     sideration, negated 155b7
91  155b7 γίγνοιτ᾽ –
92  155c1 γενόμενα 0+ here, and
     155c3: general consideration,
     affirmed 155c4–6
93  155c3 γίγνεσθαι 0+
94  155c6 γίγνεται +
95  155c7 γίγνεται –
96  155d1 γίγνεσθαι +
97  155d4 ἐγίγνετο +
98  155d4 γίγνεται +
99  155d4 γενήσεται +

S2C
1*  156a5 γίγνεσθαι 0+ general defini-
     tion, affirmed 156a7–b1
2*  156a7 γίγνεταί +
3*  156b2 γιγνόμενον +
4*  156b2 γίγνηται +
5   156b4 γιγνόμενον +
6   156b6 γίγνηται +
7*  157a1 τὸ γίγνεσθαι +
8*  157a2 γίγνεται +
9   157a3 γίγνεται –

S3
1   157e1 γεγονός +
2   158d1 γένηται +
3   158d5 γίγνεσθαι +

S4
1*  160a5 γιγνόμενα –

S5
1*  163a8 γίγνεσθαι 0+ general con-
     sideration, affirmed 163b3; 163b4
2*  163b1 γίγνεσθαι 0– general con-
     sideration, negated 163b4; 163b5
3*  163b3 γίγνεταί +
4*  163b4 γίγνεται –
5*  163b4 γίγνεταί +
6*  163b5 γίγνεται –

S6
1*  163d1 τὸ … γίγνεσθαι 0– general
     definition (cf. S2C 156a5), negated
     163d7–8
2*  163d7 γίγνεται –
3*  163e1 γίγνοιτό 0– hypothetical
     consideration, negated 163d7–8

S7
1*  165d7 γιγνομένους + in the mode
     of φαίνεσθαι (cf. 165d4)


ἀπόλλυμι
Occurrences marked with * are paired with γίγνομαι.

S2C
1*  156a6 ἀπόλλυσθαι 0+ general
     definition, affirmed 156b1
2*  156b1 ἀπόλλυται +
3*  156b2 ἀπολλύμενον +

4*  156b3 ἀπόλλυται +
5*  156b4 ἀπόλλυται +
6*  156e8 τὸ ἀπόλλυσθαι +
7*  157a3 ἀπόλλυται –

S4
1* 160a5 ἀπολλύμενα -

S5
1* 163a8 ἀπόλλυσθαι 0+ general consideration, affirmed 163b3; 163b5
2* 163b2 ἀπόλλυσθαι 0- general
consideration, negated 163b4;
163b5
3* 163b3 ἀπόλλυται +
4* 163b4 ἀπόλλυται -
5* 163b5 ἀπόλλυται +
6* 163b5 ἀπόλλυται -

S6
1* 163d1-2 τὸ ἀπόλλυσθαι 0-
here, and 163d3: general definition
(cf. S2C 156a6), negated 163d7-8
2 163d3 ἀπολλύναι 0-
3 163d4 ἀπολλύοι 0- general consideration, negated 163d7-8
4* 163d7 ἀπόλλυται -
5* 163e1 ἀπολλύοιτο 0- hypothetical
consideration, negated 163d7-8

S7
1* 165d7 ἀπολλυμένους +

μεταβάλλω, μεταβολή

S2C
1 156c2 μεταβάλλῃ +
2 156c4-5 μεταβάλλειν 0+ from
here to 156d4: general consideration, affirmed 156e3-5
3 156c7 μεταβάλλει 0+
4 156c8 τοῦ μεταβάλλειν 0+
5 156c8 μεταβάλλει 0+
6 156c9 μεταβάλλει 0+
7 156d2 μεταβάλλει 0+
8 156d4 μεταβάλλον 0+
9 156d5 μεταβάλλει 0- here, and
156d6: negated with regard to the
moment of transition, yet generally
affirmed 156e3-5
10 156d6 μεταβάλλει 0-
11 156e2 μεταβάλλει 0+ general
consideration, affirmed 156e3-5

12 156e4 μεταβάλλοι +
13 156e5 μεταβάλλον +
14 156e5 μεταβάλλει +
15 156e6 μεταβάλλει +
16 156e8 μεταβολὰς +
17 157a1 μεταβάλλῃ +

S5
1 162b9 μεταβάλλον 0+ from
here to 162c2: general consideration (162b9 is considered to be
a rhetorical question), affirmed
162c4-6
2 162c1 μεταβολὴν 0+
3 162c2 μεταβολὴ 0+
4 162c5 μεταβολὴν +

ἀλλοιόω, ἀλλοίωσις, ἀλλοῖος

S1
1 138c1 ἀλλοιοῖτο 0- hypothetical consideration und definition,
negated 138c3; 139a1-3
2 138c1-2 ἀλλοιούμενον 0-
hypothetical consideration, negated
138c3; 139a1-3
3 138c3 ἀλλοίωσίν -
4 139a2 ἀλλοιούμενον -

S2
1 142b2 ἀλλοῖον 0+ general consideration with regard to S2; counted

as positive since S2 shows obviously
something ἀλλοῖον to S1
2 148c4 ἀλλοῖον -
3 148c5 ἀλλοῖον -
4 148c6 ἀλλοῖον +
5 148c6 ἀλλοῖον +

S5
1 161a8 ἀλλοῖα 0+ here, and in
161a8 twice: rhetorical question,
affirmed 161b1-4
2 161a8 τὰ ... ἀλλοῖα 0+

3   162d6 ἀλλοιοῦταί –
4   162d7 ἠλλοιοῦτο 0– hypothetical
    formulation of another hypothesis,
    negated 162d7
5   162d9 ἀλλοιοῦταί –
6   162e4–163a1 ἀλλοιοῦσθαι +
7   162a3 ἀλλοιοῦταί +
8   162a4 ἀλλοιοῖτο 0– general
    consideration, negated 163a5
9   162a5 ἀλλοιοῦταί +
10   162a5 ἀλλοιοῦταί –
11   162a6 ἀλλοιοῦταί +
12   162a6–7 ἀλλοιοῦταί –

13   163a7 τὸ ... ἀλλοιούμενον
    0+ general consideration, affirmed
    163b2–3
14   163b1 τὸ ... ἀλλοιούμενον 0–
    general consideration, negated
    163b3–4
15   163b2–3 ἀλλοιούμενον +
16   163b3 ἀλλοιούμενον –

S6

1   163e1 ἀλλοιοῦται –
2   163e2 ἀλλοιοῦται –

## μεταβαίνω

S2

1   146a1 μεταβαῖνον 0– general con-
    sideration, negated to define rest of
    the One (cf. 145e7–8; 146a7)

S5

1   162d1 μεταβαίνειν –
2   162d9 μεταβαίνει –

S7

1   165a3 μετέβαινεν + in the mode
    of δοξάζω, the negation is rhetori-
    cal to affirm reaching ἴσος
    (cf. 165a1–2)

## μεθίστημι

S5

1   162c8 μεθίσταιτό –

## ἀπαλλάττω, ἀφίημι

S2

1   152c4 ἀφιέμενον +

S2C

1   156a2 ἀπαλλάττεται +

2   156a4 ἀφίῃ +
3   156a6 ἀπαλλάττεσθαι 0+ general
    definition, affirmed 156a7–b1
4   156a7 ἀφιὲν +

## αὐξάνω

S2C

1   156b8 αὐξάνεσθαί +

2   157b2 αὐξανόμενον –

## φθίω

S2C

1   156b8 φθίνειν +

2   157b3 φθῖνον –

φαίνω

Occurrences marked with * are those where the appearance of the subject in question is denoted.

S1

1   138d5 ἐφάνη ο from here to
    140d3: remark on the argument
2   139e9 ἐφάνη ο
3   140d3 ἐφάνη ο

S2

1   142b2 φανῇ ο here, and 143a6:
    remark on the following argument
2   143a6 ἐφάνη ο
3   143a8–9 φανήσεται ο remark on
    the present and following argument
4   146c7 ἐφάνη ο from here to
    148d3: remark on the argument
5   147c2 ἐφάνη ο
6   148a8 ἐφάνη ο
7   148b3 ἐφάνη ο
8   148d3 ἐφάνη ο
9*  148d4 φανήσεται ο+ could also be
    meant with regard to the argument
    itself (sc. 'it will turn out as';
    cf. 148d3; 148d7)
10  148d7 ἐφάνη ο remark on the
    argument itself
11* 151d6 φαίνεται +
12  153c2 ἐφάνη ο from here to
    155b3: remark on the argument
13  154c6 ἐφάνη ο
14  155a8 ἐφάνη ο
15  155b3 ἐφάνη ο

S3

1   159b1 ἐφάνη ο remark on the
    argument itself

S4

1   160a3 ἐφάνη ο here, and 160b1:
    remark on the argument itself
2   160b1 ἐφάνη ο

S5

1*  162b6 φαίνεται +
2   162c3 ἐφάνη ο from here to
    162c5: remark on the argument
3   162c4 φαίνεται ο
4   162c5 πέφανται ο

S6

1   163b8 φανεῖται ο remark on the
    forthcoming argument itself

S7

1*  164d2 φαίνεται +
2*  164d7 φαινόμενος +
3*  164e3 φαίνεται +
4*  164e5 φαίνεται +
5*  165a3–4 φαινόμενος + the
    negation refers to μετέβαινεν
    ἐκ μείζονος εἰς ἔλαττον,
    while φαινόμενος is parallel to
    δοξασθήσεται (165a2) and δόξειεν
    (165a4)
6*  165b1 φαίνεται +
7*  165c1 φαίνεσθαι +
8*  165c2 φανῆναι +
9*  165c5 φαίνεσθαι +
10* 165c7–8 φαινόμενα +
11* 165c8 φαίνεσθαι +
12* 165d4 φαίνεσθαι +

S8

1*  166a1 φαίνεται –
2*  166b6 φαινόμενα – this refers
    back to S7, still S8 clearly negates
    these appearances (cf. 166b7)
3*  166b7 φαίνεται –

δοκέω

Occurrences marked with * are those where the appearance of the subject in question is denoted.

S1

1   140e2 δοκεῖ ο directed towards
    Aristotle (sc. 'does it seem to you',
    'do you think that …'); negative
    tendency possible, cf. 141a2–4

2  141d8 δοκεῖ ο directed towards
Aristotle (sc. 'does it seem to you',
'do you think that ...'); negative
tendency could be ascribed,
cf. negation 141e3–7

S7
1* 164d1–2 τὸ ... δοκοῦν +

2* 164d3 δόξαντος 0+ the negation
refers primarily to ἑνὸς versus
πολλά since φαίνεται (164d2) still
preserves the mode of appearance
3* 164e1 δόξει +
4* 164e4 δόξει +
5* 165a4 δόξειεν +
6* 165c6 δόξει +

ὄγκος

S7
1  164d1 ὁ ὄγκος +
2  164d5 ὄγκων +
3  164d7 ὄγκοι +
4  165a2 ὄγκος +

5  165a5 ὄγκον +
6  165b6 ὄγκος +
7  165d3 τοὺς ὄγκους +

ὄναρ, ὕπνος

S7
1  164d2 ὄναρ +

2  164d2 ὕπνῳ +

φάντασμα

S7
1  165a5 φάντασμα +
2  165d2 τῷ ... φαντάσματι +

S8
1  166a5 φάντασμα –

σκιαγραφέω

S7
1  165c7 ἐσκιαγραφημένα +

κίνησις, κινέω

S1
1  138b7–8 κινεῖσθαι 0– general
consideration and question,
negated 138c3; 139a2–3; 139b3
2  138b8 κινούμενόν 0– hypothetical
consideration, negated 138c3;
139a2–3; 139b3
3  138c1 κινήσεις 0– general definition, negated 138c3; 139a2–3
4  138c3 κινεῖται –
5  138d3 κινεῖται 0– general
hypothetical consideration,
negated 139a2–3; 139b3

6  139a3 κίνησιν –
7  139a3 ἀκίνητον – counted as
negation due to *alpha privativum*
8  139b3 κινεῖται –

S2
1  145e7 κινεῖσθαι 0+ general
question, affirmed 146a6–7
2  146a6 κινεῖσθαι 0+ general
consideration, affirmed 146a6–7
3  146a7 κινεῖσθαί +

S2C

1  156c1 κινούμενόν +
2  156c1–2 τὸ κινεῖσθαι +
3  156c3 κινεῖσθαι o+ here, and
156c4: general consideration,
affirmed 156e3–5 (though also
negated 156e6–7 with regard to
the sudden transition)
4  156c4 κινούμενον o+
5  156c6 κινεῖσθαι o– general consideration, negated with regard to
not being in time at the moment of
sudden transition, cf. 156e6–7
6  156c9 κινούμενον o– negated with
regard to the moment of transition,
cf. 156e6–7
7  156d5 κινήσεως o– negated to
define the moment of sudden
transition
8  156d5 κινουμένης o– negated
to define the moment of sudden
transition
9  156d7 κινήσεώς o+ general consideration, affirmed with regard to
156e3–4
10  156e1–2 τό ... κινούμενον
o+ here, and 156e2–3: general
consideration, affirmed 156e3–5
11  156e2–3 τὸ κινεῖσθαι o+
12  156e4 κινεῖται +
13  156e6 κινοῖτ’ – negated in the
moment of sudden transition
14  157a2 κινήσεών o+ affirmed with
regard to 156e3–4

S3

1  159a7 κινούμενα +

S4

1  160a4 κινούμενα –

S5

1  162c2 κίνησις o+ general definition, affirmed 162c4–5
2  162c4–5 κινούμενον +
3  162d1 κινοῖτ’ –
4  162e1 κινοῖτο o– rhetorical
question, clear negative tendency
(though affirmed in 162e3–4)
5  162e1 τό ... ἀκίνητον o– counted
as negation of κίνητος; affirmed as
‘rest’ in 162e3
6  162e3 κινεῖται +
7  162e4 κινεῖται +
8  163a1 κινηθῇ o+ general consideration, affirmed 162e2–3; 163a2–3
9  163a2 κινούμενον +
10  163a3 κινούμενον o– general consideration, negated 163a5
11  163a4 κινεῖται +
12  163a5 κινεῖται –

S6

1  163e3 κινεῖσθαι –
2  163e6 κινεῖσθαι –

S7

1  165d6 κινουμένους + in the mode
of φαίνεσθαι (165d4)
2  165d6 κινήσεις + in the mode of
φαίνεσθαι (165d4)


φέρω, περιφέρω

S1

1  138b8 φέροιτο o– from here to
138d2: hypothetical consideration,
negated 138e7–139a2
2  138c4 τῷ φέρεσθαι o–
3  138c5 φέροιτο o–
4  138c5 περιφέροιτο o–
5  138c7 περιφερόμενον o–
6  138c8 φερόμενα o–
7  138d2 ἐνεχθῆναι o–
8  139a1–2 περιφερόμενον –

ἀλλάττω, μεταλλάττω, ἀμείβω

S1
1  138c5–6 μεταλλάττοι 0–  here,
   and 138d3: hypothetical consideration, negated 138e7–139a2

2  138d3 ἀμεῖβον 0–
3  139a1 ἀλλάττει –

στρέφω

S5
1  162d2 στρέφοιτο –
2  162d4 στρέφεσθαι –

3  162d9 στρέφεται –

στάσις, ἡσυχία, ἡσυχάζω, ἵστημι

S1
1  138b7 ἑστάναι 0–  general consideration and question, negated
   139b2–3
2  139b1 ἡσυχίαν 0–  here, and
   139b2: general consideration,
   negated 139b2–3
3  139b2 ἕστηκεν 0–
4  139b3 ἕστηκεν –

S2
1  145e8 ἑστάναι 0+  general question, affirmed 145e8; 146a6–7
2  145e8 ἕστηκε +
3  146a3 ἑστὸς 0+  general consideration, affirmed 145e8; 146a6–7
4  146a5 ἑστάναι 0–  here, and second occurrence in 146a5: difficult
   reasoning, but 'rest' is obviously
   negated to reach the affirmation of
   κίνησις in 146a6–7
5  146a5 ἑστὸς 0–
6  146a7 ἑστάναι +

S2C
1  156c1 ἵστηται +
2  156c1 ἑστὸς +
3  156c3 ἑστός 0+  here, and 156c4:
   general consideration, affirmed
   156e3–5 (though also negated
   156e6–7 with regard to the sudden
   transition)
4  156c4 ἑστάναι 0+
5  156c7 ἑστάναι 0–  general consideration, negated with regard to not

being in time at the moment of
sudden transition, cf. 156e6–7
6  156c9 ἑστὸς 0–  negated with
   regard to the moment of transition,
   cf. 156e6–7
7  156d4–5 τοῦ ἑστάναι 0–  here,
   and 156d5: negated to define the
   moment of sudden transition
8  156d5 ἑστῶτος 0–
9  156d7 στάσεως 0+  from here
   to 156e2: general consideration,
   affirmed with regard to 156e3–5
10  156e2 τὸ ἑστάναι 0+
11  156e2 τὸ ἑστὸς 0+
12  156e3 ἕστηκέ +
13  156e7 σταίη –  negated in the
   moment of sudden transition
14  157a2 στάσεων 0+  affirmed with
   regard to 156e3–4

S3
1  159a7 ἑστῶτα +

S4
1  160a4 ἑστῶτα –

S5
1  162e2 ἡσυχίαν 0+  from here to
   162e2 (twice): general consideration, affirmed 162e2–3
2  162e2 τὸ ... ἡσυχάζον 0+
3  162e2 ἑστάναι 0+
4  162e3 ἕστηκέ +

S6
1   163e3 ἑστάναι –
2   163e4 τὸ ... ἑστὸς 0– hypothetical
    negated 163e3–4; 163e5–6
3   163e6 ἑστάναι –

S7
1   165d6 ἑστῶτας + in the mode of
    φαίνεσθαι (165d4)


πόλυς

Excluding the reoccurring formula πολλὴ ἀνάγκη (cf. also 138e5).


S1
1   137c4 πολλὰ –
2   137d1 πολλὰ 0– hypothetical
    consideration, negated 137d1–2 et
    passim
3   137d2 πολλὰ –
4   137e5 πολλὰ 0– hypothetical
    consideration, negated 137d1–2;
    137d2–3
5   138a5 πολλοῖς 0– hypothetical
    consideration, negated 138a5–7
6   139d4 τοῖς πολλοῖς 0– here, and
    139d5: general hypothetical consid-
    eration, negated 139e4–5
7   139d5 πολλὰ 0–
8   140a2 πλείω 0– hypothetical
    consideration, negated immediately
    after 140a2–3
9   140a7 πλείω 0– hypothetical
    consideration, negated 140a2–3;
    cf. the negation afterwards 140b4–5
10  140c2 πλείω 0– here, and 140c8:
    hypothetical consideration, negated
    140d4–7
11  140c8 πλειόνων 0– hypothetical
    consideration, negated 140d4–7
12  140d5 πολλῶν –
13  141c5 πλείω 0– general considera-
    tion, negated 141d3–5

S2
1   143a5 πολλὰ +
2   143a9 πολλὰ 0– difficult; negated
    (only) by Aristotle; said about αὐτὸ
    τὸ ἕν (143c9); but cf. also the affir-
    mation 144e5–7 (perhaps 143a7–9
    refers back to the One of S1)
3   144a5 πολλὰ +
4   144c1 πλεῖστα + affirmed,
    but cf. 144d6–7

5   144b1 πολλὰ +
6   144d6 πλεῖστα –
7   144d7 πλείω –
8   144e4 πολλά +
9   144e5 πολλά +
10  144e7 πολλὰ +
11  145a2 πολλά +
12  145c2 πλέον –
13  145d6 τὸ πλέον 0– hypothetical
    consideration, negated directly
    afterwards 145d6
14  145d7 πλέοσιν –
15  147d4 πολλάκις 0+ from here to
    147e1: linguistic consideration;
    used affirmatively, no indication
    of negation
16  147d5 πολλάκις 0+
17  147e1 πολλάκις 0+
18  149b5 (τὸ) πλείω (εἶναι) 0+
19  151b8 πλειόνων +
20  151c2 πλειόνων +
21  151c3 πλέον +
22  151c5 πλειόνων +
23  151d1 πλειόνων +
24  151d3 πλειόνων +
25  151d3 πλέον +
26  151d6 πλέον +
27  151e1 πλέον +
28  152e3 πλείω 0– question, counted
    as negative since second alternative
    is affirmed
29  153a2 πλείω +
30  153a3 πλείω +
31  153a4 πλείονος +
32  153a6 τὰ πλείω 0– question,
    counted as negative since the sec-
    ond alternative (τὰ ἐλάττω 153a4)
    is affirmed
33  154c8 πλείω +

34  154d1 πλέονι 0+  here, and 154d3:
    difficult to decide; general consid-
    eration, counted as positive due to
    154d4–7
35  154d3 τὸ πλέον 0+

S2C
1   155e5 πολλὰ +
2   155e6 πολλὰ –
3   156b1 πολλὰ +
4   156b3 (τὸ) πολλὰ (εἶναι) –
    counted as negative due to
    ἀπόλλυται (156b3)
5   156b3 πολλά +
6   156b4 πολλὰ +
7   157a5 πολλὰ +
8   157a5 πολλῶν 0+  might also be
    counted as negative
9   157a6 πολλά –

S3
1   157c6 πολλῶν +
2   157c7 πολλῶν –
3   157c8 πολλῶν 0–  hypothetical
    consideration, negated for μόριον
    in 157c7–8
4   157d5 τῶν πολλῶν –
5   157d7 τῶν πολλῶν –
6   158b3 πολλά +
7   158b3 πλείω +  hypothetical to
    some extent, but affirmed 158b5
8   158b5 πλείω +

S4
1   159d4 πολλά –
2   159d5 πολλὰ 0–  hypothetical
    consideration, negated 159d1–4
3   159d6 πολλὰ –

S5
1   160e8 πολλῶν +
2   161a5 (ἄλλων) πολλῶν +

S7
1   164d3 πολλὰ +  in the mode of
    δόξαντος (164d3)
2   164d7 πολλοὶ (ὄγκοι) +  each one
    of them in the mode of φαινόμενος
    (164d7)
3   164e1 πολλῶν +  in the mode of
    δόξει (164e1)
4   164e5 πολλὰ +  in the mode of
    φαίνεται (164e5)
5   164e5–165a1 τῶν ... πολλῶν +  in
    the mode of φαίνεται (164e5)
6   165a2 τοῖς πολλοῖς +  in the mode
    of δοξασθήσεται (165a2)
7   165c4 πολλὰ +  in the mode of
    φαίνεσθαι (165c5)
8   165d1 πολλὰ +  in the mode of
    φαίνεσθαι (165c8)
9   165e1 πολλὰ +

S8
1   165e5 πολλά –
2   165e5 πολλοῖς 0–  here, and
    165e7: hypothetical consideration,
    negated 165e7–8
3   165e7 πολλὰ 0–
4   165e8 πολλὰ –
5   166a1 πολλά –  negation of the
    mode of φαίνεται (166a1)
6   166b1 πολλά –
7   166b1 πολλὰ 0–  hypothetical
    consideration, negated 166a7–b1
8   166b3 πολλά –


ἄπειρος, ἀπέραντος, ἀπειρία

S1
1   137d7 ἄπειρον +

S2
1   143a2 ἄπειρον +
2   144a6 ἄπειρον +
3   144a6 ἄπειρος 0+  rhetorical
    question, clearly positive

4   144c1 ἀπέραντα +
5   144e4 ἄπειρα +
6   145a3 ἄπειρον +

S3
1   158b6 ἄπειρα +
2   158c6 ἄπειρον +  said about τὴν
    ἑτέραν φύσιν τοῦ εἴδους (158c6)

3  158d6 ἀπειρίαν +
4  158d7 ἄπειρά +
5  158e2 ἄπειρά +
6  158e6 ἄπειρα +

S7
1  164d1 ἄπειρός +
2  165c2 ἄπειρον + in the mode of
   φανῆναι (165c2)
3  165c4 ἄπειρά + in the mode of
   φαίνεσθαι (165c5)

πλῆθος, πλεονάκις, πλεονεκτέω

S2
1  143a2 τὸ πλῆθος +
2  144a6 πλῆθος +
3  144a6 πλήθει + rhetorical question, clearly positive
4  144e4–5 τὸ πλῆθός +
5  145a3 πλήθει +
6  147d2–3 πλεονάκις 0+ linguistic
   consideration; used affirmatively,
   no indication of negation
7  149b3 τοῦ πλήθους 0+ from here
   to 149b6: general consideration,
   affirmed 149c2–3
8  149b4 ἐπλεονέκτησεν 0+
9  149b6 πλεονεκτεῖ 0+
10  151d3 τὸ πλῆθος +
11  151d7–8 τὸ πλῆθος +

12  153a3 πλῆθος +
13  153a4 πλῆθος +

S3
1  158b6 πλήθει +
2  158c1 πλήθη +
3  158c4 πλῆθος 0+ question,
   affirmed 158c6–7
4  158c7 πλήθει +

S7
1  164c7 πλήθη +
2  164d1 πλήθει +
3  165c2 πλήθει + in the mode of
   φανῆναι (165c2)

πέρας, περαίνω

S1
1  137d6 πέρας 0– general definition,
   negated 137d7

S2
1  144e8 πεπερασμένον +
2  145a1 πέρας 0+ general definition,
   affirmed 145a3
3  145a3 πεπερασμένον +
4  145a4 πεπερασμένον +

S3
1  158d1 πέρας +

2  158d5 πέρας +
3  158d8 πέρατος +
4  158e4 πέρατος +
5  158e5 πεπερασμένα +

S7
1  165a6 πέρας + probably in the
   mode of δόξειεν (165a4)
2  165a6 πέρας – probably in the
   mode of δόξειεν (165a4)
3  165c4 πέρας + in the mode of
   φαίνεσθαι (165c5)

ἀρχή
Excluding the reoccurring formula ἐξ ἀρχῆς (142b1; 159b4; 160d3; 163b7; 165e2).

S1
1  137d4 ἀρχὴν –
2  137d6 ἀρχὴ 0– general definition,

negated 137d4–5; 137d7–8
3  137d7 ἀρχὴν –

S2

1  145a5 ἀρχὴν 0+  question, affirmed
   145a8–b1
2  145a8 ἀρχὴν +
3  153c2 ἀρχὴν +
4  153c3 ἀρχή +
5  153c4 τὴν ἀρχὴν +
6  153d5 ἀρχὴν +

S7

1  165a6 ἀρχὴν –  probably in the
   mode of δόξειεν (165a4)
2  165a8 τῆς ἀρχῆς +  in the mode of
   φαίνεται (165b1)
3  165b1 ἀρχή +  in the mode of
   φαίνεται (165b1)

μέσος

S1

1  137d5 μέσον –
2  137e2 τοῦ μέσου 0–  here, and
   137e3: general definition, negated
   137e4–138a1
3  137e3 τὸ μέσον 0–
4  138c7 μέσου 0–  here, and 138c7:
   general, hypothetical consideration,
   negated by the rhetorical questions
   138d1–2 and 139a2–3; 139b3
5  138c8 τὸ μέσον 0–
6  138d1 μέσου 0–  here, and 138d2:
   rhetorical question, referring to the
   partless One (cf. e.g. 137d2–3) and
   thus negated
7  138d2 τοῦ μέσου 0–

3  145b1–2 τό ... μέσον 0+  here,
   and 145b2: general consideration,
   affirmed implicitly in 145b3–5
4  145b2 μέσον 0+
5  149a6 μέσῳ 0–  general consideration, negated implicitly 149a8–b1
6  153c2 μέσον +
7  153e3 μέσου +  counted as positive
   since οὔτε negates ἀπολειφθὲν
   (153e4)

S7

1  165a7 μέσον –  probably in the
   mode of δόξειεν (165a4)
2  165b2 τῷ μέσῳ +  in the mode
   φαίνεται (165b1)
3  165b2 μεσαίτερα +  in the mode
   φαίνεται (165b1)
4  165b2 τοῦ μέσου +  in the mode
   φαίνεται (165b1)

S2

1  145a6 μέσον 0+  question, affirmed
   145a8–b1
2  145b1 μέσον +

τελευτή, τέλος, τέλειος

S1

1  137d4 τελευτὴν –
2  137d6 τελευτή 0–  general definition, negated 137d4–5; 137d7–8
3  137d7–8 τελευτὴν –

S2

1  145a6 τελευτὴν 0+  question,
   affirmed 145a8–b1
2  145b1 τελευτὴν +
3  153c2 τελευτὴν +
4  153c5 τοῦ τέλους +
5  153c7 τῇ τελευτῇ +
6  153c8 τελευτὴ +

7  153d2 τελευτῇ +

S3

1  157e1 (ἐν) τέλειον +
2  157e4 (ἐν ... ὅλον) τέλειον +

S5

1  162a6 τελέως 0+  from here to
   162b3: general consideration,
   despite the chiasm of being and
   non-being, τελέως remains affirmed throughout
2  162b1 τελέως 0+
3  162b3 τελέως 0+

**S7**

1  165b1 τὴν τελευτὴν + in the mode     2  165b2 τελευτή + in the mode of
   of φαίνεται (165b1)                        φαίνεται (165b1)

ἔσχατος

**S1**

1  137e2 τὰ ἔσχατα 0- general          2  145b2 τῶν ἐσχάτων 0+ general
   definition, negated 137e4–138a1        definition, affirmed implicitly
2  137e4 τοῖν ἐσχάτοιν 0- general          145b3–5
   definition, negated 137e4–138a1     3  153e3 τὸ ἔσχατον +
                                        4  153e4 ἐσχάτου + counted as
**S2**                                      positive since οὔτε negates
1  145a4 ἔσχατα +                          ἀπολειφθὲν (153e4)

ὅλος

**S1**

1   137c5 ὅλον –                        8   144e9 τοῦ ὅλου 0+ rhetorical
2   137c6 ὅλου 0- from here to 137c9:       question, obviously positive
    definition, general and hypothetical  9   145a3 ὅλον +
    consideration, negated 137c5–6;     10  145a5 ὅλον 0+ from here to 145a8:
    137d2–3                                 question, affirmed 145a2–3
3   137c7 τὸ ὅλον 0-                     11  145a6 ὅλον 0+
4   137c7 ὅλον 0-                        12  145a8 ὅλον 0+
5   137c9 ὅλον 0-                        13  145b7 τῷ ὅλῳ 0+ from here
6   137d2 ὅλον –                             to 145c1: general consideration,
7   138b3 ὅλον 0- hypothetical con-          affirmed 142d4; 142d8–9 et passim;
    sideration, negated before (137c5–6;     used affirmatively also once more
    137d2–5) and 138b5–6                     in 145c4–7
8   138e4 ὅλον 0- from here to 138e7:   14  145b8 τοῦ ὅλου 0+
    general hypothetical consideration, 15  145b8–c1 τοῦ ὅλου 0+
    negated before (137c5–6; 137d2–5)   16  145c3 τὸ ὅλον 0+ rhetorical
    and 139a2–3                              question, obviously positive
9   138e5 ὅλον 0-                        17  145c4 ὅλῳ +
10  138e7 ὅλον 0-                        18  145c5 τὸ ὅλον +
                                         19  145c5 τοῦ ὅλου +
**S2**                                   20  145c7–8 τό … ὅλον 0+ from here
1   142d4 τὸ … ὅλον +                        to 145e2: general consideration,
2   142d7 τοῦ ὅλου 0+ general                affirmed 145e3
    consideration, affirmed 142d4–5;    21  145d3 τὸ … ὅλον 0+
    142d8–9                             22  145d5 τὸ ὅλον 0+
3   142d8 ὅλον +                        23  145d8 τὸ ὅλον 0+
4   144d1 ὅλον 0+ general question,     24  145e2 ὅλον 0+
    negated in 144d2, but ultimately    25  145e3 ὅλον +
    affirmed 144e5–145a3                26  146b5 ὅλον 0- general considera-
5   144d2 ὅλον –                            tion, negated 146b6–7
6   144e8 ὅλον +                        27  146b7 ὅλον –
7   144e9 τὸ ὅλον +                     28  146c3 ὅλον –

29  147b1 ὅλον 0-  from here to
    147b4: difficult; general consider-
    ation, counted as negative since its
    consequence is affirmed 147b5–8
30  147b2 ὅλα 0-
31  147b4 ὅλα 0-
32  148d7 ὅλῳ +
33  150a2 ὅλῳ 0-  from here to 150a4
    and 150b4: general consideration,
    negated for σμικρότης 150b1–2
34  150a3 ὅλῳ 0-
35  150a4 ὅλου 0-
36  150b1 ὅλῳ –
37  150b3–4 τὸ ὅλον 0-
38  150b6 ὅλῳ –
39  153c6 τοῦ ὅλου +
40  153c7 ὅλον +
41  153e3 ὅλον +

S3
1   157c5 ὅλον +

2   157c6 τό ... ὅλον +
3   157c8 ὅλου +
4   157e1 ὅλου +
5   157e3 τοῦ ὅλου +
6   157e4 ὅλον +
7   158a7 τῷ ... ὅλῳ +
8   158a7 τὸ ... (ἐν) ὅλον +
9   158a8 τοῦ ὅλου +
10  158b1 ὅλου +
11  158b6 τοῦ (ἑνὸς) ὅλου +
12  158d2 τὸ ὅλον +
13  158d2 τὸ ὅλον +
14  158d7 ὅλα +

S4
1   159c6 ὅλον –
2   159d2 ὅλον –
3   159d5 τοῦ ὅλου 0-  hypothetical
    consideration, negated before in
    159d1–4
4   159d6 ὅλον –

## μέρος

S1
1   137c5 μέρος –
2   137c6 τὸ μέρος 0-  from here
    to 137c9: definition, general and
    hypothetical consideration, negated
    137c5–6; 137d2–3
3   137c6 μέρος 0-
4   137c7 μέρος 0-
5   137c8 μερῶν 0-
6   137c9 μέρη 0-
7   137d3 μέρη –
8   137d4 μέρη –
9   137d5 μέρη 0-  hypothetical
    consideration, negated 137c5–6;
    137d2–3
10  137e4 μέρη 0-  hypothetical
    consideration, negated 137c5–6;
    137d2–3; 137e6–138a1
11  138a1 μέρη –
12  138a6 ἀμεροῦς –  counted as nega-
    tion due to alpha privativum
13  138c8 μέρη 0-  general hypothe-
    tical consideration, negated by the
    rhetorical question 138d1–2 and
    139a2–3

14  138d1 μερῶν 0-  rhetorical ques-
    tion, referring to the partless One
    (cf. e.g. 137d2–3) and thus negated
15  138e1 μέρη 0-  from here to
    138e6: general hypothetical consid-
    eration, negated before (137c5–6;
    137d2–5) and 139a2–3
16  138e3 μέρη 0-
17  138e5 μέρη 0-
18  138e6 μέρη 0-
19  140c9 μερῶν 0-  hypothetical
    consideration, negated before
    (137c5–6; 137d2–5) and 140d4–7

S2
1   142d1 μέρη 0+  question, affirmed
    142d1–5
2   144c1 μέρη +
3   144c2 τὰ μέρη + πλεῖστα is cor-
    rected 144d5–7, yet μέρη remains
    affirmed
4   144c3 μέρος 0+  here, and second
    occurrence in 144c3: general
    consideration, affirmed 144c6–8

5  144c3 μέρος 0+ question, affirmed
   144c6–8
6  144c6 τῷ ... μέρει +
7  144c8 μέρους +
8  144d3 τοῖς ... μέρεσιν 0+ hypothetical consideration, affirmed
   144e1–3
9  144d5 μέρη +
10 144d6 μέρη + πλεῖστα negated,
   yet μέρη remains affirmed
11 145b7 τῶν μερῶν +
12 145b8 τὰ μέρη +
13 145c1 μέρη +
14 145c4 τὰ μέρη +
15 145c8 τοῖς μέρεσίν 0– from here
   to 145d8: difficult to judge; general
   consideration, negation is used in
   145e3; yet also affirmed in 145e4
16 145d5 τῶν μερῶν 0–
17 145d8 τοῖς μέρεσι 0–
18 145e4 τὰ ... μέρη +
19 146b4 μέρος 0– from here to
   146b6: general consideration,
   negated 146b6–c4
20 146b5 μέρος 0–

21 146b6 μέρος 0–
22 146b6 μέρος –
23 146b7 μέρος –
24 146c3 μέρος –
25 150a2 μέρει 0– from here to
   150b4: general consideration,
   negated for σμικρότης 150b6
26 150b2 μέρει 0–
27 150b3 τῷ μέρει 0–
28 150b4 τοῦ μέρους 0–
29 150b6 μέρει –
30 151c1 μερῶν +
31 151c6 μερῶν +
32 151d2 μερῶν +
33 151d2 μερῶν +
34 153c1 μέρη +
35 153c2 μέρη +
36 153d5 μέρος +
37 153d6 μέρος +
38 153d7 μέρη –
39 153d7 μέρος +

S8
1  166a4 μέρος –


μόριον

S2
1  142d5 μόρια +
2  142d6 τῶν μορίων +
3  142d6 μόριον 0+ from here to
   142d7 (twice): general consideration, affirmed 142d4–5; 142d8–9
4  142d7 μόριον 0+
5  142d7 τό ... μόριον 0+
6  142d9 μόριον +
7  142d9 τῶν μορίων 0+ from here
   to 142e2: general question, affirmed
   142e3–143a1
8  142e2 τοῦ ... μορίου 0+
9  142e2 τοῦ ... μορίου 0+
10 142e3 τῶν μορίων +
11 142e5 μορίοιν +
12 142e5 τὸ μόριον +
13 142e6 μόριον +
14 142e6 τὼ μορίω +
15 144a8 τὸ μόριον +
16 144e8 τὰ μόρια +

17 144e8 μόρια +
18 144e9–145a1 τὰ μόρια 0+ rhetorical question, obviously positive
19 145a3 μόρια +
20 147a7 μόριά 0– from here to
   147b3: difficult passage; general
   consideration, counted as negative
   since its consequence is affirmed
   147b5–8
21 147b1 μόριον 0–
22 147b2 μορίων 0–
23 147b2 μόρια 0–
24 147b3 μορίῳ 0–
25 147b3 τὰ ... μόρια 0–
26 153c5 μόριά +
27 154d2 τῷ ... μορίῳ 0+ general
   question, counted as positive since
   μόριον is implicitly used in both
   alternatives in 154d3
28 155b8 ἄλλῳ ... μορίῳ +

## S3

| | |
|---|---|
| 1 | 157c3 μόρια + |
| 2 | 157c4 μόρια 0+ hypothetical negation, affirmed 157c3; 157c4–5 |
| 3 | 157c4 μόρια + |
| 4 | 157c6 μόρια + |
| 5 | 157c7 τὰ μόρια + |
| 6 | 157c7 τῶν μορίων + |
| 7 | 157c7 μόριον + πολλῶν is negated, while being μόριον remains affirmed |
| 8 | 157c8 μόριον 0+ from here to 157d6: difficult, general consideration; counted as positive since – while being negated with regard to multitude and the Others – μόριον is ultimately affirmed 157d7–e1; and even affirmed for the Others in 157e4–5 |
| 9 | 157d1 μόριον 0+ |
| 10 | 157d3 μόριον 0+ |
| 11 | 157d4 μόριον 0+ |
| 12 | 157d4 μόριον 0+ |
| 13 | 157d6 μόριον 0+ |
| 14 | 157d8 τὸ μόριον + counted as positive since affirmed for μιᾶς τινὸς ἰδέας καὶ ἑνός τινος ὃ καλοῦμεν ὅλον (157d8–e1) |
| 15 | 157d8 μόριον + |
| 16 | 157e2 μόριον + |
| 17 | 157e2 τὸ μόριον + |
| 18 | 157e3 μόρια + |
| 19 | 157e4 μόρια + |
| 20 | 157e5 τοῦ μορίου + |
| 21 | 158a1 μόριόν + |
| 22 | 158a7 τῷ μορίῳ + |
| 23 | 158a8 μόρια + |
| 24 | 158a8 τὰ μόρια + |
| 25 | 158a8 μόριον + |
| 26 | 158b1 μόριον + |
| 27 | 158b5 τοῦ ... μορίου + |
| 28 | 158d1 μόριον + |
| 29 | 158d1 μόριον + |
| 30 | 158d2 τὰ μόρια + |
| 31 | 158d7 μόρια + |

## S4

| | |
|---|---|
| 1 | 159c5 μόριά – |
| 2 | 159c6 μόρια – |
| 3 | 159c7 μόρια – |
| 4 | 159d2 μόριόν – |
| 5 | 159d5 μόριον 0– hypothetical consideration, negated 159d1–4 |
| 6 | 159d6 μόριά – |

## μερίζω

### S2

| | |
|---|---|
| 1 | 144b6 μεμέρισται + |
| 2 | 144d2 μεμερισμένον 0+ from here to 144d4: hypothetical consideration, affirmed 144e1–3 |
| 3 | 144d4 μεμερισμένον 0+ |
| 4 | 144d4 τό ... μεριστὸν 0+ |

## μέτρον

### S1

| | |
|---|---|
| 1 | 140b7–8 τῶν ... μέτρων 0– from here to 140c5: general consideration, negated later in 140c6–d7 |
| 2 | 140c2 μέτρα 0– |
| 3 | 140c4 μέτρων 0– |
| 4 | 140c5 μέτρων 0– |
| 5 | 140c7 τῶν ... μέτρων – |
| 6 | 140c8 μέτρων 0– from here to 140d3: hypothetical consideration, negated 140d4–5 |
| 7 | 140c9 μέτρων 0– |
| 8 | 140d2 τὰ μέτρα 0– |
| 9 | 140d2 μέτρου 0– |
| 10 | 140d3 τῷ μέτρῳ 0– |
| 11 | 140d4 μέτρου – |

S2

| | | | | |
|---|---|---|---|---|
| 1 | 151b8 μέτρων + | | 5 | 151c6 μέτρων + |
| 2 | 151c1 μέτρων + | | 6 | 151d1 μέτρων + |
| 3 | 151c2 μέτρων + | | 7 | 151d1 μέτρων + |
| 4 | 151c6 μέτρων + | | | |

# APPENDIX C

| | S1 | S2 | S2C | S3 | S4 | S5 | S6 | S7 | S8 | **S1–8** | IS | TP | FS | **Total** |
|---|---|---|---|---|---|---|---|---|---|---|---|---|---|---|
| ἄγω | 1 | 0 | 0 | 0 | 0 | 1 | 0 | 0 | 0 | **2** | 0 | 0 | 0 | **2** |
| ἀδύνατος | 12 | 4 | 0 | 3 | 3 | 2 | 0 | 0 | 1 | **25** | 0 | 0 | 0 | **25** |
| ἀεί | 3 | 28 | 0 | 2 | 0 | 2 | 1 | 3 | 0 | **39** | 0 | 0 | 0 | **39** |
| ἀθρέω | 0 | 1 | 0 | 0 | 0 | 0 | 0 | 0 | 0 | **1** | 0 | 0 | 0 | **1** |
| αἰσθάνομαι | 1 | 0 | 0 | 0 | 0 | 0 | 0 | 0 | 0 | **1** | 0 | 0 | 0 | **1** |
| αἴσθησις | 1 | 1 | 0 | 0 | 0 | 0 | 1 | 0 | 0 | **3** | 0 | 0 | 0 | **3** |
| ἀκίνητος | 1 | 0 | 0 | 0 | 0 | 1 | 0 | 0 | 0 | **2** | 0 | 0 | 0 | **2** |
| ἀληθής | 0 | 1 | 0 | 0 | 1 | 3 | 0 | 1 | 0 | **6** | 0 | 0 | 0 | **6** |
| ἀλλά | 25 | 39 | 2 | 5 | 0 | 9 | 1 | 1 | 0 | **82** | 0 | 0 | 0 | **82** |
| ἀλλάττω | 1 | 0 | 0 | 0 | 0 | 0 | 0 | 0 | 0 | **1** | 0 | 0 | 0 | **1** |
| ἀλλήλων | 0 | 15 | 0 | 7 | 1 | 1 | 0 | 5 | 0 | **29** | 0 | 0 | 1 | **30** |
| ἄλλοθι | 1 | 0 | 0 | 0 | 0 | 0 | 0 | 0 | 0 | **1** | 0 | 0 | 0 | **1** |
| ἀλλοῖος | 0 | 5 | 0 | 0 | 0 | 2 | 0 | 0 | 0 | **7** | 0 | 0 | 0 | **7** |
| ἀλλοιόω | 3 | 0 | 0 | 0 | 0 | 14 | 2 | 0 | 0 | **19** | 0 | 0 | 0 | **19** |
| ἀλλοίωσις | 1 | 0 | 0 | 0 | 0 | 0 | 0 | 0 | 0 | **1** | 0 | 0 | 0 | **1** |
| ἄλλος | 22 | 135 | 3 | 21 | 22 | 20 | 9 | 24 | 12 | **268** | 1 | 4 | 1 | **274** |
| ἄλλοτε | 1 | 0 | 0 | 0 | 0 | 0 | 0 | 0 | 0 | **1** | 0 | 0 | 0 | **1** |
| ἄλογος | 0 | 1 | 0 | 0 | 0 | 0 | 0 | 0 | 0 | **1** | 0 | 0 | 0 | **1** |
| ἅμα | 6 | 11 | 1 | 0 | 0 | 0 | 0 | 0 | 0 | **18** | 0 | 0 | 0 | **18** |
| ἀμβλύς | 0 | 0 | 0 | 0 | 0 | 0 | 0 | 1 | 0 | **1** | 0 | 0 | 0 | **1** |
| ἀμείβω | 1 | 0 | 0 | 0 | 0 | 0 | 0 | 0 | 0 | **1** | 0 | 0 | 0 | **1** |
| ἀμερής | 1 | 0 | 0 | 0 | 0 | 0 | 0 | 0 | 0 | **1** | 0 | 0 | 0 | **1** |
| ἀμφότερος | 2 | 6 | 1 | 2 | 2 | 1 | 0 | 0 | 0 | **14** | 0 | 0 | 0 | **14** |
| ἄμφω | 2 | 4 | 0 | 0 | 0 | 0 | 0 | 0 | 0 | **6** | 0 | 0 | 0 | **6** |
| ἄν | 47 | 115 | 9 | 17 | 7 | 25 | 7 | 9 | 3 | **239** | 0 | 2 | 0 | **241** |
| ἀναγκαῖος | 0 | 1 | 0 | 0 | 0 | 0 | 0 | 0 | 0 | **1** | 0 | 0 | 0 | **1** |
| ἀνάγκη | 6 | 36 | 2 | 6 | 0 | 9 | 1 | 3 | 0 | **63** | 0 | 0 | 0 | **63** |
| ἄνευ | 1 | 2 | 2 | 0 | 0 | 0 | 0 | 1 | 1 | **7** | 0 | 0 | 0 | **7** |
| ἀνίημι | 0 | 0 | 0 | 0 | 0 | 1 | 0 | 0 | 0 | **1** | 0 | 0 | 0 | **1** |
| ἄνισος | 1 | 2 | 0 | 0 | 0 | 5 | 0 | 0 | 0 | **8** | 0 | 0 | 0 | **8** |
| ἀνισότης | 1 | 0 | 0 | 0 | 0 | 2 | 0 | 0 | 0 | **3** | 0 | 0 | 0 | **3** |
| ἀνόμοιος | 4 | 10 | 4 | 4 | 4 | 6 | 1 | 3 | 1 | **37** | 0 | 0 | 0 | **37** |
| ἀνομοιότης | 1 | 0 | 0 | 0 | 2 | 4 | 0 | 0 | 0 | **7** | 0 | 0 | 0 | **7** |

|  | S1 | S2 | S2C | S3 | S4 | S5 | S6 | S7 | S8 | **S1–8** | IS | TP | FS | **Total** |
|---|---|---|---|---|---|---|---|---|---|---|---|---|---|---|
| ἀνομοιόω | 0 | 1 | 2 | 0 | 0 | 0 | 0 | 0 | 0 | **3** | 0 | 0 | 0 | **3** |
| ἀντί | 0 | 0 | 0 | 0 | 0 | 0 | 0 | 2 | 0 | **2** | 0 | 0 | 0 | **2** |
| ἀπαλλακτέος | 0 | 0 | 0 | 0 | 0 | 0 | 1 | 0 | 0 | **1** | 0 | 0 | 0 | **1** |
| ἀπάλλαττω | 0 | 0 | 2 | 0 | 0 | 0 | 0 | 0 | 0 | **2** | 0 | 0 | 0 | **2** |
| ἅπαξ | 0 | 4 | 0 | 0 | 0 | 0 | 0 | 0 | 1 | **5** | 0 | 0 | 0 | **5** |
| ἅπας | 0 | 11 | 0 | 2 | 0 | 0 | 0 | 0 | 1 | **14** | 0 | 0 | 0 | **14** |
| ἄπειμι | 1 | 0 | 0 | 0 | 0 | 0 | 0 | 0 | 0 | **1** | 0 | 0 | 0 | **1** |
| ἀπείργω | 0 | 1 | 0 | 0 | 0 | 0 | 0 | 0 | 0 | **1** | 0 | 0 | 0 | **1** |
| ἀπειρία | 0 | 0 | 0 | 1 | 0 | 0 | 0 | 0 | 0 | **1** | 0 | 0 | 0 | **1** |
| ἄπειρος | 1 | 5 | 0 | 5 | 0 | 0 | 0 | 3 | 0 | **14** | 0 | 0 | 0 | **14** |
| ἀπέραντος | 0 | 1 | 0 | 0 | 0 | 0 | 0 | 0 | 0 | **1** | 0 | 0 | 0 | **1** |
| ἀπέχω | 1 | 1 | 0 | 0 | 0 | 0 | 0 | 0 | 0 | **2** | 0 | 0 | 0 | **2** |
| ἁπλός | 0 | 0 | 0 | 0 | 0 | 0 | 1 | 0 | 0 | **1** | 0 | 0 | 0 | **1** |
| ἀπό | 1 | 0 | 0 | 0 | 0 | 0 | 0 | 0 | 0 | **1** | 0 | 0 | 0 | **1** |
| ἀπολείπω | 0 | 5 | 0 | 0 | 0 | 0 | 0 | 0 | 0 | **5** | 0 | 0 | 0 | **5** |
| ἀπόλλυμι | 0 | 0 | 7 | 0 | 1 | 6 | 5 | 1 | 0 | **20** | 0 | 0 | 0 | **20** |
| ἀποστατέω | 0 | 3 | 0 | 0 | 0 | 0 | 0 | 0 | 0 | **3** | 0 | 0 | 0 | **3** |
| ἀπουσία | 0 | 0 | 0 | 0 | 0 | 0 | 1 | 0 | 0 | **1** | 0 | 0 | 0 | **1** |
| ἅπτω | ? | 18 | 0 | 0 | 0 | 1 | 0 | 1 | 1 | **23** | 0 | 0 | 0 | **23** |
| ἄρα | 35 | 71 | 1 | 4 | 11 | 19 | 6 | 3 | 4 | **154** | 0 | 1 | 0 | **155** |
| ἆρα | 3 | 31 | 8 | 1 | 2 | 4 | 1 | 0 | 0 | **50** | 0 | 3 | 0 | **53** |
| ἀριθμός | 0 | 24 | 0 | 0 | 0 | 0 | 0 | 1 | 0 | **25** | 0 | 0 | 0 | **25** |
| ἄρτι | 0 | 1 | 0 | 0 | 0 | 0 | 0 | 0 | 0 | **1** | 0 | 0 | 0 | **1** |
| ἀρτιάκις | 0 | 2 | 0 | 0 | 0 | 0 | 0 | 0 | 0 | **2** | 0 | 0 | 0 | **2** |
| ἄρτιος | 0 | 3 | 0 | 0 | 1 | 0 | 0 | 1 | 0 | **5** | 0 | 0 | 0 | **5** |
| ἀρχή | 3 | 8 | 0 | 0 | 1 | 1 | 1 | 3 | 1 | **18** | 0 | 0 | 0 | **18** |
| ἅτε | 0 | 0 | 0 | 0 | 0 | 0 | 0 | 1 | 0 | **1** | 0 | 0 | 0 | **1** |
| ἄτοπος | 0 | 0 | 2 | 0 | 0 | 0 | 0 | 0 | 0 | **2** | 0 | 0 | 0 | **2** |
| αὖ | 3 | 13 | 1 | 1 | 0 | 3 | 1 | 0 | 0 | **22** | 0 | 0 | 0 | **22** |
| αὖθις | 0 | 1 | 0 | 0 | 0 | 0 | 1 | 0 | 0 | **2** | 0 | 0 | 0 | **2** |
| αὐξάνω | 0 | 0 | 2 | 0 | 0 | 0 | 0 | 0 | 0 | **2** | 0 | 0 | 0 | **2** |
| αὐτός | 41 | 112 | 7 | 12 | 12 | 23 | 10 | 12 | 3 | **232** | 0 | 1 | 1 | **234** |
| ἀφαιρέω | 0 | 0 | 0 | 2 | 0 | 0 | 0 | 0 | 0 | **2** | 0 | 0 | 0 | **2** |
| ἀφίημι | 0 | 1 | 2 | 0 | 0 | 0 | 0 | 0 | 0 | **3** | 0 | 0 | 0 | **3** |
| ἀφίστημι | 0 | 0 | 0 | 0 | 0 | 1 | 0 | 1 | 0 | **2** | 0 | 0 | 0 | **2** |
| ἀφορίζω | 0 | 0 | 0 | 1 | 0 | 0 | 0 | 0 | 0 | **1** | 0 | 0 | 0 | **1** |
| ἄψις | 0 | 13 | 0 | 0 | 0 | 0 | 0 | 0 | 0 | **13** | 0 | 0 | 0 | **13** |
| βαίνω | 1 | 0 | 0 | 0 | 0 | 0 | 0 | 0 | 0 | **1** | 0 | 0 | 0 | **1** |

| | S1 | S2 | S2C | S3 | S4 | S5 | S6 | S7 | S8 | **S1–8** | IS | TP | FS | **Total** |
|---|---|---|---|---|---|---|---|---|---|---|---|---|---|---|
| βούλομαι | 0 | 2 | 0 | 0 | 0 | 0 | 0 | 0 | 0 | **2** | 0 | 0 | 0 | **2** |
| γάρ | 10 | 32 | 5 | 9 | 5 | 11 | 3 | 6 | 4 | **85** | 0 | 1 | 0 | **86** |
| γε | 29 | 49 | 5 | 13 | 3 | 14 | 4 | 7 | 3 | **127** | 0 | 0 | 0 | **127** |
| γένεσις | 0 | 1 | 0 | 0 | 0 | 0 | 0 | 0 | 0 | **1** | 0 | 0 | 0 | **1** |
| γίγνομαι | 43 | 90 | 9 | 3 | 1 | 6 | 3 | 1 | 0 | **156** | 0 | 0 | 0 | **156** |
| γιγνώσκω | 1 | 0 | 0 | 0 | 0 | 1 | 0 | 0 | 0 | **2** | 0 | 1 | 0 | **3** |
| γνωστός | 0 | 0 | 0 | 0 | 0 | 0 | 0 | 0 | 0 | **0** | 0 | 1 | 0 | **1** |
| γοῦν | 0 | 1 | 0 | 0 | 0 | 0 | 0 | 0 | 0 | **1** | 0 | 0 | 0 | **1** |
| δέ | 30 | 117 | 9 | 15 | 7 | 24 | 8 | 11 | 2 | **223** | 0 | 2 | 0 | **225** |
| δεσμός | 0 | 0 | 0 | 0 | 0 | 1 | 0 | 0 | 0 | **1** | 0 | 0 | 0 | **1** |
| δεύτερος | 0 | 1 | 0 | 0 | 0 | 0 | 0 | 0 | 0 | **1** | 0 | 0 | 0 | **1** |
| δέω | 4 | 7 | 1 | 0 | 0 | 7 | 2 | 2 | 0 | **23** | 0 | 0 | 0 | **23** |
| δή | 5 | 26 | 7 | 7 | 1 | 7 | 3 | 8 | 1 | **65** | 1 | 1 | 0 | **67** |
| δῆλος | 0 | 0 | 0 | 1 | 0 | 2 | 0 | 0 | 0 | **3** | 0 | 0 | 0 | **3** |
| δηλόω | 0 | 0 | 0 | 0 | 0 | 0 | 0 | 0 | 0 | **0** | 0 | 2 | 0 | **2** |
| δήπου | 1 | 1 | 1 | 2 | 0 | 0 | 0 | 0 | 0 | **5** | 0 | 0 | 0 | **5** |
| διά | 0 | 3 | 0 | 0 | 0 | 0 | 0 | 1 | 0 | **4** | 0 | 0 | 0 | **4** |
| διακρίνω | 0 | 0 | 2 | 0 | 0 | 0 | 0 | 0 | 0 | **2** | 0 | 0 | 0 | **2** |
| διανέμω | 0 | 1 | 0 | 0 | 0 | 0 | 0 | 0 | 0 | **1** | 0 | 0 | 0 | **1** |
| διάνοια | 0 | 1 | 0 | 1 | 0 | 0 | 0 | 2 | 0 | **4** | 0 | 0 | 0 | **4** |
| διαφέρω | 1 | 10 | 0 | 0 | 0 | 0 | 0 | 0 | 0 | **11** | 0 | 2 | 0 | **13** |
| διάφορος | 3 | 0 | 0 | 0 | 0 | 0 | 0 | 0 | 0 | **3** | 0 | 1 | 0 | **4** |
| διαφορότης | 1 | 0 | 0 | 0 | 0 | 0 | 0 | 0 | 0 | **1** | 0 | 0 | 0 | **1** |
| διέρχομαι | 0 | 1 | 1 | 0 | 0 | 0 | 0 | 1 | 1 | **4** | 0 | 0 | 0 | **4** |
| διό | 0 | 1 | 0 | 0 | 0 | 0 | 0 | 0 | 0 | **1** | 0 | 0 | 0 | **1** |
| διομολογητέος | 0 | 1 | 0 | 0 | 0 | 0 | 0 | 0 | 0 | **1** | 0 | 0 | 0 | **1** |
| δίς | 0 | 7 | 0 | 0 | 0 | 0 | 0 | 0 | 0 | **7** | 0 | 0 | 0 | **7** |
| δοκέω | 2 | 0 | 0 | 0 | 0 | 0 | 0 | 6 | 0 | **8** | 0 | 0 | 0 | **8** |
| δόξα | 1 | 1 | 0 | 0 | 0 | 0 | 1 | 0 | 1 | **4** | 0 | 0 | 0 | **4** |
| δοξάζω | 1 | 0 | 0 | 0 | 0 | 0 | 0 | 1 | 4 | **6** | 0 | 0 | 0 | **6** |
| δυάς | 0 | 2 | 0 | 0 | 0 | 0 | 0 | 0 | 0 | **2** | 0 | 0 | 0 | **2** |
| δύναμαι | 1 | 1 | 0 | 0 | 0 | 1 | 1 | 1 | 0 | **5** | 0 | 0 | 0 | **5** |
| δύναμις | 0 | 1 | 0 | 0 | 0 | 0 | 0 | 0 | 0 | **1** | 0 | 0 | 0 | **1** |
| δυνατός | 3 | 2 | 0 | 0 | 0 | 0 | 0 | 0 | 0 | **5** | 0 | 0 | 0 | **5** |
| δύο | 1 | 21 | 0 | 0 | 5 | 0 | 0 | 0 | 0 | **27** | 0 | 0 | 0 | **27** |
| ἐάν | 1 | 9 | 1 | 0 | 0 | 0 | 0 | 0 | 0 | **11** | 0 | 0 | 0 | **11** |
| ἐάνπερ | 0 | 2 | 0 | 0 | 0 | 0 | 0 | 0 | 0 | **2** | 0 | 0 | 0 | **2** |
| ἐάντε | 0 | 4 | 0 | 0 | 0 | 0 | 0 | 0 | 0 | **4** | 0 | 0 | 0 | **4** |

| | S1 | S2 | S2C | S3 | S4 | S5 | S6 | S7 | S8 | S1–8 | IS | TP | FS | Total |
|---|---|---|---|---|---|---|---|---|---|---|---|---|---|---|
| ἑαυτοῦ | 42 | 77 | 0 | 11 | 3 | 4 | 1 | 4 | 0 | **142** | 1 | 0 | 1 | **144** |
| ἐάω | 0 | 0 | 0 | 0 | 1 | 0 | 0 | 0 | 0 | **1** | 0 | 0 | 0 | **1** |
| ἐγγίγνομαι | 0 | 4 | 0 | 0 | 0 | 0 | 0 | 0 | 0 | **4** | 0 | 0 | 0 | **4** |
| ἐγγύθεν | 0 | 0 | 0 | 0 | 0 | 0 | 0 | 1 | 0 | **1** | 0 | 0 | 0 | **1** |
| ἐγκάθημαι | 0 | 0 | 1 | 0 | 0 | 0 | 0 | 0 | 0 | **1** | 0 | 0 | 0 | **1** |
| ἐγώ | 0 | 1 | 0 | 0 | 0 | 0 | 0 | 0 | 0 | **1** | 0 | 0 | 0 | **1** |
| ἕδρα | 0 | 1 | 0 | 0 | 0 | 0 | 0 | 0 | 0 | **1** | 0 | 0 | 0 | **1** |
| ἐθέλω | 0 | 3 | 0 | 1 | 0 | 0 | 0 | 0 | 0 | **4** | 0 | 0 | 0 | **4** |
| εἰ | 17 | 41 | 2 | 8 | 7 | 17 | 4 | 7 | 7 | **110** | 1 | 8 | 0 | **119** |
| εἶδος | 0 | 2 | 0 | 1 | 2 | 0 | 0 | 0 | 0 | **5** | 0 | 0 | 0 | **5** |
| εἶεν | 1 | 0 | 0 | 0 | 0 | 0 | 0 | 0 | 0 | **1** | 0 | 1 | 0 | **2** |
| εἰμί | 136 | 369 | 27 | 54 | 22 | 111 | 30 | 42 | 24 | **815** | 3 | 15 | 4 | **837** |
| εἶμι | 1 | 2 | 3 | 0 | 0 | 0 | 1 | 0 | 0 | **7** | 0 | 0 | 0 | **7** |
| εἴπερ | 4 | 19 | 1 | 3 | 1 | 8 | 0 | 4 | 0 | **40** | 0 | 0 | 0 | **40** |
| εἶπον | 0 | 7 | 0 | 0 | 0 | 2 | 0 | 0 | 3 | **12** | 0 | 3 | 0 | **15** |
| εἴρω | 0 | 1 | 0 | 0 | 2 | 0 | 0 | 0 | 0 | **3** | 0 | 0 | 1 | **4** |
| εἰς | 0 | 4 | 5 | 0 | 0 | 1 | 0 | 2 | 0 | **12** | 0 | 0 | 0 | **12** |
| εἷς | 63 | 240 | 15 | 48 | 25 | 38 | 4 | 21 | 15 | **469** | 3 | 7 | 1 | **480** |
| εἴτε | 2 | 3 | 0 | 0 | 0 | 0 | 0 | 0 | 0 | **5** | 0 | 2 | 2 | **9** |
| ἐκ | 2 | 11 | 11 | 4 | 1 | 4 | 0 | 2 | 0 | **35** | 0 | 0 | 0 | **35** |
| ἕκαστος | 2 | 10 | 0 | 10 | 1 | 0 | 0 | 9 | 0 | **32** | 0 | 1 | 0 | **33** |
| ἑκάτερος | 0 | 8 | 2 | 1 | 0 | 0 | 0 | 0 | 0 | **11** | 0 | 0 | 0 | **11** |
| ἐκεῖνος | 8 | 29 | 1 | 2 | 0 | 11 | 2 | 0 | 0 | **53** | 0 | 0 | 0 | **53** |
| ἐκτέος | 0 | 0 | 0 | 0 | 0 | 0 | 1 | 0 | 0 | **1** | 0 | 0 | 0 | **1** |
| ἐκτός | 0 | 2 | 0 | 0 | 0 | 0 | 0 | 0 | 0 | **2** | 0 | 0 | 0 | **2** |
| ἐκφεύγω | 0 | 1 | 0 | 0 | 0 | 0 | 0 | 0 | 0 | **1** | 0 | 0 | 0 | **1** |
| ἐλαχύς | 6 | 35 | 1 | 0 | 1 | 0 | 0 | 1 | 0 | **44** | 0 | 0 | 0 | **44** |
| ἐν | 28 | 89 | 8 | 4 | 8 | 5 | 1 | 4 | 3 | **150** | 0 | 0 | 0 | **150** |
| ἐναντίος | 0 | 9 | 1 | 4 | 2 | 0 | 0 | 0 | 0 | **16** | 0 | 1 | 0 | **17** |
| ἔνειμι | 3 | 10 | 0 | 0 | 2 | 0 | 0 | 1 | 2 | **18** | 0 | 0 | 0 | **18** |
| ἐντός | 1 | 0 | 0 | 0 | 0 | 0 | 0 | 0 | 0 | **1** | 0 | 0 | 0 | **1** |
| ἐντυγχάνω | 0 | 3 | 0 | 0 | 0 | 0 | 0 | 0 | 0 | **3** | 0 | 0 | 0 | **3** |
| ἐξαίφνης | 0 | 0 | 4 | 0 | 0 | 0 | 0 | 1 | 0 | **5** | 0 | 0 | 0 | **5** |
| ἐξῆς | 0 | 1 | 0 | 0 | 0 | 0 | 0 | 0 | 0 | **1** | 0 | 0 | 0 | **1** |
| ἕξις | 0 | 0 | 0 | 0 | 0 | 2 | 0 | 0 | 0 | **2** | 0 | 0 | 0 | **2** |
| ἐξισόω | 0 | 1 | 0 | 0 | 0 | 0 | 0 | 0 | 0 | **1** | 0 | 0 | 0 | **1** |
| ἔξω | 3 | 0 | 0 | 0 | 0 | 0 | 0 | 0 | 0 | **3** | 0 | 0 | 0 | **3** |
| ἔξωθεν | 0 | 1 | 0 | 0 | 0 | 0 | 0 | 0 | 0 | **1** | 0 | 0 | 0 | **1** |

| | S1 | S2 | S2C | S3 | S4 | S5 | S6 | S7 | S8 | **S1–8** | IS | TP | FS | **Total** |
|---|---|---|---|---|---|---|---|---|---|---|---|---|---|---|
| ἔοικα | 5 | 6 | 2 | 1 | 0 | 4 | 0 | 1 | 0 | **19** | 0 | 0 | 1 | **20** |
| ἐπάνειμι | 0 | 1 | 0 | 0 | 0 | 0 | 0 | 0 | 0 | **1** | 0 | 0 | 0 | **1** |
| ἐπανέρχομαι | 0 | 1 | 0 | 0 | 0 | 0 | 0 | 0 | 0 | **1** | 0 | 0 | 0 | **1** |
| ἐπεί | 0 | 0 | 0 | 1 | 0 | 0 | 0 | 0 | 0 | **1** | 0 | 0 | 0 | **1** |
| ἐπειδάν | 1 | 3 | 0 | 1 | 0 | 0 | 0 | 0 | 0 | **5** | 0 | 0 | 0 | **5** |
| ἐπειδή | 0 | 9 | 0 | 0 | 1 | 3 | 1 | 0 | 0 | **14** | 0 | 0 | 0 | **14** |
| ἐπειδήπερ | 0 | 1 | 0 | 0 | 0 | 0 | 0 | 0 | 0 | **1** | 0 | 0 | 0 | **1** |
| ἐπείπερ | 1 | 4 | 0 | 2 | 0 | 2 | 1 | 0 | 0 | **10** | 0 | 0 | 0 | **10** |
| ἔπειτα | 2 | 7 | 0 | 0 | 0 | 0 | 1 | 0 | 0 | **10** | 0 | 1 | 0 | **11** |
| ἐπέχω | 0 | 1 | 0 | 0 | 0 | 0 | 0 | 0 | 0 | **1** | 0 | 0 | 0 | **1** |
| ἐπί | 2 | 10 | 10 | 0 | 0 | 1 | 1 | 1 | 2 | **27** | 0 | 1 | 0 | **28** |
| ἐπιδίδωμι | 0 | 1 | 0 | 0 | 0 | 0 | 0 | 0 | 0 | **1** | 0 | 0 | 0 | **1** |
| ἐπιλαμβάνω | 0 | 1 | 0 | 0 | 0 | 0 | 0 | 0 | 0 | **1** | 0 | 0 | 0 | **1** |
| ἐπίπροσθεν | 1 | 0 | 0 | 0 | 0 | 0 | 0 | 0 | 0 | **1** | 0 | 0 | 0 | **1** |
| ἐπισκοπέω | 0 | 0 | 0 | 0 | 1 | 0 | 0 | 0 | 0 | **1** | 0 | 0 | 0 | **1** |
| ἐπιστήμη | 1 | 1 | 0 | 0 | 0 | 2 | 1 | 0 | 0 | **5** | 0 | 0 | 0 | **5** |
| ἐπίσχω | 0 | 2 | 0 | 0 | 0 | 0 | 0 | 0 | 0 | **2** | 0 | 0 | 0 | **2** |
| ἔρομαι | 0 | 1 | 0 | 0 | 0 | 0 | 0 | 0 | 0 | **1** | 0 | 0 | 0 | **1** |
| ἔρχομαι | 0 | 0 | 0 | 0 | 0 | 0 | 0 | 1 | 1 | **2** | 0 | 0 | 0 | **2** |
| ἔσχατος | 2 | 4 | 0 | 0 | 0 | 0 | 0 | 0 | 0 | **6** | 0 | 0 | 0 | **6** |
| ἑτεροῖος | 0 | 0 | 0 | 0 | 0 | 2 | 0 | 1 | 0 | **3** | 0 | 0 | 0 | **3** |
| ἑτεροιότης | 0 | 0 | 0 | 0 | 0 | 2 | 1 | 0 | 0 | **3** | 0 | 0 | 0 | **3** |
| ἕτερος | 34 | 80 | 0 | 5 | 4 | 7 | 2 | 9 | 1 | **142** | 0 | 3 | 0 | **145** |
| ἑτέρωθι | 0 | 2 | 0 | 0 | 0 | 0 | 0 | 0 | 0 | **2** | 0 | 0 | 0 | **2** |
| ἔτι | 6 | 9 | 3 | 0 | 1 | 2 | 0 | 2 | 1 | **24** | 0 | 0 | 0 | **24** |
| εὐθύς | 4 | 3 | 0 | 0 | 0 | 1 | 0 | 0 | 0 | **8** | 0 | 0 | 0 | **8** |
| εὐπετής | 0 | 0 | 0 | 0 | 0 | 0 | 0 | 1 | 0 | **1** | 0 | 0 | 0 | **1** |
| εὑρίσκω | 0 | 0 | 0 | 1 | 0 | 0 | 0 | 0 | 0 | **1** | 0 | 0 | 0 | **1** |
| ἐφεξῆς | 0 | 3 | 0 | 0 | 0 | 0 | 0 | 0 | 0 | **3** | 0 | 0 | 0 | **3** |
| ἔχω | 18 | 34 | 3 | 5 | 6 | 12 | 1 | 3 | 1 | **83** | 0 | 0 | 0 | **83** |
| ἕως | 1 | 2 | 0 | 0 | 0 | 0 | 0 | 0 | 0 | **3** | 0 | 0 | 0 | **3** |
| ἕωσπερ | 0 | 1 | 0 | 0 | 0 | 0 | 0 | 0 | 0 | **1** | 0 | 0 | 0 | **1** |
| ἤ (comp.) | 4 | 14 | 0 | 1 | 0 | 3 | 2 | 0 | 0 | **24** | 0 | 0 | 0 | **24** |
| ἤ (disj.) | 26 | 44 | 3 | 0 | 3 | 4 | 17 | 2 | 0 | **99** | 0 | 4 | 0 | **103** |
| ᾗ | 1 | 2 | 0 | 0 | 0 | 0 | 0 | 0 | 0 | **3** | 0 | 0 | 0 | **3** |
| ἦ | 0 | 16 | 0 | 3 | 0 | 2 | 0 | 0 | 0 | **21** | 0 | 0 | 0 | **21** |
| ἤδη | 8 | 6 | 0 | 2 | 1 | 1 | 2 | 1 | 0 | **21** | 0 | 0 | 0 | **21** |
| ἡλικία | 5 | 8 | 0 | 0 | 0 | 0 | 0 | 0 | 0 | **13** | 0 | 0 | 0 | **13** |

|  | S1 | S2 | S2C | S3 | S4 | S5 | S6 | S7 | S8 | **S1–8** | IS | TP | FS | **Total** |
|---|---|---|---|---|---|---|---|---|---|---|---|---|---|---|
| ἡμεῖς | 0 | 2 | 0 | 0 | 0 | 2 | 1 | 1 | 0 | **6** | 0 | 0 | 0 | **6** |
| ἡσυχάζω | 0 | 0 | 0 | 0 | 0 | 1 | 0 | 0 | 0 | **1** | 0 | 0 | 0 | **1** |
| ἡσυχία | 1 | 0 | 0 | 0 | 0 | 1 | 0 | 0 | 0 | **2** | 0 | 0 | 0 | **2** |
| ἤτοι | 1 | 2 | 0 | 0 | 0 | 0 | 0 | 0 | 0 | **3** | 0 | 0 | 0 | **3** |
| ἥττων | 0 | 2 | 0 | 0 | 0 | 0 | 0 | 0 | 0 | **2** | 0 | 1 | 0 | **3** |
| θρύπτω | 0 | 0 | 0 | 0 | 0 | 0 | 0 | 1 | 0 | **1** | 0 | 0 | 0 | **1** |
| ἰδέα | 0 | 0 | 0 | 1 | 0 | 0 | 0 | 0 | 0 | **1** | 0 | 0 | 0 | **1** |
| ἵνα | 0 | 0 | 0 | 0 | 0 | 1 | 0 | 0 | 0 | **1** | 0 | 0 | 0 | **1** |
| ἴσος | 9 | 39 | 3 | 0 | 1 | 5 | 0 | 1 | 0 | **58** | 0 | 0 | 0 | **58** |
| ἰσότης | 2 | 2 | 0 | 0 | 0 | 4 | 1 | 1 | 0 | **10** | 0 | 0 | 0 | **10** |
| ἰσόω | 0 | 0 | 2 | 0 | 0 | 0 | 0 | 0 | 0 | **2** | 0 | 0 | 0 | **2** |
| ἵστημι | 3 | 6 | 12 | 1 | 1 | 2 | 3 | 1 | 0 | **29** | 0 | 0 | 0 | **29** |
| ἴσχω | 0 | 5 | 0 | 0 | 0 | 0 | 0 | 0 | 0 | **5** | 0 | 0 | 0 | **5** |
| καί | 54 | 285 | 43 | 38 | 14 | 53 | 3 | 38 | 2 | **530** | 3 | 4 | 7 | **544** |
| καλέω | 0 | 2 | 1 | 1 | 0 | 0 | 0 | 1 | 0 | **5** | 0 | 0 | 0 | **5** |
| κατά | 5 | 22 | 1 | 7 | 2 | 2 | 0 | 2 | 0 | **41** | 0 | 0 | 0 | **41** |
| κατακερματίζω | 0 | 1 | 0 | 0 | 0 | 0 | 0 | 0 | 0 | **1** | 0 | 0 | 0 | **1** |
| κατέχω | 0 | 2 | 0 | 0 | 0 | 0 | 0 | 0 | 0 | **2** | 0 | 0 | 0 | **2** |
| κεῖμαι | 0 | 3 | 0 | 0 | 0 | 0 | 0 | 0 | 0 | **3** | 0 | 0 | 0 | **3** |
| κερματίζω | 0 | 1 | 0 | 0 | 0 | 0 | 0 | 2 | 0 | **3** | 0 | 0 | 0 | **3** |
| κινέω | 5 | 3 | 11 | 1 | 1 | 10 | 2 | 1 | 0 | **34** | 0 | 0 | 0 | **34** |
| κίνησις | 2 | 0 | 3 | 0 | 0 | 1 | 0 | 1 | 0 | **7** | 0 | 0 | 0 | **7** |
| κοινωνέω | 0 | 0 | 0 | 1 | 0 | 0 | 0 | 0 | 0 | **1** | 0 | 0 | 0 | **1** |
| κοινωνία | 0 | 1 | 0 | 0 | 0 | 0 | 0 | 0 | 1 | **2** | 0 | 0 | 0 | **2** |
| κύκλος | 6 | 0 | 0 | 0 | 0 | 0 | 0 | 0 | 0 | **6** | 0 | 0 | 0 | **6** |
| κωλύω | 0 | 0 | 0 | 0 | 0 | 1 | 0 | 0 | 0 | **1** | 0 | 0 | 0 | **1** |
| λαμβάνω | 0 | 3 | 2 | 0 | 0 | 0 | 1 | 5 | 0 | **11** | 0 | 0 | 0 | **11** |
| λέγω | 3 | 12 | 1 | 1 | 1 | 12 | 3 | 2 | 0 | **35** | 0 | 6 | 0 | **41** |
| λείπω | 0 | 0 | 0 | 0 | 0 | 0 | 0 | 1 | 0 | **1** | 0 | 0 | 0 | **1** |
| λεκτέος | 0 | 0 | 0 | 0 | 0 | 1 | 0 | 0 | 0 | **1** | 0 | 0 | 0 | **1** |
| λόγος | 2 | 5 | 1 | 1 | 0 | 3 | 1 | 1 | 0 | **14** | 0 | 0 | 0 | **14** |
| λοιπός | 0 | 1 | 0 | 0 | 0 | 0 | 0 | 0 | 0 | **1** | 0 | 0 | 0 | **1** |
| μάλα | 0 | 4 | 0 | 0 | 0 | 1 | 0 | 0 | 0 | **5** | 0 | 0 | 0 | **5** |
| μέγας | 4 | 26 | 3 | 0 | 1 | 1 | 0 | 2 | 0 | **37** | 0 | 0 | 0 | **37** |
| μέγεθος | 0 | 14 | 0 | 0 | 0 | 5 | 1 | 0 | 0 | **20** | 0 | 1 | 0 | **21** |
| μέθεξις | 1 | 1 | 0 | 1 | 0 | 0 | 0 | 0 | 0 | **3** | 0 | 0 | 0 | **3** |
| μεθίστημι | 0 | 0 | 0 | 0 | 0 | 1 | 0 | 0 | 0 | **1** | 0 | 0 | 0 | **1** |
| μέλλω | 6 | 7 | 0 | 0 | 0 | 2 | 0 | 1 | 0 | **16** | 0 | 0 | 0 | **16** |

| | S1 | S2 | S2C | S3 | S4 | S5 | S6 | S7 | S8 | **S1–8** | IS | TP | FS | **Total** |
|---|---|---|---|---|---|---|---|---|---|---|---|---|---|---|
| μέν | 15 | 44 | 4 | 6 | 4 | 7 | 1 | 5 | 1 | **87** | 0 | 1 | 0 | **88** |
| μέντοι | 0 | 2 | 0 | 0 | 0 | 2 | 0 | 0 | 0 | **4** | 0 | 0 | 0 | **4** |
| μερίζω | 0 | 3 | 0 | 0 | 0 | 0 | 0 | 0 | 0 | **3** | 0 | 0 | 0 | **3** |
| μεριστός | 0 | 1 | 0 | 0 | 0 | 0 | 0 | 0 | 0 | **1** | 0 | 0 | 0 | **1** |
| μέρος | 18 | 39 | 0 | 0 | 0 | 0 | 0 | 0 | 1 | **58** | 0 | 0 | 0 | **58** |
| μέσος | 7 | 7 | 0 | 0 | 0 | 0 | 0 | 4 | 0 | **18** | 0 | 0 | 0 | **18** |
| μετά | 0 | 6 | 0 | 0 | 0 | 0 | 0 | 1 | 0 | **7** | 0 | 1 | 0 | **8** |
| μεταβαίνω | 0 | 1 | 0 | 0 | 0 | 2 | 0 | 1 | 0 | **4** | 0 | 0 | 0 | **4** |
| μεταβάλλω | 0 | 0 | 16 | 0 | 0 | 1 | 0 | 0 | 0 | **17** | 0 | 0 | 0 | **17** |
| μεταβολή | 0 | 0 | 1 | 0 | 0 | 3 | 0 | 0 | 0 | **4** | 0 | 0 | 0 | **4** |
| μεταλαμβάνω | 0 | 0 | 2 | 3 | 0 | 0 | 1 | 0 | 0 | **6** | 0 | 0 | 0 | **6** |
| μεταληπτέος | 0 | 0 | 0 | 0 | 0 | 0 | 1 | 0 | 0 | **1** | 0 | 0 | 0 | **1** |
| μεταλλάττω | 1 | 0 | 0 | 0 | 0 | 0 | 0 | 0 | 0 | **1** | 0 | 0 | 0 | **1** |
| μεταξύ | 0 | 2 | 2 | 0 | 0 | 3 | 0 | 1 | 0 | **8** | 0 | 0 | 0 | **8** |
| μέτειμι | 3 | 0 | 0 | 0 | 0 | 5 | 1 | 0 | 0 | **9** | 0 | 0 | 0 | **9** |
| μετέχω | 13 | 22 | 11 | 12 | 8 | 5 | 5 | 0 | 0 | **76** | 0 | 0 | 0 | **76** |
| μέτρον | 11 | 7 | 0 | 0 | 0 | 0 | 0 | 0 | 0 | **18** | 0 | 0 | 0 | **18** |
| μέχρι | 0 | 1 | 0 | 0 | 0 | 0 | 0 | 0 | 0 | **1** | 0 | 0 | 0 | **1** |
| μή | 11 | 45 | 6 | 4 | 1 | 54 | 13 | 10 | 11 | **155** | 0 | 14 | 1 | **170** |
| μηδαμός | 3 | 3 | 0 | 0 | 0 | 2 | 1 | 0 | 0 | **9** | 0 | 0 | 0 | **9** |
| μηδέ | 0 | 4 | 1 | 0 | 1 | 2 | 1 | 1 | 0 | **10** | 0 | 0 | 0 | **10** |
| μηδείς | 3 | 3 | 0 | 1 | 0 | 0 | 2 | 1 | 1 | **11** | 0 | 0 | 0 | **11** |
| μηδέποτε | 1 | 4 | 0 | 0 | 0 | 0 | 0 | 0 | 0 | **5** | 0 | 0 | 0 | **5** |
| μηδέτερος | 0 | 0 | 0 | 0 | 0 | 0 | 0 | 1 | 0 | **1** | 0 | 0 | 0 | **1** |
| μήν | 22 | 26 | 2 | 5 | 1 | 10 | 3 | 2 | 2 | **73** | 0 | 0 | 0 | **73** |
| μήτε | 16 | 28 | 4 | 2 | 2 | 9 | 2 | 0 | 0 | **63** | 0 | 0 | 0 | **63** |
| μηχανή | 1 | 1 | 0 | 0 | 0 | 0 | 0 | 0 | 0 | **2** | 0 | 0 | 0 | **2** |
| μικτός | 0 | 1 | 0 | 0 | 0 | 0 | 0 | 0 | 0 | **1** | 0 | 0 | 0 | **1** |
| μιμνήσκω | 0 | 1 | 0 | 0 | 0 | 0 | 0 | 0 | 0 | **1** | 0 | 0 | 0 | **1** |
| μόνος | 3 | 6 | 2 | 0 | 1 | 0 | 0 | 0 | 0 | **12** | 0 | 1 | 0 | **13** |
| μόριον | 0 | 28 | 0 | 31 | 6 | 0 | 0 | 0 | 0 | **65** | 0 | 0 | 0 | **65** |
| νέμω | 0 | 3 | 0 | 0 | 0 | 0 | 0 | 0 | 0 | **3** | 0 | 0 | 0 | **3** |
| νέος | 8 | 40 | 0 | 0 | 0 | 0 | 0 | 0 | 0 | **48** | 0 | 0 | 0 | **48** |
| νοέω | 0 | 0 | 0 | 0 | 0 | 0 | 0 | 1 | 0 | **1** | 0 | 0 | 0 | **1** |
| νῦν | 2 | 16 | 0 | 1 | 1 | 0 | 2 | 0 | 0 | **22** | 0 | 1 | 0 | **23** |
| ὁ, ἡ, τό | 122 | 603 | 34 | 75 | 41 | 106 | 26 | 41 | 21 | **1,069** | 2 | 13 | 1 | **1,085** |
| ὄγκος | 0 | 0 | 0 | 0 | 0 | 0 | 0 | 7 | 0 | **7** | 0 | 0 | 0 | **7** |
| ὅδε | 0 | 7 | 0 | 0 | 0 | 0 | 0 | 0 | 0 | **7** | 0 | 1 | 0 | **8** |

| | S1 | S2 | S2C | S3 | S4 | S5 | S6 | S7 | S8 | **S1–8** | IS | TP | FS | **Total** |
|---|---|---|---|---|---|---|---|---|---|---|---|---|---|---|
| οἶδα | 0 | 0 | 0 | 0 | 0 | 0 | 0 | 0 | 0 | **0** | 0 | 1 | 0 | **1** |
| οἴομαι | 1 | 4 | 0 | 0 | 0 | 0 | 0 | 1 | 0 | **6** | 0 | 0 | 0 | **6** |
| οἷος | 4 | 6 | 5 | 2 | 0 | 3 | 0 | 2 | 0 | **22** | 0 | 0 | 0 | **22** |
| ὀλίγος | 1 | 2 | 0 | 1 | 0 | 0 | 0 | 0 | 0 | **4** | 0 | 0 | 0 | **4** |
| ὅλος | 10 | 41 | 0 | 14 | 4 | 0 | 0 | 0 | 0 | **69** | 0 | 0 | 0 | **69** |
| ὅμοιος | 5 | 12 | 4 | 3 | 4 | 2 | 1 | 3 | 1 | **35** | 0 | 0 | 0 | **35** |
| ὁμοιότης | 2 | 0 | 0 | 0 | 2 | 2 | 1 | 0 | 0 | **7** | 0 | 0 | 0 | **7** |
| ὁμοιόω | 0 | 2 | 2 | 0 | 0 | 0 | 0 | 0 | 0 | **4** | 0 | 0 | 0 | **4** |
| ὄναρ | 0 | 0 | 0 | 0 | 0 | 0 | 0 | 1 | 0 | **1** | 0 | 0 | 0 | **1** |
| ὄνομα | 1 | 9 | 0 | 0 | 0 | 0 | 1 | 0 | 0 | **11** | 0 | 0 | 0 | **11** |
| ὀνομάζω | 1 | 2 | 0 | 0 | 0 | 0 | 0 | 0 | 0 | **3** | 0 | 0 | 0 | **3** |
| ὀξύς | 0 | 0 | 0 | 0 | 0 | 0 | 0 | 1 | 0 | **1** | 0 | 0 | 0 | **1** |
| ὅπη | 0 | 0 | 0 | 0 | 0 | 1 | 0 | 0 | 0 | **1** | 0 | 0 | 0 | **1** |
| ὁποῖος | 0 | 1 | 0 | 0 | 0 | 0 | 0 | 0 | 0 | **1** | 0 | 0 | 0 | **1** |
| ὁπότε | 2 | 0 | 0 | 0 | 0 | 0 | 0 | 0 | 0 | **2** | 0 | 0 | 0 | **2** |
| ὁπότερος | 0 | 1 | 0 | 0 | 0 | 0 | 0 | 0 | 0 | **1** | 0 | 0 | 0 | **1** |
| ὅπως | 1 | 0 | 0 | 0 | 0 | 0 | 1 | 0 | 0 | **2** | 0 | 0 | 0 | **2** |
| ὁράω | 1 | 4 | 0 | 2 | 0 | 0 | 1 | 1 | 0 | **9** | 0 | 0 | 0 | **9** |
| ὀρθός | 0 | 2 | 0 | 0 | 0 | 0 | 0 | 0 | 1 | **3** | 0 | 0 | 0 | **3** |
| ὅρος | 0 | 1 | 0 | 0 | 0 | 0 | 0 | 0 | 0 | **1** | 0 | 0 | 0 | **1** |
| ὅς, ἥ, ὅ | 12 | 24 | 2 | 10 | 4 | 4 | 2 | 3 | 0 | **61** | 0 | 1 | 0 | **62** |
| ὅσος | 1 | 3 | 0 | 1 | 0 | 0 | 0 | 0 | 1 | **6** | 0 | 0 | 0 | **6** |
| ὁσοσπερ | 2 | 3 | 0 | 0 | 0 | 0 | 0 | 0 | 0 | **5** | 0 | 0 | 0 | **5** |
| ὅσπερ | 2 | 6 | 0 | 0 | 0 | 0 | 1 | 0 | 0 | **9** | 0 | 0 | 0 | **9** |
| ὅστις | 2 | 5 | 0 | 0 | 0 | 1 | 0 | 0 | 0 | **8** | 0 | 0 | 0 | **8** |
| ὅταν | 0 | 7 | 7 | 0 | 1 | 2 | 2 | 1 | 0 | **20** | 0 | 2 | 0 | **22** |
| ὅτανπερ | 0 | 1 | 0 | 0 | 0 | 0 | 0 | 0 | 0 | **1** | 0 | 0 | 0 | **1** |
| ὅτε | 0 | 0 | 6 | 1 | 0 | 0 | 0 | 0 | 0 | **7** | 0 | 0 | 0 | **7** |
| ὅτι | 6 | 16 | 2 | 3 | 1 | 3 | 1 | 1 | 1 | **34** | 0 | 3 | 1 | **38** |
| ὁτιοῦν | 0 | 2 | 0 | 1 | 0 | 0 | 1 | 0 | 0 | **4** | 0 | 0 | 0 | **4** |
| ὅτιπερ | 0 | 3 | 0 | 0 | 0 | 0 | 0 | 0 | 0 | **3** | 0 | 0 | 0 | **3** |
| οὐ | 31 | 81 | 11 | 11 | 4 | 29 | 4 | 8 | 1 | **180** | 0 | 2 | 2 | **184** |
| οὐδαμός | 6 | 2 | 0 | 0 | 2 | 2 | 8 | 0 | 4 | **24** | 0 | 0 | 0 | **24** |
| οὐδέ | 28 | 25 | 4 | 3 | 16 | 10 | 6 | 0 | 18 | **110** | 1 | 0 | 0 | **111** |
| οὐδείς | 6 | 14 | 3 | 4 | 3 | 2 | 0 | 0 | 5 | **37** | 0 | 1 | 0 | **38** |
| οὐδέποτε | 1 | 3 | 0 | 0 | 1 | 0 | 0 | 0 | 0 | **5** | 0 | 0 | 0 | **5** |
| οὐκέτι | 1 | 0 | 0 | 1 | 0 | 1 | 0 | 0 | 0 | **3** | 0 | 0 | 0 | **3** |
| οὐκοῦν | 7 | 31 | 1 | 5 | 1 | 4 | 1 | 5 | 2 | **57** | 0 | 1 | 0 | **58** |

| | S1 | S2 | S2C | S3 | S4 | S5 | S6 | S7 | S8 | S1–8 | IS | TP | FS | Total |
|---|---|---|---|---|---|---|---|---|---|---|---|---|---|---|
| οὖν | 6 | 27 | 4 | 1 | 1 | 3 | 1 | 1 | 0 | **44** | 0 | 1 | 0 | **45** |
| οὐσία | 3 | 34 | 5 | 0 | 0 | 7 | 8 | 0 | 0 | **57** | 0 | 0 | 0 | **57** |
| οὔτε | 73 | 63 | 21 | 1 | 13 | 6 | 18 | 3 | 6 | **204** | 0 | 0 | 0 | **204** |
| οὗτος | 13 | 48 | 7 | 11 | 4 | 8 | 9 | 4 | 1 | **105** | 0 | 2 | 1 | **108** |
| οὕτως | 11 | 29 | 3 | 4 | 2 | 10 | 2 | 1 | 0 | **62** | 1 | 0 | 0 | **63** |
| πάθημα | 1 | 0 | 1 | 0 | 0 | 0 | 0 | 0 | 0 | **2** | 0 | 0 | 0 | **2** |
| πάθος | 0 | 3 | 0 | 4 | 0 | 0 | 0 | 0 | 0 | **7** | 0 | 0 | 0 | **7** |
| πάλιν | 0 | 4 | 0 | 0 | 1 | 0 | 1 | 0 | 1 | **7** | 0 | 0 | 0 | **7** |
| παμμεγέθης | 0 | 0 | 0 | 0 | 0 | 0 | 0 | 1 | 0 | **1** | 0 | 0 | 0 | **1** |
| παντάπασι | 1 | 1 | 0 | 1 | 0 | 0 | 0 | 0 | 0 | **3** | 0 | 0 | 0 | **3** |
| πανταχῇ | 1 | 0 | 0 | 0 | 1 | 0 | 0 | 0 | 0 | **2** | 0 | 0 | 0 | **2** |
| πανταχῶς | 0 | 2 | 0 | 0 | 0 | 0 | 0 | 0 | 0 | **2** | 0 | 0 | 0 | **2** |
| παντελής | 0 | 0 | 0 | 1 | 0 | 0 | 0 | 0 | 0 | **1** | 0 | 0 | 0 | **1** |
| πάντῃ | 0 | 2 | 0 | 0 | 1 | 0 | 0 | 1 | 0 | **4** | 0 | 0 | 0 | **4** |
| παρά | 0 | 4 | 0 | 0 | 1 | 0 | 0 | 0 | 2 | **7** | 0 | 0 | 0 | **7** |
| παράπαν | 2 | 0 | 0 | 0 | 0 | 0 | 0 | 0 | 0 | **2** | 0 | 0 | 0 | **2** |
| πάρειμι | 1 | 3 | 0 | 0 | 0 | 0 | 0 | 0 | 0 | **4** | 0 | 0 | 0 | **4** |
| παρέρχομαι | 0 | 2 | 0 | 0 | 0 | 0 | 0 | 0 | 0 | **2** | 0 | 0 | 0 | **2** |
| παρέχω | 0 | 0 | 0 | 1 | 0 | 0 | 0 | 0 | 0 | **1** | 0 | 0 | 0 | **1** |
| πᾶς | 1 | 31 | 1 | 6 | 2 | 2 | 0 | 4 | 0 | **47** | 1 | 1 | 2 | **51** |
| πάσχω | 12 | 11 | 2 | 8 | 3 | 0 | 1 | 2 | 0 | **39** | 0 | 0 | 0 | **39** |
| περαίνω | 0 | 3 | 0 | 1 | 0 | 0 | 0 | 0 | 0 | **4** | 0 | 0 | 0 | **4** |
| πέρας | 1 | 1 | 0 | 4 | 0 | 0 | 0 | 3 | 0 | **9** | 0 | 0 | 0 | **9** |
| περί | 2 | 10 | 0 | 1 | 0 | 6 | 2 | 2 | 0 | **23** | 0 | 0 | 0 | **23** |
| περιέχω | 5 | 11 | 0 | 0 | 0 | 0 | 0 | 0 | 0 | **16** | 0 | 0 | 0 | **16** |
| περιττάκις | 0 | 2 | 0 | 0 | 0 | 0 | 0 | 0 | 0 | **2** | 0 | 0 | 0 | **2** |
| περιττός | 0 | 3 | 0 | 0 | 1 | 0 | 0 | 1 | 0 | **5** | 0 | 0 | 0 | **5** |
| περιφερής | 2 | 0 | 0 | 0 | 0 | 0 | 0 | 0 | 0 | **2** | 0 | 0 | 0 | **2** |
| περιφέρω | 3 | 0 | 0 | 0 | 0 | 0 | 0 | 0 | 0 | **3** | 0 | 0 | 0 | **3** |
| πῃ | 0 | 1 | 0 | 1 | 0 | 3 | 1 | 0 | 0 | **6** | 0 | 0 | 0 | **6** |
| πιστεύω | 1 | 0 | 0 | 0 | 0 | 0 | 0 | 0 | 0 | **1** | 0 | 0 | 0 | **1** |
| πλεονάκις | 0 | 1 | 0 | 0 | 0 | 0 | 0 | 0 | 0 | **1** | 0 | 0 | 0 | **1** |
| πλεονεκτέω | 0 | 2 | 0 | 0 | 0 | 0 | 0 | 0 | 0 | **2** | 0 | 0 | 0 | **2** |
| πλῆθος | 0 | 10 | 0 | 4 | 0 | 0 | 0 | 3 | 0 | **17** | 0 | 0 | 0 | **17** |
| πλήν | 0 | 2 | 0 | 2 | 0 | 0 | 0 | 0 | 0 | **4** | 0 | 0 | 0 | **4** |
| ποθεν | 0 | 0 | 0 | 0 | 0 | 1 | 0 | 0 | 0 | **1** | 0 | 0 | 0 | **1** |
| ποι | 1 | 0 | 0 | 0 | 0 | 1 | 0 | 0 | 0 | **2** | 0 | 0 | 0 | **2** |
| ποιέω | 1 | 3 | 1 | 0 | 0 | 0 | 0 | 0 | 0 | **5** | 0 | 0 | 0 | **5** |

| | S1 | S2 | S2C | S3 | S4 | S5 | S6 | S7 | S8 | **S1–8** | IS | TP | FS | **Total** |
|---|---|---|---|---|---|---|---|---|---|---|---|---|---|---|
| ποιός | 0 | 1 | 0 | 0 | 0 | 0 | 0 | 0 | 0 | **1** | 0 | 0 | 0 | **1** |
| πολλάκις | 0 | 3 | 0 | 0 | 0 | 0 | 0 | 0 | 0 | **3** | 0 | 0 | 0 | **3** |
| πολλαχῇ | 1 | 0 | 0 | 0 | 0 | 0 | 0 | 0 | 0 | **1** | 0 | 0 | 0 | **1** |
| πολλαχοῦ | 1 | 1 | 0 | 0 | 0 | 0 | 0 | 0 | 0 | **2** | 0 | 0 | 0 | **2** |
| πολύς | 14 | 35 | 9 | 8 | 3 | 2 | 0 | 9 | 8 | **88** | 0 | 0 | 0 | **88** |
| πορεύω | 0 | 2 | 0 | 0 | 0 | 0 | 0 | 0 | 0 | **2** | 0 | 0 | 0 | **2** |
| πόρρωθεν | 0 | 0 | 0 | 0 | 0 | 0 | 0 | 1 | 0 | **1** | 0 | 0 | 0 | **1** |
| ποτε | 6 | 8 | 4 | 0 | 0 | 0 | 2 | 0 | 0 | **20** | 0 | 0 | 0 | **20** |
| πότερος | 0 | 2 | 0 | 0 | 0 | 0 | 1 | 0 | 0 | **3** | 0 | 0 | 0 | **3** |
| που | 12 | 16 | 0 | 4 | 2 | 2 | 0 | 4 | 0 | **40** | 0 | 0 | 0 | **40** |
| πράττω | 0 | 2 | 0 | 0 | 0 | 0 | 0 | 0 | 0 | **2** | 0 | 0 | 0 | **2** |
| πρέσβυς | 11 | 55 | 0 | 0 | 0 | 0 | 0 | 0 | 0 | **66** | 0 | 0 | 0 | **66** |
| πρίν | 0 | 0 | 0 | 0 | 0 | 0 | 0 | 1 | 0 | **1** | 0 | 0 | 0 | **1** |
| πρό | 0 | 0 | 0 | 0 | 0 | 0 | 0 | 1 | 0 | **1** | 0 | 0 | 0 | **1** |
| προαίρεσις | 0 | 1 | 0 | 0 | 0 | 0 | 0 | 0 | 0 | **1** | 0 | 0 | 0 | **1** |
| προαιρέω | 0 | 2 | 0 | 0 | 0 | 0 | 0 | 0 | 0 | **2** | 0 | 0 | 0 | **2** |
| πρόειμι | 0 | 2 | 0 | 0 | 0 | 0 | 0 | 0 | 0 | **2** | 0 | 0 | 0 | **2** |
| προέρχομαι | 0 | 1 | 0 | 0 | 0 | 0 | 0 | 0 | 0 | **1** | 0 | 0 | 0 | **1** |
| πρός | 0 | 23 | 1 | 4 | 0 | 5 | 2 | 4 | 0 | **39** | 2 | 0 | 2 | **43** |
| προσαγορεύω | 0 | 2 | 0 | 0 | 0 | 0 | 0 | 0 | 0 | **2** | 0 | 0 | 0 | **2** |
| προσγίγνομαι | 0 | 5 | 0 | 0 | 0 | 0 | 0 | 0 | 0 | **5** | 0 | 0 | 0 | **5** |
| πρόσειμι | 0 | 2 | 0 | 0 | 0 | 0 | 0 | 0 | 0 | **2** | 0 | 0 | 0 | **2** |
| προσερέω | 0 | 1 | 0 | 0 | 0 | 0 | 0 | 0 | 0 | **1** | 0 | 0 | 0 | **1** |
| προσέρχομαι | 0 | 0 | 0 | 0 | 0 | 0 | 0 | 1 | 0 | **1** | 0 | 0 | 0 | **1** |
| προσήκω | 2 | 0 | 0 | 1 | 0 | 0 | 0 | 0 | 0 | **3** | 0 | 0 | 0 | **3** |
| πρόσθεν | 0 | 3 | 0 | 0 | 0 | 0 | 0 | 0 | 1 | **4** | 0 | 0 | 0 | **4** |
| προσρητέος | 0 | 1 | 0 | 0 | 0 | 0 | 0 | 0 | 0 | **1** | 0 | 0 | 0 | **1** |
| προστίθημι | 0 | 2 | 0 | 0 | 0 | 0 | 0 | 0 | 0 | **2** | 0 | 1 | 0 | **3** |
| πρότερος | 0 | 13 | 2 | 0 | 0 | 2 | 0 | 0 | 0 | **17** | 0 | 0 | 0 | **17** |
| πρῶτος | 0 | 10 | 0 | 0 | 0 | 1 | 0 | 0 | 0 | **11** | 0 | 1 | 0 | **12** |
| πω | 2 | 0 | 0 | 0 | 0 | 0 | 0 | 0 | 0 | **2** | 0 | 0 | 0 | **2** |
| πως | 0 | 0 | 0 | 0 | 0 | 1 | 3 | 0 | 0 | **4** | 0 | 0 | 0 | **4** |
| πῶς | 1 | 3 | 1 | 0 | 0 | 0 | 0 | 0 | 0 | **5** | 0 | 0 | 0 | **5** |
| σημαίνω | 1 | 2 | 1 | 1 | 0 | 1 | 2 | 0 | 0 | **8** | 0 | 0 | 0 | **8** |
| σκεπτέος | 0 | 0 | 0 | 1 | 0 | 0 | 0 | 0 | 0 | **1** | 0 | 1 | 0 | **2** |
| σκιαγραφέω | 0 | 0 | 0 | 0 | 0 | 0 | 0 | 1 | 0 | **1** | 0 | 0 | 0 | **1** |
| σκοπέω | 0 | 3 | 0 | 1 | 0 | 0 | 0 | 0 | 0 | **4** | 0 | 0 | 0 | **4** |
| σμικρός | 1 | 7 | 2 | 0 | 0 | 0 | 0 | 6 | 0 | **16** | 0 | 0 | 0 | **16** |

| | S1 | S2 | S2C | S3 | S4 | S5 | S6 | S7 | S8 | **S1–8** | IS | TP | FS | **Total** |
|---|---|---|---|---|---|---|---|---|---|---|---|---|---|---|
| σμικρότης | 0 | 16 | 0 | 0 | 0 | 5 | 1 | 0 | 0 | **22** | 0 | 1 | 0 | **23** |
| στάσις | 0 | 0 | 2 | 0 | 0 | 0 | 0 | 0 | 0 | **2** | 0 | 0 | 0 | **2** |
| στέρομαι | 0 | 0 | 0 | 1 | 2 | 0 | 0 | 1 | 0 | **4** | 0 | 0 | 0 | **4** |
| στρέφω | 0 | 0 | 0 | 0 | 0 | 3 | 0 | 0 | 0 | **3** | 0 | 0 | 0 | **3** |
| στρογγύλος | 2 | 1 | 0 | 0 | 0 | 0 | 0 | 0 | 0 | **3** | 0 | 0 | 0 | **3** |
| σύ | 0 | 1 | 0 | 0 | 0 | 0 | 0 | 0 | 0 | **1** | 0 | 0 | 0 | **1** |
| συγκρίνω | 0 | 0 | 2 | 0 | 0 | 0 | 0 | 0 | 0 | **2** | 0 | 0 | 0 | **2** |
| συζυγία | 0 | 1 | 0 | 0 | 0 | 0 | 0 | 0 | 0 | **1** | 0 | 0 | 0 | **1** |
| συλλήβδην | 0 | 1 | 0 | 0 | 0 | 0 | 0 | 0 | 1 | **2** | 0 | 0 | 0 | **2** |
| συμβαίνω | 0 | 5 | 0 | 1 | 0 | 0 | 1 | 0 | 0 | **7** | 0 | 1 | 0 | **8** |
| σύμμετρος | 2 | 0 | 0 | 0 | 0 | 0 | 0 | 0 | 0 | **2** | 0 | 0 | 0 | **2** |
| σύνδυο | 0 | 1 | 0 | 0 | 0 | 0 | 0 | 0 | 0 | **1** | 0 | 0 | 0 | **1** |
| συντίθημι | 0 | 1 | 0 | 0 | 0 | 0 | 0 | 0 | 0 | **1** | 0 | 0 | 0 | **1** |
| σχῆμα | 2 | 1 | 0 | 0 | 0 | 0 | 0 | 0 | 0 | **3** | 0 | 0 | 0 | **3** |
| ταὐτός | 18 | 27 | 0 | 1 | 1 | 3 | 0 | 1 | 0 | **51** | 0 | 0 | 0 | **51** |
| τε | 9 | 76 | 17 | 14 | 3 | 13 | 1 | 8 | 0 | **141** | 1 | 0 | 4 | **146** |
| τείνω | 0 | 1 | 0 | 0 | 0 | 0 | 0 | 0 | 0 | **1** | 0 | 0 | 0 | **1** |
| τέλειος | 0 | 0 | 0 | 2 | 0 | 3 | 0 | 0 | 0 | **5** | 0 | 0 | 0 | **5** |
| τελευτή | 3 | 6 | 0 | 0 | 0 | 0 | 0 | 2 | 0 | **11** | 0 | 0 | 0 | **11** |
| τέλος | 0 | 1 | 0 | 0 | 0 | 0 | 0 | 0 | 0 | **1** | 0 | 0 | 0 | **1** |
| τις | 22 | 34 | 4 | 6 | 3 | 9 | 6 | 6 | 4 | **94** | 0 | 5 | 0 | **99** |
| τίς | 5 | 23 | 0 | 3 | 1 | 2 | 3 | 2 | 1 | **40** | 0 | 4 | 0 | **44** |
| τοίνυν | 0 | 0 | 0 | 0 | 0 | 0 | 0 | 0 | 0 | **0** | 0 | 0 | 1 | **1** |
| τοιόσδε | 1 | 0 | 1 | 0 | 0 | 0 | 0 | 0 | 0 | **2** | 0 | 0 | 0 | **2** |
| τοιοῦτος | 7 | 4 | 0 | 1 | 2 | 4 | 0 | 3 | 0 | **21** | 0 | 1 | 0 | **22** |
| τοσόσδε | 0 | 1 | 0 | 0 | 0 | 0 | 0 | 0 | 0 | **1** | 0 | 0 | 0 | **1** |
| τοσοῦτος | 2 | 1 | 0 | 0 | 0 | 1 | 0 | 0 | 0 | **4** | 0 | 0 | 0 | **4** |
| τότε | 0 | 5 | 7 | 1 | 0 | 0 | 0 | 0 | 0 | **13** | 0 | 0 | 0 | **13** |
| τρία | 0 | 10 | 0 | 0 | 2 | 0 | 0 | 0 | 0 | **12** | 0 | 0 | 0 | **12** |
| τρίς | 0 | 6 | 0 | 0 | 0 | 0 | 0 | 0 | 0 | **6** | 0 | 0 | 0 | **6** |
| τρίτος | 0 | 2 | 1 | 0 | 0 | 0 | 0 | 0 | 0 | **3** | 0 | 0 | 0 | **3** |
| τρόπος | 1 | 0 | 0 | 0 | 1 | 0 | 0 | 0 | 0 | **2** | 0 | 0 | 0 | **2** |
| τυγχάνω | 1 | 5 | 0 | 0 | 0 | 0 | 0 | 0 | 0 | **6** | 0 | 0 | 0 | **6** |
| ὑπάρχω | 0 | 2 | 0 | 0 | 0 | 1 | 0 | 0 | 0 | **3** | 0 | 0 | 0 | **3** |
| ὑπερβαίνω | 0 | 1 | 0 | 0 | 0 | 0 | 0 | 0 | 0 | **1** | 0 | 0 | 0 | **1** |
| ὑπερέχω | 0 | 9 | 0 | 0 | 0 | 0 | 0 | 0 | 0 | **9** | 0 | 0 | 0 | **9** |
| ὕπνος | 0 | 0 | 0 | 0 | 0 | 0 | 0 | 1 | 0 | **1** | 0 | 0 | 0 | **1** |
| ὑπό | 1 | 7 | 0 | 0 | 0 | 0 | 0 | 0 | 0 | **8** | 0 | 0 | 0 | **8** |

| | S1 | S2 | S2C | S3 | S4 | S5 | S6 | S7 | S8 | **S1–8** | IS | TP | FS | **Total** |
|---|---|---|---|---|---|---|---|---|---|---|---|---|---|---|
| ὑπόθεσις | 0 | 3 | 0 | 0 | 0 | 1 | 0 | 0 | 0 | **4** | 0 | 1 | 0 | **5** |
| ὑπόκειμαι | 0 | 0 | 0 | 0 | 0 | 1 | 0 | 0 | 0 | **1** | 0 | 0 | 0 | **1** |
| ὑπολείπω | 0 | 1 | 0 | 0 | 0 | 0 | 0 | 1 | 0 | **2** | 0 | 0 | 0 | **2** |
| ὑπομένω | 0 | 0 | 0 | 0 | 1 | 0 | 0 | 0 | 0 | **1** | 0 | 0 | 0 | **1** |
| ὑποτίθημι | 0 | 1 | 0 | 0 | 0 | 0 | 0 | 0 | 0 | **1** | 0 | 0 | 0 | **1** |
| ὕστερος | 0 | 8 | 2 | 0 | 0 | 0 | 0 | 0 | 0 | **10** | 0 | 0 | 0 | **10** |
| φαίνω | 3 | 15 | 0 | 1 | 2 | 4 | 1 | 12 | 3 | **41** | 0 | 0 | 2 | **43** |
| φανερός | 0 | 0 | 0 | 0 | 1 | 0 | 0 | 0 | 0 | **1** | 0 | 0 | 0 | **1** |
| φάντασμα | 0 | 0 | 0 | 0 | 0 | 0 | 0 | 2 | 1 | **3** | 0 | 0 | 0 | **3** |
| φέρω | 5 | 0 | 0 | 0 | 0 | 0 | 0 | 0 | 0 | **5** | 0 | 0 | 0 | **5** |
| φημί | 2 | 10 | 0 | 1 | 1 | 3 | 5 | 2 | 0 | **24** | 0 | 0 | 0 | **24** |
| φθέγγομαι | 0 | 2 | 0 | 0 | 0 | 1 | 0 | 0 | 0 | **3** | 0 | 0 | 0 | **3** |
| φθίω | 0 | 0 | 2 | 0 | 0 | 0 | 0 | 0 | 0 | **2** | 0 | 0 | 0 | **2** |
| φύσις | 2 | 4 | 1 | 3 | 0 | 0 | 0 | 0 | 0 | **10** | 0 | 0 | 0 | **10** |
| φύω | 0 | 4 | 0 | 0 | 0 | 0 | 0 | 0 | 0 | **4** | 0 | 0 | 0 | **4** |
| χαλεπός | 0 | 0 | 0 | 1 | 0 | 0 | 0 | 0 | 0 | **1** | 0 | 0 | 0 | **1** |
| χρή | 0 | 1 | 0 | 2 | 1 | 1 | 1 | 1 | 1 | **8** | 0 | 1 | 0 | **9** |
| χρόνος | 10 | 19 | 8 | 0 | 0 | 0 | 0 | 0 | 0 | **37** | 0 | 0 | 0 | **37** |
| χώρα | 3 | 2 | 0 | 0 | 0 | 0 | 0 | 0 | 0 | **5** | 0 | 0 | 0 | **5** |
| χωρίς | 2 | 2 | 0 | 0 | 4 | 0 | 0 | 1 | 1 | **10** | 0 | 0 | 0 | **10** |
| ὧδε | 1 | 4 | 0 | 1 | 0 | 1 | 0 | 0 | 0 | **7** | 0 | 0 | 0 | **7** |
| ὡς | 5 | 17 | 2 | 3 | 2 | 7 | 0 | 3 | 1 | **40** | 0 | 0 | 1 | **41** |
| ὡσαύτως | 0 | 7 | 0 | 0 | 0 | 1 | 0 | 0 | 0 | **8** | 1 | 0 | 0 | **9** |
| ὥσπερ | 0 | 3 | 0 | 0 | 0 | 1 | 0 | 1 | 0 | **5** | 0 | 0 | 0 | **5** |
| ὥστε | 2 | 4 | 0 | 0 | 0 | 0 | 0 | 0 | 1 | **7** | 0 | 0 | 0 | **7** |

# BIBLIOGRAPHY

## A. Primary Sources

*Platonis Opera*. Recognovit brevique adnotatione critica
  instruxit I. Burnet. 5 vol. Oxford ²1905–1913 [1900–1907].
Platon. *Parménide* (= Œuvres complètes. Vol. viii/1). Texte établi et
  traduit par A. Diès. Paris ³1956 [1923].
*Platonis Parmenides Phaedrus*. Recognovit brevique adnotatione critica
  instruxit C. Moreschini. Rome 1966.

Aristoteles. *Über die Seele. De anima*. Übersetzt, mit einer Einleitung
  und Anmerkungen herausgegeben von K. Corcilius. Hamburg 2017.
  [Source of Greek text by A. Förster, Budapest 1912.]
*Aristotelis Ethica Eudemia*. Recensverunt brevique adnotatione critica
  instruxerunt R. R. Walzer et J. M. Mingay. Oxford 1991.
*Aristotelis Metaphysica*. Recognovit brevique adnotatione critica
  instruxit W. Jaeger. Oxford 1957.
*Aristotelis Physica*. Recognovit brevique adnotatione critica
  instruxit W. D. Ross. Oxford 1950.
Aristoteles. *Über die Bewegung der Lebewesen. De motu animalium*.
  Historisch-kritische Edition des griechischen Textes und philologische
  Einleitung von O. Primavesi. Deutsche Übersetzung, philosophische
  Einleitung und erklärende Anmerkungen von K. Corcilius. Hamburg 2018.

Alexander of Aphrodisias. *Commentary on Aristotle*, Metaphysics (Books i–iii).
  Critical edition with Introduction and Notes. Edited by P. Golitsis.
  Berlin, Boston 2022.
*Die Fragmente der Vorsokratiker*. Griechisch und Deutsch von H. Diels.
  Herausgegeben von W. Kranz. 3 vol. Hildesheim ⁶1951–1952 [1903].
*Procli In Platonis Parmenidem commentaria*. Edidit C. Steel.
  3 vol. Oxford 2007–2009.
*Simplicii In Aristotelis Physicorum libros quattuor priores commentaria*.
  Edidit H. Diels. Berlin 1882.
*The Hellenistic Philosophers*. Edited by A. A. Long and D. N. Sedley.
  2 vol. Cambridge 1987.

## B. Secondary Literature

ACERBI, F. 2000. "Plato: *Parmenides* 149a7–c3. A Proof by Complete Induction?" *Archive for History of Exact Sciences* 55: 57–76.

ADAM, J. ²1963 [1902]. *The Republic of Plato.* 2 vol. Cambridge et al.

ALLEN, R. E. ²1997 [1983]. *Plato's Parmenides.* New Haven.

AUBENQUE, P. 1992. "De l'égalité des segments intermédiaires dans la Ligne de la *République.*" In: GOULET-CAZÉ, M.-O.; MADEC, G.; O'BRIEN, D. (eds.). Σοφίης μαιήτορες. *"Chercheurs de sagesse".* Hommage à Jean Pépin. Paris. 37–44.

BRANDWOOD, L. 1992. "Stylometry and chronology." In: KRAUT, R. (ed.). *The Cambridge Companion to Plato.* Cambridge. 90–120.

BRISSON, L. ²1977 [1975]. "La question du statut de Parm. 155e4–157b5 dans la seconde partie du *Parménide* de Platon examinée à l'aide de l'informatique et de la statistique lexicale." In: BERTIER, J.; BRISSON, L.; COMBÈS, J.; TROUILLARD, J. *Recherches sur la tradition platonicienne (Platon, Aristote, Proclus, Damascius).* Paris. 9–29.

BRISSON, L. 1978. "La répartition des négations dans la seconde partie du *Parménide* de Platon (Le discours de Parménide)." *Informatique et statistique lexicale. Revue de l'Organisation Internationale pour l'Études des Langues Anciennes par Ordinateur* 1: 45–62.

BRISSON, L. 1984. "Les réponses du jeune Aristote dans la seconde partie du *Parménide* de Platon. Essai de classification." *Revue informatique et statistique dans les sciences humaines* 20: 59–79.

BRISSON, L.; BENZÉCRI, J.-P. 1989. "Structure de la seconde partie du *Parménide* de Platon et répartition des vocables." *Les Cahiers de l'analyse des données* 14: 117–126.

BRISSON, L. 2002. "Is the world one? A new interpretation of Plato's *Parmenides.*" *Oxford Studies in Ancient Philosophy* 22: 1–20.

BRISSON, L. 2005. "Réponse à Denis O'Brien." In: HAVLÍČEK/KARFÍK 2005, 257–262.

BRISSON, L.; MACÉ, A.; RENAUT, O. (eds.). *Plato's Parmenides. Selected Papers of the Twelfth Symposium Platonicum.* Baden-Baden.

BRUMBAUGH, R. S. 1961. *Plato on the One. The Hypotheses in the Parmenides.* Port Washington.

BRUNSCHWIG, J. ²2018 [1971]. "*Éthique à Eudème* I 8, 1218 A 15–32 et le ΠΕΡΙ ΤΑΓΑΘΟΥ." In: AUFFRET, TH.; RASHED, M. (eds.). *Les Études philosophiques* N° 181. *L'interprétation mathématique de Platon.* 15–36.

BURNET, J. 1914. *Greek Philosophy.* London et al.

BURNYEAT, M. F. ²2022 [2001]. "Plato." In: BURNYEAT, M. F. *Explorations in Ancient and Modern Philosophy.* Vol. 3. Cambridge. 241–263.

CHERNISS, H. F. 1956. "A Much Misread Passage of the *Timaeus* (*Timaeus* 49 C 7–50 B 5)." *The American Journal of Philology* 75: 113–130.

CHERNISS, H. F. 1957. "The Relation of the *Timaeus* to Plato's Later Dialogues." *The American Journal of Philology* 78: 225–266.

COHEN, S. M. 1971. "The Logic of the Third Man." *Philosophical Review* 80: 448–475.

COMBÈS, J. 1997. "Introduction." In: *Damascius. Commentaire du Parménide de Platon.* Texte établit par L. G. WESTERINK. Introduit, traduit et annoté par J. COMBÈS. Paris. IX–XXXVII.

CORNFORD, F. M. 1932. "Mathematics and Dialectic in the *Republic* VI.-VII. (II.)." *Mind* 41: 173–190.

CORNFORD, F. M. 1939. *Plato and Parmenides. Parmenides' Way of Truth and Plato's Parmenides.* London.

CORRIGAN, K. 2010. "The Place of the *Parmenides* in Plato's Thought and in the Subsequent Tradition." In: TURNER, J. D.; CORRIGAN, K. (ed.). *Plato's Parmenides and Its Heritage.* Vol. 1: *History and Interpretation From the Old Academy to Later Platonism and Gnosticism.* Atlanta. 23–36.

COXON, A. H. 1999. *The philosophy of forms. An analytical and historical commentary on Plato's Parmenides. With a new English translation.* Assen.

CUMMING, G. 2014. "The new statistics." *Psychological Science* 25: 7–29.

CURD, P. 1989. "Some problems of unity in the first hypothesis of the *Parmenides*." *The Southern Journal of Philosophy* 27: 347–359.

DILLON, J. 2003. *The Heirs of Plato. A Study of the Old Academy* (347–274 BC). Oxford.

DILLON, J. 2005. "Speusippus and the Ontological Interpretation of the *Parmenides*." In: HAVLÍČEK/KARFÍK 2005, 296–311.

DESJARDINS, R. 2004. *Plato and the Good. Illuminating the Darkling Vision.* Leiden, Boston.

DODDS, E. R. 1928. "The *Parmenides* of Plato and the Origin of the Neoplatonic 'One'." *The Classical Quarterly* 22: 129–142.

DÖRRIE, H.; BALTES, M. 1996. *Der Platonismus in der Antike.* Vol. IV: *Die philosophische Lehre des Platonismus. Einige grundlegende Axiome, platonische Physik (im antiken Verständnis)* 1. Bausteine 101–124. Text, Übersetzung, Kommentar. Stuttgart-Bad Cannstatt.

DORTER, K. 1994. *Form and Good in Plato's Eleatic Dialogues. The Parmenides, Theaetetus, Sophist, and Statesman.* Berkeley.

ENGELS, B. 2015. *XNomial: Exact Goodness-of-Fit Test for Multinomial Data with Fixed Probabilities.* R Package Version 1.0.4. https://cran.r-project.org/package=XNomial/

ERLER, M. 2007. *Platon.* Basel.

FERRARI, F. 2000. "Teoria delle idee e ontologia." In: VEGETTI, M. (ed.). *La Repubblica. Traduzione e commento.* Vol. IV: *Libro* V. Naples. 365–391.

FERRARI, F. ⁸2019 [2004]. *Platone. Parmenide.* Milan.

FERRARI, F. 2022. "La maschera di Parmenide: riduzionismo ed equiparazionismo nella prima parte del *Parmenide* di Platone." *Philologia Philosophica* 1: 63–89.

FINE, G. 1980. "The One Over Many." *The Philosophical Review* 89: 197–240.

FINE, G. 1993. *On Ideas. Aristotle's Criticism of Plato's Theory of Forms.* Oxford.

FRANCES, B. 1996. "Plato's Response to the Third Man Argument in the Paradoxical Exercise of the *Parmenides*." *Ancient Philosophy* 16: 47–64.

FRIEDLÄNDER, P. ³1964 [1928]. *Platon.* Vol. 1: *Seinswahrheit und Lebenswirklichkeit.* Berlin.

VON FRITZ, K. ²1969 [1932]. *Platon, Theaetet und die antike Mathematik.* Darmstadt.

FRONTEROTTA, F. 1998. *Guida alla lettura del Parmenide di Platone*. Rome, Bari.

FRONTEROTTA, F. 2016. "ΑΝΑΛΟΓΙΑ in Platone. Occorrenze e significato." *Archivio di Filosofia* 84: 49–64.

FUJISAWA, N. 1974. "Ἔχειν, μετέχειν, and Idioms of 'Paradigmatism' in Plato's Theory of Forms." *Phronesis* 19: 30–58.

GABRIEL, M. 2009. *Skeptizismus und Idealismus in der Antike*. Frankfurt/Main.

GADAMER; H.-G. 1978. *Die Idee des Guten zwischen Platon und Aristoteles*, Heidelberg.

GAISER, K. 1974. *Name und Sache in Platons "Kratylos"*. Heidelberg.

GEACH, P. T. 1956. "The Third Man Again." *Philosophical Review* 65: 72–82.

GERLACH, S. 2008. "Die Fügung der Welt. Mathematik und Ontologie der Proportionenlehre im platonischen *Timaios*." *Philosophisches Jahrbuch* 115: 21–43.

GERSON, L. P. 1984. Review of ALLEN 1983. *Phoenix* 38: 377–381.

GERSON, L. P. 2013. *From Plato to Platonism*. Ithaca.

GERSON, L. P. 2020. *Platonism and Naturalism. The Possibility of Philosophy*. Ithaca.

GLEEDE, B. 2008. "Die vierzehnstufige Theogonie des *Parmenides*. Syrians und Proklos' Beitrag zur Interpretation des rätselhaftesten von Platons Dialogen." *Zeitschrift für Antikes Christentum* 12: 135–149.

GILL, M. L. 1996. "Introduction." In: GILL, M. L.; RYAN, P. *Plato. Parmenides*. Indianapolis, Cambridge. 1–109.

GILL, M. L. 2014. "Design of the Exercise in Plato's *Parmenides*." *Dialogue* 53: 495–520.

GONZALEZ, F. J. 2022. "'Let us say the third.' The Meaning of τὸ τρίτον in the Deductions of Plato's *Parmenides*." In: BRISSON/MACÉ/RENAUT 2022, 379–391.

GRAESER, A. 1996. "Wie uber Ideen sprechen? *Parmenides*." In: KOBUSCH, TH.; MOJSISCH, B. (eds.). *Platon. Seine Dialoge in der Sicht neuer Forschung*. Darmstadt. 146–166.

GRAESER, A. 2002. "*Parmenides*' 132a1–b2 und Speusipp." *Museum Helveticum* 59: 133–136.

GRAESER, A. 2003. *Platons Parmenides*. Stuttgart.

GREGORY, A. 2012. "Kennedy and Stichometry – Some Methodological Considerations." *Apeiron* 45: 157–179.

GRIES, S. TH. 2008. "Dispersions and adjusted frequencies in corpora." *International Journal of Corpus Linguistics* 13: 403–437.

GRIES, S. TH. 2010. "Dispersions and adjusted frequencies in corpora: further explorations." In: GRIES, S. TH.; WULFF, S.; DAVIES, M. (eds.). *Corpus-linguistic applications. Current studies, new directions*. Amsterdam, New York. 197–212.

GRIES, S. TH. ³2021 [2009]. *Statistics for Linguistics with R. A Practical Introduction*. Berlin, Boston.

GUTIÉRREZ, R. 2017. *El Arte de la Conversión. Un estudio sobre la República de Platón*. Lima.

HÄGLER, R.-P. 1983. *Platons 'Parmenides'. Probleme der Interpretation*. Berlin.

HALFWASSEN, J. 1993. "Speusipp und die metaphysische Deutung von Platons 'Parmenides'." In: HAGEMANN, L.; GLEY, R. (eds.). *Hen kai plêthos – Einheit und Vielheit. Festschrift für Karl Bormann zum 65. Geburtstag*. Würzburg, Altenberge. 339–373.

HALFWASSEN, J. ²2006 [1992]. *Der Aufstieg zum Einen. Untersuchungen zu Platon und Plotin*. Munich, Leipzig.

HARDIE, W. F. R. 1936. *A Study in Plato*. Oxford.

HAVLÍČEK, A.; KARFÍK, F. (eds.). 2005. *Plato's Parmenides. Proceedings of the Fourth Symposium Platonicum Pragense*. Prague.

HÖSLE, V. 2018. *Kritik der verstehenden Vernunft. Eine Grundlegung der Geisteswissenschaften*. Munich.

HÖSLE, V. 2019. "The Tübingen School." In: KIM, A. (ed.). *Brill's Companion to German Platonism*. Leiden, Boston. 328–348.

HORN, CH. 1995. "Der Platonische *Parmenides* und die Möglichkeit seiner prinzipientheoretischen Interpretation." *Antike und Abendland* 41: 95–114.

HUNT, D. 1997. "How (not) Exempt Platonic Forms from Parmenides's Third Man." *Phronesis* 42: 1–20.


KAHN, CH. H. 2001. *Pythagoras and the Pythagoreans. A Brief History*. Indianapolis, Cambridge.

KARFÍK, F. 2004. *Die Beseelung des Kosmos. Untersuchungen zur Kosmologie, Seelenlehre und Theologie in Platons Phaidon und Timaios*. Munich, Leipzig.

KARFÍK, F. 2005. "Par rapport à soi-même et par rapport aux autres. Une distinction clef dans le *Parménide* de Platon." In: HAVLÍČEK / KARFÍK 2005, 141–164.

KENNEDY, J. B. 2010. "Plato's Forms, Pythagorean Mathematics, and Stichometry." *Apeiron* 43: 1–32.

KIRK, R. E. 2003. "The importance of effect magnitude." In: DAVIS, S. F. (ed.). *Handbook of Research Methods in Experimental Psychology*. Malden. 83–105.

KOCH, D.; MÄNNLEIN-ROBERT, I.; WEIDTMANN, N. (eds.). 2019. *Platon und die Physis*. Tübingen.

VON KUTSCHERA, F. 1995. *Platons "Parmenides"*. Berlin.


LAKMAN, M.-L. 2017. *Platonici minores. 1. Jh. v. Chr. – 2. Jh. n. Chr.* Leiden, Boston.

LIENEMANN, B. 2010. *Die Argumente des Dritten Menschen in Platons Dialog "Parmenides". Rekonstruktion und Kritik aus analytischer Perspektive*. Göttingen.

LIJFFIJT, J.; GRIES, S. TH. 2012. "Correction to Stefan Th. Gries' 'Dispersions and adjusted frequencies in corpora'." *International Journal of Corpus Linguistics* 17: 147–149.

LUCARINI, C. M. 2021. "De Platonis Parmenidis Codicibus Quaestiones." *Rheinisches Museum für Philologie* 164: 241–268.

LUTOSŁAWSKI, W. 1897. *The Origin and Growth of Plato's Logic. With an account of Plato's style and of the chronology of his writings*. London, New York, Bombay.

LYNCH, W. F. 1959. *An approach to the metaphysics of Plato through the Parmenides*. Washington.


MÄNNLEIN-ROBERT, I. 2022. "Der ferne Gott – Ideen auf Distanz? Die siebte Aporie im Kontext (Prm. 133b4–135b4)." In: BRISSON / MACÉ / RENAUT 2022, 269–277.

MARINESCU, R. I. 2021. "Plato on Self-Motion in *Laws* x." *Rhizomata* 9: 96–122.

MARTENS, E. ²2001 [1987]. *Platon. Parmenides*. Stuttgart.

MEINWALD, C. C. 1991. *Plato's Parmenides*. New York et al.

MEINWALD, C. C. 1992. "Good-bye to the Third Man." In: KRAUT, R. (ed.). *The Cambridge Companion to Plato*. Cambridge. 365–396.

MIGLIORI, M. 1990. *Dialettica e Verità. Commentario filosofico al "Parmenide" di Platone*. Milan.

MIGNUCCI, M. 1990. "Plato's Third Man Arguments in the *Parmenides*."
*Archiv für Geschichte der Philosophie* 72: 143–184.
MILLER, D. 2003. *The third kind in Plato's Timaeus*. Göttingen.
MILLER, M. H. 1986. *Plato's Parmenides. The Conversion of the Soul*.
Princeton.
MULLER, CH. 1973. *Initiation aux méthodes de la statistique linguistique*. Paris.
MORAVCSIK, J. M. E. 1963. "The 'Third Man' Argument and Plato's
Theory of Forms." *Phronesis* 8: 50–62.

NIEWÖHNER, F. W. 1971. *Dialog und Dialektik in Platons "Parmenides"*.
*Untersuchungen zur sogenannten Platonischen "Esoterik"*. Meisenheim
am Glan.

O'BRIEN, D. 2005A. "Einai copulatif et existentiel dans le *Parménide* de Platon."
*Revue des études grecques* 118: 229–245.
O'BRIEN, D. 2005B. "Le Parménide historique et le *Parménide* de Platon."
In: HAVLÍČEK/KARFÍK 2005, 234–256.
OPSOMER, J. 2020. "The Platonic Soul, from the Early Academy to the
First Century CE." In: INWOOD, B.; WARREN, J. (eds.). *Body and Soul
in Hellenistic Philosophy*. Cambridge. 171–198.
OWEN, G. E. L. 1953. "The Place of the *Timaeus* in Plato's Dialogues."
*The Classical Quarterly* 3: 79–95.

PALMER, J. A. 1999. *Plato's Reception of Parmenides*. Oxford.
PARPOLA, A. ³2009 [1994]. *Deciphering the Indus script*. Cambridge.
PENNER, T. 1987. *The Ascent from Nominalism. Some Existence Arguments
in Plato's Middle Dialogues*. Dordrecht et al.
PETERSON, S. 1973. "A Reasonable Self-Predication Premise for the Third Man
Argument." *Philosophical Review* 82: 451–470.
PETERSON, S. 1996. "Plato's *Parmenides*. A Principle of Interpretation and Seven
Arguments." *Journal of the History of Philosophy* 34: 167–192.
POETSCH, CH. 2019. *Platons Philosophie des Bildes. Systematische Untersuchungen
zur platonischen Metaphysik*. Frankfurt/Main.
POETSCH, CH. 2021A. "Die Logoi der platonischen Sonnenanalogie."
*Zeitschrift für philosophische Forschung* 75: 235–273.
POETSCH, CH. 2021B. "Das *Thothbuch*: eine ägyptische Vorlage der platonischen
Schriftkritik im *Phaidros*?" *Archiv für Geschichte der Philosophie* 103: 195–220.
POETSCH, CH. 2022. "Dimensions of Pleasure. A first Detailed Reconstruction of
Plato's 'Tyrant Number'." *Apeiron* 55: 391–416.
PRIOU, A. 2018. *Becoming Socrates. Political philosophy in Plato's Parmenides*.
Rochester.

R CORE TEAM. 2020. *R: A language and environment for statistical computing*.
R Foundation for Statistical Computing, Vienna, Austria.
https://www.r-project.org/
RICKLESS, S. C. 2007. *Plato's forms in transition. A reading of the Parmenides*.
Cambridge et al.
ROBINSON, R. ²1953 [1941]. *Plato's Earlier Dialectic*. Oxford.
RUNCIMAN, W. G. 1959. "Plato's Parmenides." *Harvard Studies in Classical
Philology* 64: 89–120.

SAFFREY, H. D.; WESTERINK, L. G. 1968. "Introduction." In: *Proclus. Théologie Platonicienne*. Texte établi et traduit par H. D. SAFFREY et L. G. WESTERINK. Paris. I–LXXXIX.

SANDAY, E. 2015. *A study of dialectic in Plato's Parmenides*. Evanston.

SAYRE, K. M. 1983. *Plato's Late Ontology. A riddle resolved*. Princeton.

SAYRE, K. M. 1996. *Parmenides' Lesson. Translation and Explication of Plato's Parmenides*. Notre Dame.

SAYRE, K. M. 2005. "The Method Revisited: *Parmenides*, 135e9–136c6." In: HAVLÍČEK/KARFÍK 2005, 125–140.

SCHADEWALDT, W. ²1970 [1960]. "Platon und Kratylos. Ein Hinweis." In: SCHADEWALDT, W. *Hellas und Hesperien*. Vol. I. Zurich. 626–632.

SCHUDOMA, I. 2001. *Platons Parmenides. Kommentar und Deutung*. Würzburg.

SCHWABE, W. 2001. "Der Geistcharakter des 'überhimmlischen Raumes'. Zur Korrektur der herrschenden Auffassung von *Phaidros* 247 c–e." In: SZLEZÁK, TH. A. (ed.). *Platonisches Philosophieren. Zehn Vorträge zu Ehren von Hans Joachim Krämer*. Hildesheim et al. 181–332.

SCOLNICOV, S. 2003. *Plato's Parmenides*. Berkeley et al.

SÉGUY-DUCLOT, A. 1998. *Le Parménide des Platon ou le jeu des hypothèses*. Paris.

SELLARS, W. 1955. "Vlastos and 'The Third Man'." *Philosophical Review* 64: 405–437.

SPEISER, A. ²1959 [1937]. *Ein Parmenideskommentar. Studien zur Platonischen Dialektik*. Leipzig, Stuttgart.

ŠPINKA, Š. 2005. "Relation, Sein und Zeit." In: HAVLÍČEK/KARFÍK 2005, 181–199.

STROBEL, B. 2007. *"Dieses" und "So etwas". Zur ontologischen Klassifikation platonischer Formen*. Göttingen.

STROBEL, B. 2018. Review of LIENEMANN 2010. *Gnomon* 90: 200–214.

SZAIF, J. 2022. "Pseudo-Objects in a World of Seeming (Prm. 164b–165e)." In: BRISSON/MACÉ/RENAUT, 439–451.

SZLEZÁK, TH. A. 1988. "Gespräche unter Ungleichen. Zur Struktur und Zielsetzung der platonischen Dialoge." *Antike und Abendland* 34: 99–116.

SZLEZÁK, TH. A. 2021. *Platon. Meisterdenker der Antike*. Munich.


TABAK, M. 2015. *Plato's Parmenides reconsidered*. New York et al.

TARRANT, H. 1983. "Middle Platonism and the Seventh Epistle." *Phronesis* 28: 75–103.

TARRANT, H. 1993. *Thrasyllan Platonism*. Ithaca.

TAYLOR, A. E. 1934. *The 'Parmenides' of Plato*. Oxford.

TORNAU, CH. 2000. "Die Prinzipienlehre des Moderatos von Gades. Zu Simplikios in Ph. 230,34–231,24 DIELS." *Rheinisches Museum für Philologie* 143: 197–220.

TURNBULL, R. 1998. *The Parmenides and Plato's Late Philosophy*. Translation of and Commentary on the *Parmenides* with Interpretative Chapters on the *Timaeus*, the *Theaetetus*, the *Sophist*, and the *Philebus*. Toronto.


VLASTOS, G. 1954. "The Third Man Argument in the *Parmenides*." *The Philosophical Review* 63: 319–349.

VLASTOS, G. 1955. "Addenda to the Third Man Argument. A Reply to Professor Sellars." *Philosophical Review* 64: 438–448.

VLASTOS, G. 1969. "Plato's 'Third Man'-Argument (Prm. 132a1–b2). Text and Logic." *Philosophical Quarterly* 19: 289–301.

WAHL, J. ²1951 [1926]. *Étude sur le Parménide de Platon*. Paris.

WALTER, D. (forthcoming.) "The Definitional Structure and the Role of the Same, the Different and the Part-Whole-Relations in Plato's *Parmenides* 137c–166c." Forthcoming in: *Ancient Philosophy*.

WASSERSTEIN, R. L.; LAZAR, N. A. 2016. "The ASA Statement on *p*-Values: Context, Process, and Purpose." *The American Statistician* 70: 129–133.

VON WEIZSÄCKER, C. F. ²2002 [1981]. *Ein Blick auf Platon. Ideenlehre, Logik und Physik*. Stuttgart.

WICKHAM H. 2016. *ggplot2. Elegant Graphics for Data Analysis*. New York. https://ggplot2.tidyverse.org

WILPERT, P. 1941. "Das Argument vom 'dritten' Menschen." *Philologus* 94: 51–64.

WINTER, B. 2020. *Statistics for Linguists. An Introduction Using R*. New York, London.

WUNDT, M. 1935. *Platons Parmenides*. Stuttgart, Berlin.

WYLLER, E. A. ²2006 [1960]. *Platons Parmenides in seinem Zusammenhang mit Symposion und Politeia*. Würzburg.

# INDEX NOMINUM

The following index lists all ancient and modern persons. Characters from Plato's dialogues are not included. Authors of secondary literature are only listed if they are named in the main text, quoted verbatim in the main text or in the notes, or further commented on or discussed in the notes. Mere references are generally not listed.

# INDEX RERUM

# INDEX LOCORUM